The English Companion

with compliments from

✳ **BANK OF SCOTLAND**
CORPORATE

The
English
Companion

An idiosyncratic A to Z of
England and Englishness

Godfrey Smith

Old House Books

First Published in England in 1984 by Pavilion Books Ltd
This revised and updated version published in 1996 by
Old House Books, Moretonhampstead, Devon TQ13 8NA
Copyright © Godfrey Smith 1984, 1988 and 1996
Illustrations © John Lawrence

The right of Godfrey Smith to be identified as the author
of this work has been asserted by him in accordance with
The Copyright, Design and Patents Act 1988.

British Cataloguing in Publication Data
A CIP catalogue record for this book is available from the
British Library

ISNB 1 873590 – 21 – 0

Printed in Spain by Gráficas Santamaría S.A.
by arrangement with Associated Agencies, Oxford

for Asa

Introduction

Companions nowadays take a capital initial letter. They have scholarly editors, and thousands of pages. They are designed to guide us through dauntingly complex landscapes: art, film, literature, science and theatre. Yet when the first, *The Oxford Companion to English Literature*, was originally discussed, it took a small 'c'. It was intended to be an unassuming friend who would stroll with the reader, pointing out an interesting tree here, a shrub there, a pleasing valley or refreshing stream. It would tell you a yarn or two on your journey, but would not chuck its weight about.

In putting together *The English Companion* I have tried to follow this modest first plan. It is an informal ramble through English things. It makes no pretensions to original thought, academic distinction, or comprehensive sweep. Indeed, not to put too fine a point on it, it is subjective, idiosyncratic, and, some would say, perversely capricious. Thus Auden is included but not Eliot, Winchester is discussed but not Canterbury, Fortnums but not Selfridges. There was of course no choice about this piecemeal policy: to attempt to deal exhaustively with English preoccupations would need a dozen volumes and defeat the object of the exercise, for if a companion cannot go unobtrusively where the reader goes, what is the use of it?

Nevertheless, I hope the subjects I have included will divert readers and perhaps even occasionally tell them something new; certainly I have learned a lot about my native country, and my fellow countrymen, in putting it together. The English are curiously neglected. Until George Orwell sat down to write on the English people, as his biographer Bernard Crick points out, there was really very little in the language on the theme apart from the orotund guff of Winston Churchill, Arthur Bryant, and A.L. Rowse. What we might call the Whitbread view of England – a smiling land full of wheatfields and wenches, gaffers and gumboots, cakes and ale – had its heyday in Edwardian England and lingered on between the wars. It can still be detected residually, but happily a new spirit of realism is abroad and the English now take themselves far less seriously than they did. Over and again in putting this book together I have been struck by the way in which words and ideas once taken quite literally and solemnly are now used increasingly in an ironic and mocking sense.

To take just one obvious example: it is increasingly hard in modern England to use the word gentleman four-square. It is introduced, if at all in a flip way which seems to say: I'm using this word but of course you realise I'm not to be taken seriously when I do so. Are we then to assume that the national character is changing? Marginally and gradually, perhaps it is; but I think it is the *perception* of England which is changing. The world sees us differently; we see ourselves differently. Ancient stereotypes have been stood on their heads. The UK, once the richest country in the world, now ranks fifteenth in terms of real income, well behind Norway and Sweden, and roughly on a par with Italy. The English, once seen as the coldest fish in Europe, now show clear signs of becoming one of the randiest races on the earth. On the other hand certain English attributes seem never to change: a daunting philistinism, a shaky grip on hygiene, an obsession with animals, a predilection for gambling, a gift with gardens, a passion for sport, an incomprehension of foreigners and a huge sense of humour.

There remains too the English preoccupation with class. I have argued under that heading in this companion that though class has been the English pox, increasingly what really preoccupies the English is not so much class as style. I may be wrong, but it does seem to me this is one way in which the texture of English life has changed most radically. The collapse of the old deference structure is in my mind one of the best developments in modern England, and through I have tried not to flinch at English failings, no reader will be left in much doubt where my affections really lie. I find England so overwhelmingly the best country in the world that it is really rather bad form to say how much. Nevertheless Arcadias are precarious places that must be perennially guarded and things could go very wrong in England very quickly. So perhaps it is not a bad idea to stop and take stock of our credit balance every now and then.

A final word: this is an English companion, not a British one. The Scots, the Welsh and the Irish have long been adept at blowing their own trumpets, and I admire them for it. In this book, however, we are giving two cheers for England. I like to think that only an Englishman could have thought of giving just those two cheers.

Godfrey Smith
Malmesbury
Summer 1984

The Revised Edition

Twelve years may seem no time at all in the story of a country as old as England. Yet, revising and updating *The English Companion* for this 1996 edition, a surprisingly thorough re-working of the original material was necessary; and many new words and phrases forced their way in. The rise and fall of Thatcherism changed many tenses; the collapse of Soviet communism many moods and attitudes. The opening of the Channel Tunnel subtly undermined traditional English insularity; the launch of the National Lottery underwrote the old English predilection for gambling. It was a pleasure to welcome Channel 4 to the book; an unhappy duty to record the onset of AIDS. New ninnies like the wet and the wimp seemed worth a mention; and how could we resist noting, with resignation, the rise of the ubiquitous yuppie in the land?

Andrew Lloyd Webber's phenomenal show *Cats* has now grossed over £2 billion. Meanwhile the Aston Martin, a mere £40,000 twelve years ago, is now a sobering £82,500; the cheapest Rolls-Royce is £118,557.50 now against £55,000 then. The return air fare on Concorde from London to New York will set you back £4,845 now against a trifling £2,200 then.

One critic felt the book too masculine in flavour, and suggested, *inter alia*, entries for such enduring English heroines as Gracie Fields and Vera Lynn. I thought this an excellent idea. Nor could I resist a new entry for a lady who cheered the nation inordinately for weeks on end: so Cynthia Payne is now in too. Another critic felt I had been too critical in the RAF entry on the role of Bomber Command. I agree, having learned much more about the dramatic improvement in our bombing accuracy as the war went on; and I have softened somewhat too my summing up of the Falklands Conflict. As so often, we were given, not one good and one bad option, but several lousy ones, and we did our best in the unpleasant circumstances.

I am particularly grateful to Mr A.J.P. Taylor for pointing out to me that it was T.F. Tout and not L.B. Namier who gave the Manchester history school its international réclame; and to my old friend John Fraser, a professional linguist, for sorting out the spelling of black pudding in a bewildering variety of foreign tongues. I was grateful, too, to the scientifically minded reader who pointed out to me that in the entry for Sherlock Holmes, I describe the historic first meeting with Dr Watson as taking place by the flickering blue light of a Bunsen burner. A flickering Bunsen flame, he pointed out with some reason, is yellow, while blue denotes the full jet. Here, though, I had simply quoted the words of

Conan Doyle himself. Clearly it is not up to me to tamper with the Great man's words, so flickering blue light it must remain.

Finally, I must record an enormous debt to my daughter, Amanda Smith, who tackled both fresh research and pernickety checking with her usual zing. It was, as always, a pleasure to work with her.

> Godfrey Smith
> Malmesbury
> Summer 1996

Bread and Butter Letter

Acknowledgements are notoriously the most boring part of any book, so in this *English Companion* I thought we would substitute the fine old English institution of the bread and butter letter.

My thanks are due first to Colin Webb, managing director of Pavilion Books. In my experience publishers are not usually good at coming up with irresistibly good ideas, but this book was totally Colin's; and he had no sooner outlined it than I had agreed to do it. I should like to thank too my agent Anne McDermid who suggested the lunch with Colin from which the idea sprang; it is just this kind of catalyst that a good agent should be.

Once again I am grateful to Oscar Turnill, that prince among editors, who has put this book, like to many others, though the fine mesh of his mill. Since even Oscar is not omniscient I shall not claim that he has obviated every error; but he has certainly taken out a great many while tightening up the bolts of my prose, and I would not dream of committing a book like this to the press unless it first had the benefit of his wisdom, humour and common sense. I am equally grateful to Judy Dauncey, who saw the book through to press at Pavilion Books, and to John Lawrence for his elegant drawings.

I should like to thank my wife, Mary Schoenfeld Smith, for much valuable research and for many suggestions throughout the writing. I am grateful to Judith Woolliams, who researched and typed for me so cheerfully in the country, and my daughter, Amanda Smith, who performed the same function so briskly in London.

When it comes to books I feel like Gerald Asher – who introduced his enchanting book, *On Wine*, with the disarming disclaimer that if he were to thank everybody who had helped him understand wine he would really have to tell the story of his life. And which reader is going to wait to hear his – or mine? Still, I cannot end without naming a few key titles.

First, of course, no one in his right mind would take on a book like this without the *Oxford English Dictionary* at his side. I also found the three volumes of the *Supplement* continuously useful, and my old friend Robert Burchfield, then chief editor of the *OED,* sportingly let me see many galleys from his final volume.

The *Dictionary of National Biography* has been another stalwart friend, and at the point it then ran out, in 1970, the three volumes of *Obituaries from the Times* often came gallantly to my rescue. I have looked into many other books of reference but should like to single out one that has proved as readable as it is reliable: the third edition of A.C. Wards *Longman's Companion to Twentieth Century Literature.* I am sorry it is now out of print, for the press of new writing never diminishes, and we need his light touch at our elbow to guide us through it.

Finally, there was hardly a town or a shop, a club or a sport, a society or a company discussed in this companion that did not give me unstinted help in seeing that my facts and figures were as up-to-date as they could be: and many supplied reams of fascinating material on their histories and quiddities too. I have tried to thank each individually; let me end by giving them one great heartfelt thank-you here. There is little kindness in the world, remarks Sidney Greenstreet as he topples dramatically down the stairs to his death in *The Mask of Dimitrios*; but there is much kindness yet in England; to that I can testify.

G.S.

An asterisk indicates a cross-reference
to a separate subject heading.

Abroad   Nothing conveys the ambivalence of the English quite so much as their attitude to being abroad. On the one hand, abroad is the place where the island race made their names and fortunes. It was as natural for your young Englishman to make his way abroad as it was for him to breathe. 'Go out and govern New South Wales!' exhorted Hilaire Belloc in a celebrated verse. On the other hand, foreigners were suspect, and all wogs began at Calais.

For the English writer the temptations of abroad were manifest. He needed no office or factory to make his living, the pound was strong and the Mediterranean sun beckoned him south. Besides, he could throw off abroad what seemed the repressive *moeurs* of his native land (Norman Douglas, D.H. Lawrence). There is a famous remark made by a celebrated actress on entering Somerset Maugham's* living room at the Villa Mauresque in the South of France. In the room were Noël Coward*, Godfrey Winn and Beverley Nichols. 'Why,' she exclaimed, 'this is fairyland!'

Interestingly, though, a new race of English writers have matured who cannot be doing with abroad, and will go there only when they must (Kingsley Amis* was one). On balance, abroad has probably done the Englishman more good than harm, and the fact that some six hundred million now speak his lingo bears eloquent testimony to the peripatetic restlessness of his forbears; even as it makes him one of the world's worst linguists.

It must also be faced that in the eyes of the world the Englishman is at his worst abroad: with his buck teeth, baggy shorts, braying voice and

14

dowdy memsahib he's a twerp at best, a thug at worst, and a pain in the arse at most times.

Accent   It is now over eighty years since Professor Henry Higgins first boasted to Colonel Pickering in Bernard Shaw's play *Pygmalion* that he could take a flower girl like Eliza Doolittle and in three months pass her off as a duchess (or get her a place as a shop assistant, which required – and requires – better English). Bernard Shaw had seized on the crashingly obvious point that no Englishman can open his mouth without being despised by some other Englishman.

The years since the claim was first made have seen remarkably little change in that basic proposition. Employers still speak the lingo of Winchester and New College (Oxford), or Shrewsbury and Peterhouse (Cambridge); the trade union leaders with the accents they learned in Ebbw Vale or Heckmondwike, Jarrow or Poplar. We are still two nations. Subtle changes, however, have complicated the old clean-cut divisions.

Certain varieties of upper class inflection are now archaic. Mayfair cockney has almost gone, though it lingered on in the mouths of the Mitford girls. Gaumont British newsreel gung-ho has given way to television *Newsnight* neutral. There is a middle English now that anyone with half an ear can acquire. It is the language of Robin Day (Oxford Union extra-clear) and Kate Adie (Sunderland plainsong), of Bernard Levin (with a dash of Christ's Hospital school still obtruding) and Jeremy Paxman (Malvern New Brutalist).

Meanwhile the young have acquired their own secret code: a kind of pop-culture cockney, into which they can switch from their parental accent and back at the drop of an aspirate. It has even been learned by at least one of the Queen's children (Prince Edward). The lesson Higgins taught us has been well learned. Margaret Thatcher (with her duchess drawl) is perhaps his most striking disciple.

Acting   It is frankly amazing that there has been any good acting in England when one considers the eccentric and chaotic ragbag of talents that have made up the *soi-disant* profession. Through the gallimaufry of Hooray Henrys*, superannuated subalterns, peripatetic alcoholics, plum-faced actor-managers and (*pace* Noël Coward*) unrepentant Miss Worthingtons, there nevertheless always ran a thin thread of excellence: among the buffoons, the odd Olivier*, Gielgud, Richardson or Redgrave.

Today if you take a boat down the Thames* from Westminster Pier you will pass some of the best acting in the world on your starboard bow, and do so again a mile down to port: the National Theatre is on the south bank; the Royal Shakespeare is still entrenched in its metropolitan headquarters at the Barbican. Meanwhile, Broadway is in the thrall of the British musical, and Andrew Lloyd Webber is the toast of New York.

Fringe theatre abounds, lunchtime theatre booms, student theatre escalates, and with the mushrooming of commercial radio and cable television, there seems plenty of scope for any aspirant English actor who can lay hands on an Equity card – by no means an easy trick, by the way.

The chances for the young actor outside London proliferate. To take just three towns at random: in Manchester the Royal Exchange theatre flourishes under a lively management; in Bath the Theatre Royal has been sparklingly refurbished and still attracts the metropolitan talents on their way into town; at Chichester the theatre festival thrives in what Olivier called its concrete hexagon.

Afters   There is no word for what an Englishman eats after his meat that does not make some other Englishman wince. The upper class say pudding (or 'pud') – a patent misnomer if what comes up is sorbet or grapes. Dessert, which all Americans use without bother, strikes English ears as pretentious, whereas sweet – which after all explains most nearly what it is – puts middle-class teeth on edge. So in many a trendy English bistro nowadays, the profiteroles and rum babas are improbably described as afters. It is a good old-fashioned working-class word, pressed into middle-class service to cover an absurd and quite unnecessary difficulty.

AIDS   or, to give its daunting full name, Acquired Immune Deficiency Syndrome, is no nearer a cure in England than anywhere else. It has, however, already had a curious and profound effect on the social life of the country. The permissive society may be fairly said to have begun late in 1962, when the Family Planning Association decided to recommend the Pill as a safe, everyday method of birth control, and it was in that year too that it could be first dispensed under the National Health Service. Homosexual men had to wait a further five years before the Sexual Offences Act of 1967 legalised their mode of love between consenting adults. These two enormous catalysts seemed to offer a vast new sexual liberty; it was the onset twenty years later of the sinister and terrifying new affliction called AIDS that brought a sudden quietus to the new freedom. Promiscuity might seem fun to the young; but it was hardly worth giving your life for it, and AIDS has no cure yet. One safe, known partner seemed the only safe bet. The condom, once furtively sold in men's barber shops, and apparently doomed to extinction, became the hero of government pamphlets. Television commercials taught the bashful young not to be shy about ordering their condoms in chemists. Pockets for your condoms even became a modish feature of designer clothes. Monogamous or condomous copulation was now the name of the game. It was as if a window had been opened on a new liberty and lifestyle, only to be abruptly shut again.

Aldershot   This ugly little Hampshire town has two claims to fame: firstly, it is the home of the British army*. The brainchild of Victoria's husband Albert, it has seen many generations of British soldiers knocked into shape. Though much of its old Victorian grandeur has gone, the officers' library, stocked with treatises on the art of war, and the garrison church, replete with the loot of empire, survive, while the Duke of Wellington's huge statue still gazes down on the drilling, the cussing, the boozing and the wenching. It is an artefact of empire, a sweatshop for the craft of arms, and a repository for spit and polish.

Secondly, however, it is the setting for a famous romance. One day in the 1939–45 war John Betjeman* was sitting in the canteen at the Ministry of Information, where he worked. Then he saw a young assistant manageress who was the very exemplar of an English rose. Smitten, Betjeman asked someone her name. On hearing that she was a Miss Joan Hunter Dunn, he underwent a revelation not dissimilar to St Paul's on the road to Damascus.

The quintessentially English name at once unlocked a flood of images in his mind. He divined instantly that she would come from Aldershot, and that her people would be connected with the army. He was uncannily right: her family did live near there, and her father had been an army doctor. Betjeman, on hearing how near he had been, at once sat down and wrote *A Subaltern's Love Song,* with its celebrated opening couplet: 'Miss Joan Hunter Dunn, Miss Joan Hunter Dunn / Furnish'd and burnish'd by Aldershot sun' and its magnificent dénouement: 'We sat in the car-park till quarter past one / And now I'm engaged to Miss Joan Hunter Dunn.'

The scene of Second Lt Betjeman's proposal — if we may blur fact with fantasy for a moment – was nearby 'nine o'clock Camberley, heavy with bells / And mushroomy, pinewoody, evergreen smells'. Every Englishman knows that sandy terrain, the moss, heath, scrubland and conifers, by a kind of osmosis, even if he has not physically set foot in the place. Aldershot is embedded deep in our collective memory, and as James Morris observes in the opening volume of his trilogy on the British empire, *Heaven's Command*: 'When, at one o'clock precisely each day,

The Aldershot time gun was fired electronically from the Royal Observatory at Greenwich, it was like a time-check for the entire Raj.'

Ale   The English type of beer. Unlike most foreign beers, it is made by allowing the yeast to ferment at the top. It should mature naturally in its cask in the cellar of a pub. Unhappily the giant breweries have found it convenient to filter, pasteurise or chill their beer so that it no longer matures, but is stable or dead, and is then delivered to the glass by gas pressure from a cylinder of carbon dioxide.

It was antipathy to this dead but artificially fizzed beer which precipitated the Campaign for Real Ale (CAMRA). This is beer made from the traditional ingredients – malted barley, liquor (water) and yeast – matured in casks and delivered to the glass by any method that does not involve gas; generally by a simple suction hand pump, or drawn by gravity straight from the barrel. CAMRA, despite some vexing internal political troubles, has been a great populist movement, and the nearest English male equivalent to Women's Lib.

For the English love of ale is true and deep. 'Good ale, the true and proper drink of Englishmen,' declared George Borrow; and every Englishman feels with the Boy in Shakespeare's *Henry V* at the battle: 'Would I were in a alehouse in London: I would give all my fame for a pot of ale and safety.' Yet the best single remark on the matter was made by Alfred, Lord Tennyson, then Poet Laureate, on the occasion of his visit to the International Exhibition of 1862. Having written an ode to be sung by a choir of four thousand at its opening he enquired: 'Is there anywhere in this damned place where we can get a decent bottle of Bass?'

Hence the innate thrall of the great real ale brewers to the Englishman, reverberating through his mind like a litany: Adnams of Southwold, Ruddles of Rutland, Theakston of Masham, Vaux of Sunderland, Thwaites of Blackburn, and Tennyson's favourite, four-square tipple, Bass of Burton.

Alma Mater   Foster mother, the name given by the English middle class to their schools or universities, is now rather going out of use, though the actual cult of the alma mater still flourishes. It is probably strongest, by dint of sheer longevity, at Oxbridge and the older public schools, and is notoriously more prevalent among men than women. It is quite possible to meet men in England who have still not gone down from their old Oxbridge alma mater after a hundred and twenty terms; and a college appeal for funds to rebuild the stonework or endow new fellowships will meet with a response out of all proportion to numbers.

An Oxford college, for example, with three hundred in residence at any one time and perhaps four thousand living old members, will have no difficulty at all in raising three or four million from them. Graham Greene perfectly caught the seamy underside of the alma mater cult in *England Made Me:* 'I see you were at the old place ... Those were the days eh? ... I don't suppose you'd remember old Tester (six months for indecent assault). I try to keep up with them. Whose house were you in?' But see also under *Old Boy Network* and *Old School Tie.*

Ambition 'It is important in this world to be pushing,' said the great Benjamin Jowett, 'but it is fatal to seem so.' That really sums up the English position about ambition.

Amis, Kingsley (1922–95) 'A fair-haired young man came down staircase three and paused on the bottom step. Norman instantly pointed his right hand at him in the semblance of a pistol and uttered a short coughing bark to signify a shot... The young man's reaction was immediate. Clutching his chest in a rictus of agony, he threw one arm up against the archway and began slowly crumpling downwards, fingers scoring the stonework.' The future poet, novelist and critic Philip Larkin, an eighteen-year-old wartime undergraduate at St John's College, Oxford, had just met another – the future novelist, critic and poet Kingsley Amis. Amis's gift for mimicry was thus early noted and celebrated. He was to use it in his first published novel, *Lucky Jim,* when the ghastly Bertrand Welch is made to say 'you sam' when he means 'you see' and 'hostelram' when he means 'hostelry'. This curious verbal hallmark of the saloon-bar shitface was well established, but it had never been nailed in print.

Malcolm Bradbury has drawn parallels between Amis and Evelyn Waugh*, noting that each began as a Young Turk writing for his own generation and signalling a change in social values through what he calls 'a cleansing comic version'. Perhaps; and both were Oxford-educated former Army officers with two wives apiece (and a predilection for looking on the wine when it was red). Each had a gifted writer as a son. Still, the parallels cannot be pushed too far. Waugh was no lover of jazz or science fiction; Amis was not noted for his views on painting or architecture. Waugh was a globe-trotter, travel-writer, and war correspondent; Amis liked it here. Still, Waugh in his sixty-two years and Amis in his fecund seventy-three each produced a body of vastly entertaining work in which the easy reading is made by hard writing. Yet Amis had the wider range: from picaresque comedy to sexual satire; from his primer on booze to scholarly essays on Jane Austen*, Tennyson, and Kipling; from a mordant evocation of geriatric horrors *(Ending Up)* to a loving pastiche of the thirties thriller *(The Riverside Villas Murder)*.

Nor should we forget that Amis was a formidable critic (he rapped the chief editor of the *OED* over the knuckles for an inadequate definition of the Immelmann turn) and a skilful poet. In *Songs of Experience*, for example, he told the story of a commercial traveller regaling a pub with accounts of his amatory conquests: 'He tried all colours, white, black and coffee / Though quite a few were chary, more were bold / Some took it like the host, some like a toffee / The two or three who wept were soon consoled.'

Anthony Burgess* noted in the loosely grouped fifties writers, Amis, Osborne, and Braine, a common tendency to what he called hypergamy: 'bedding a woman of a social class superior to one's own'. That was forty years ago, though; and as Amis himself moved across the political spectrum from communism to conservatism so his heroes moved across the sexual spectrum from philandering to misogyny. Miscast as an Angry Young Man, Amis grew more atrabilious with age; but the acid precipitated some pearls. 'More will mean worse' elegantly crystallises his position and can be applied to virtually any aspect of the modern world he so distrusted and disliked, except, oddly, his own work. He won the Booker Prize in 1987.

Anon   One of the most prolific and gifted writers the English language has ever known, he is responsible for the serene words of 'Greensleeves' and the ironic lines of 'Nice One Cyril'. He wrote 'My name is George Nathaniel Curzon' and 'Would you like to Sin with Elinor Glyn?' He it was at the Battle of Blenheim who composed the prayer: 'O God, if there is a God, save my soul if I have a soul.' He it was at the beaches on D-Day* who summed it all up so magisterially: 'My dear, the noise ... and the people!' He it was who described Oxford as the Latin Quarter of Morris Cowley and coined the hippie slogan 'Make love not war'. He dreamed up phrases like 'the eternal triangle' and 'the king over the water'. He devised some of the greatest advertising slogans: this is the age of the train, and whiter than white. He sometimes lays claim to lines which one could have sworn belong to Benjamin Disraeli or Oscar Wilde ('The Church of England is the Tory Party at prayer') and then proves to have clear title. In an increasingly sophisticated audio-visual world where everything is recorded and banked away on tapes, it seems hard to believe that he should continue to flourish. But he does. As he once remarked: the future is not what it was.

Apples It is so self-evident to your Englishman that his apples are the best in the world that he considers it unnecessary to labour the point. The determined French campaign to flood England with Golden Delicious merely fortifies his resolution that there is no other fruit quite so clean, hard, sweet and true as the Cox's Orange Pippin.

Note that there are at least five hundred further varieties grown in our little island, which is just as well, for the Cox's, world-famous though its flavour remains, is a temperamental fruit that does not take kindly even to the English midlands, let alone north. Fortunately there are other varieties just about as good: notably the James Grieve, Ellison Orange, and Ribston Pippin.

Note again that in some subconscious mental process, the Englishman sees the apple as a symbol of wholesomeness, and even goodness. When something is amiss with his apples, it is amiss with the world too. During the sporadic alarms about police corruption, images of rotten apples spreading their disease through the whole barrel abound, and contrariwise.

'I said to Heart, how goes it?' proclaimed Belloc in one of his celebrated couplets. 'Heart replied / Right as a Ribston Pippin. But Heart lied.'

Archer, Jeffrey (born 1940) An author celebrated wherever English is spoken for the enormity of his sales and the fragrance of his wife.

Aristocracy 'The stately homes of England' sang Noël Coward*, 'How beautiful they stand/ To prove the upper classes have still the upper hand.' How right he was and is. Land is still the attribute which underwrites the survival of the English upper classes, and though there are poor peers (Earl Nelson of Trafalgar, descendent of the great admiral, was at one stage a police sergeant called Pete Nelson) there are plenty of rich ones (the dukes of Westminster, Devonshire and Bedford are together probably worth about a billion pounds).

A survey of landed wealth undertaken on the telephone by the *Spectator* magazine was able to reveal that one peer they rang was dead, another drunk, and a third could not remember whether he owned ten or a hundred thousand acres. This eccentricity, however, should not be taken *au pied de la lettre*. The English aristocracy were still hunting, shooting, wenching and wining in the shires while their French cousins were having their heads cut off. It is impossible to make any generalisation that will cover the whole class except to say that they are all exempt from jury service, a privilege they share with convicted felons,

MPs, barristers, bankrupts and lunatics.

As aristos go, the English are probably a better bet than any other lot. They had at one point the only communist in either House of Parliament. They have won the Nobel Prize for Literature (Winston Churchill* and Bertrand Russell) and the VC (Lord de Lisle and Dudley). They have competed in the Olympic Games (Lord Burghley). They have founded new political movements (Lord Weymouth's Wessex party) and formed their own jazz bands (Humphrey Lyttelton).

Indeed, frankly they survive by offering the English unstinted and continuing entertainment these many centuries. It was Lord Home himself who told, in his autobiography, the story of the footnote to a ministerial brief that was inadvertently read out in the House of Lords: 'This is a rotten argument, but it should be good enough for their lordships on a hot summer afternoon.'

Army Insofar as the Englishman thinks about his army at all, he usually dwells on its follies and disasters: Dunkirk* and the Dardanelles, the fall of Singapore and the Charge of the Light Brigade. Yet the truth is that the real modes of war – long periods of boredom broken by hectic spells of chaos – suit the English soldier. Over the centuries he has cussed and plodded his way through well-nigh unbelievable hardships for king and country; and in a quiet way, done it uncommonly well.

'My Lord, we are dreadfully cut up; can you not relieve us for a little while?' asked General Halkett at Waterloo. 'Impossible,' returned the Duke of Wellington. 'Very well, my Lord, we'll stand till the last man falls.' And they did. Afterwards Wellington summed up: 'Our loss is immense particularly in that best of all Instruments, British Infantry.' In the Crimea, stricken with cholera, fever, bowel and lung disease, the British infantry fought their way uphill against vastly superior forces and hacked their way through Cossacks ten times their number. In 1914 they marched to the bloody slaughter singing self-deprecatory and often obscene songs. 'No other army,' wrote A.J.P. Taylor*, 'has ever gone to war proclaiming its own incompetence and reluctance to fight, and no army has fought better.' In the Second World War, led by General Slim, the unknown Fourteenth Army fought its way through the dysentery and monsoon of the Burmese jungle and smashed the apparently invincible Japanese.

Through all this the Poor Bloody Infantry (as it dubbed itself) has been led by some extremely eccentric officers: Gordon of Khartoum; Montgomery of Alamein; Orde Wingate, creator of the Chindits; David Stirling, creator of the SAS. They have doubled as Fellows of All Souls like Lawrence of Arabia and professors of classics like General Sir John

Hackett. They have been poetry-lovers like Field Marshal Wavell, who published a best-selling anthology of verse at the height of the 1939–45 war; and music-lovers like Marine General Jeremy Moore, commander of land forces in the Falklands* conflict, whose previous qualifications for the job included an improbable stint as Purveyor of Music to the Royal Navy•. One thing all these officers had in common; not one of them could by any stretch of the imagination be called dull. Whether any of them would pass a modern selection board is a moot point. Most Englishmen would like to think so, but would not put too much money on it.

Arse   One of the primal chasms that separate us from our American cousins is that which yawns between our terms for the human fundament. To Americans, it is the ass: a niminy-piminy word, blurred by being used equally for the donkey, and confusingly for the female pudenda or even sexual coition itself. To Englishmen it is the arse: a round, honest and unambiguous word which says what it means.

Infinitely proliferating among all schoolboys and soldiers, it is one of the key verbal bricks in the construction of contempt. 'This goddam place is the asshole of the universe,' says the drunken GI of London in the old wartime canard. 'Yus mate,' replies the Tommy, 'and you're just passing through it.' A vivid and precise index of spatial reference, it was used in the last war both for the pilot who weaved in his plane at the rear of the squadron and for the tail-gunner in a bomber – 'arse-end Charlie'. It is also powerfully employed in images of complacency; notably in Louis MacNeice's* great poem *Bagpipe Music*: 'Sit on your arse for fifty years and hang your hat on a pension.'

We must allow our American cousins, however, the development of the colourful phrase for somebody whose company we would rather do without – 'he's a pain in the ass'. The word has also been effectively disguised by one of those wits who seek perpetually to penetrate the gravitas of *The Times** letters page: a sober letter printed by that great newspaper purported to be from R. Supwards.

The temptation to rhyme arsehole with castle has given rise to some rich vernacular verse, notably the charming ditty: 'My name is fair Lily / I'm a whore in Piccadilly / My mother is another in the Strand / My father hawks his arsehole / Round the Elephant and Castle / Don't you think that as a family / We're grand?

A further compound of infinite power is afforded by the coinage for one of the least popular sports known to the English, the 'arse-crawl', or more arcanely, for the unpleasant character defect known as 'arse-licking'. Such people, as far as your average Englishman is concerned, are best rewarded metaphorically, and if possible literally too, by that most salutary of all remedies, 'a good kick up the arse'.

Artists   It came out only after the death of Sir Winston Churchill's wife Clementine that, at some point in 1955 or 1956, she had ordered the destruction of Graham Sutherland's portrait of her husband. There was some protest in artistic circles, but the great British public overwhelmingly endorsed her right to destroy a picture which had caused her husband distress. Nor was this the first time Clementine had exercised her right of personal veto against artists of whom she disapproved. She put her foot in 1917 through a sketch Sickert had done of Winston and she even persuaded President Roosevelt to destroy a charcoal sketch of her husband in the presidential museum. Thus does England deal with her artists.

'Remember I'm an artist,' says Gulley Jimson in Joyce Cary's *The Horse's Mouth,* 'and you know what that means in a court of law. Next worst to an actress.' Both Cary's trilogy and Somerset Maugham's *The Moon and Sixpence* are powerful accounts of the artist outside society, which is where the Englishman perceives him to be. 'The artist,' said Osbert Sitwell, 'like the idiot or clown, sits on the edge of the world, and a push may send him over it.' It must be allowed, on the other hand, that many English artists have seemed inspired by extreme states of the human condition: 'It sounds like angels shrieking with joy,' said the visionary English painter Stanley Spencer, taken as a boy by his elder brother to hear Bach's *St Anne Prelude and Fugue,* and images of the human scream occur over and over again in the bizarre and compelling *oeuvre* of Francis Bacon.

Perhaps James McNeill Whistler was right when he said there never was an art-loving nation. Still, among the non-lovers, the English have something larger than a walk-on part. Only taken unawares will the Englishman give his artists their grudging due: as when walking in a Paris street and finding young French artists at an exhibition in the Latin Quarter queuing to sign the visitor's book in homage to the miraculous line of Bradford-born David Hockney. After all, he reflects, if these Frogs see something in an *English* artist, he must be all right

Ascot   'Everyone who should be heah is heah,' sing the gorgeously attired chorus in the Ascot scene from *My Fair Lady.* In fact a great many people who should not be theah are theah, according to that seasoned social commentator Nigel Dempster, gossip columnist of the *Daily Mail,* who has more than once launched an impassioned onslaught in his newspaper against the phonies, the hustlers, the poseurs and the shysters who in his view were ruining a gracious and select English occasion. Yet there have always been outsiders at Ascot. A morning suit and a grey topper from Moss Bros can hide a multitude of sins, and if big business is more in evidence than it used to be it was always there somewhere; indeed, the occasion would perish without it. It is a quintessentially royal occasion, with the Queen* opening the jollities in style as she bowls down the straight mile in her open landau; it is hard indeed to believe, as a forest of gleaming toppers are doffed and an ocean of foaming curtsies made, that Queen Victoria was once booed as she rode down this course. Yet she was, early in her reign, for accusing a royal lady-in-waiting, the unmarried Lady Flora Hastings, of being pregnant when what she in fact had was inoperable cancer. All that is long forgotten, and if the preposterous Mrs Shilling always got mountains of gash publicity every Ascot from her increasingly gigantic and outrageous hats, it seemed a small price to pay for so much bubbly, lobster, strawberries and cream, and so many pretty women in their floppy Ascot hats. The racing is all right too. See also *Derby*.

Aston Martin It was born in 1913 when two Singer dealers, Lionel Martin and Robert Bamford, decided to build their own car. They called it Aston after the hill climb in which both competed with distinction; Martin after Lionel Martin.

Even today, Astons make only 20 cars a week. Each goes from rest to 60 mph in 5.5 seconds. Nor may you extend it to even half its top whack on an English road without breaking the law.

Not that you would need to do anything so vulgar; the true beauty of the Aston lies in its well-bred discretion; in its colossal reserves of pace and power. Even in these mad days, about a third of all Astons are sold to the British, a third in America, and a third elsewhere; Germany is an increasingly important market. Whoever you are, you will need to pay the £82,500 which the least costly Aston – the DB7 – will set you back.

It is the favoured transport of Prince Charles and England rugby ace Will Carling and is famously driven by James Bond, who renewed his love affair with it by driving a DB5 in his last film, *Goldeneye*. It is an exquisite piece of English folly. See also *Rolls-Royce*.

Auden, Wystan Hugh (1907–73)   Asked by his tutor at Oxford, Nevill Coghill, what he wanted to be, Auden replied simply: a poet. Ah, yes, returned Coghill, that is the right way to start reading English. 'You don't understand at all,' Auden reproved him. 'I mean a *great* poet.' He became just that. He is, indeed the greatest English poet of this century. (T.S. Eliot, even after he became a naturalised British subject remained inaccessible, as Auden never was.)

Distinctly odd in his everyday persona (he once replied, when reproved for burning a hole in his host's grand piano with a cigarette, that it wouldn't affect the sound), Auden was able to fashion miracles out of plain words. He was an avowed homosexual ('Lay your sleeping head, my love / Human on my faithless arm' is deliberately ambiguous in its sexual pitch), a maverick Christian, a socialist of sorts, and an inspired teacher. His range is remarkable: from pure lyricism ('Earth, receive an honoured guest / William Yates is laid to rest') to black comedy ('They laid her out on the table / The students began to laugh / And Mr Rose the surgeon / He cut Miss Gee in half'). He is at his most formidable when his unblinking and unsentimental gaze is focused on the everyday world: 'Happy Birthday, Johnny / Live beyond your income / Follow your own nose.' He described himself as a mid-Atlantic Goethe; and was not too far out.

Austen, Jane (1785–1817)   'It is a truth universally acknowledged that a single man in possession of a good fortune must be in want of a wife.' The first sentence of *Pride and Prejudice* is not only the best opening in English literature; it is also a perfect microcosm of the world Jane Austen inhabits. The elegant shape of the epigram precisely forecasts the graceful architecture of the novel; its worldly tone announces the rules by which the beguiling game will be played; and its delicious irony at once alerts the reader to the fun in store.

Jane Austen has been criticised for writing as if the worlds of power and politics, war and want did not exist; in fact she is simply obeying the first rule of any writer's school and staying firmly inside the ambit of what she knows. None of her characters is drawn from outside the ranks of the English country gentry into which she was born; no two men ever converse in her books without a woman present.

It was not only impractical for a woman of her time to talk politics; it would have been impolite, which was much worse. We are fortunate however, in the change in public taste, which when she was born held it ill-bred for a woman to write, but thought it quite natural by the time she died. Still, in her own time she never put her name to her books, and the famous squeaking door in the house at Chawton was never oiled, so that she could hide her manuscripts from prying eyes.

Her fame rests on just six novels. *Pride and Prejudice* is the most accomplished; Benjamin Disraeli read it seventeen times; Winston Churchill*, laid low by illness when wartime prime minister, had his actress daughter Sarah read the whole book to him in bed. Jane has had a few detractors (notably Charlotte Brontë*) but her books caught on at once and have been best-sellers ever since. 'Let other pens dwell on guilt and misery,' she characteristically declared in *Mansfield Park*. No one understood better the delicate steps of the marital minuet; but she never married herself, though not for want of suitors.

'I think I may boast myself to be, with all possible vanity, the most unlearned and uninformed female who ever dared to be an authoress,' she confessed. She told her sister she thought *Pride and Prejudice* 'too light and bright and sparkling'. They are faults any writer should be glad to cultivate. Somerset Maugham paid her the fellow-writer's ultimate compliment: 'When you reach the bottom of a page you eagerly turn it in order to know what will happen next; nothing very much does and again you turn the page with the same eagerness.'

Australians   While most Australians cordially dislike the English, the emotion is not reciprocated, if only because the English have not paused to think sufficiently long and clearly about their Antipodean cousins to take a view of them. The trouble with Englishmen or Poms, the Aussies claim, is that when they arrive down under they tend to whinge, swank and pong, three highly unattractive character faults if true. Australians who make the long trip to England on the other hand tend to be high achievers who thrive, rise and shine.

Ask an Englishman what the word Australian means to him, and he will think of entertainers like Rolf Harris and Barry Humphries, cricketers like Dennis Lillee and Greg Chappell, businessmen like Robert Holmes a'Court and Rupert Murdoch, and writers like Clive James and Germaine Greer. Clearly a good case could be made out against any Aussie on that list, but your average Englishman does not let a vague sense of the pervasive brashness that informs the sample congeal into a brooding race hatred.

Besides, much harmless amusement has been gained from collating the hideous Australian accent into a formal dialect called Strine ('Emma Chizzit' is not a newly discovered novel by Dickens but Strine for 'How much is it?'); and Englishmen nowadays will readily concede that it is an unpardonable canard to assume that all Aussies are descendants of the old convicts deported to penal servitude; they only sound as if they are.

Autumn   The quick of the English year, autumn never short-changes us as spring does. Here is Cyril Connolly*, apostle of autumn: 'Fallen leaves lying on grass in November sun bring more happiness than daffodils. Spring is a call to action, hence to disillusion, therefore is April called the cruellest month. Autumn is the mind's true spring.'

To all English politicians, publishers, schoolboys and soldiers autumn is the true start of the year; the time for new laws, new books, new terms, and new wars. When the crop is safely in, tanks may surely roll. The magnificent *Autumn Journal* of Louis MacNeice*, written in the false reprieve of 1938, perfectly catches the sense of foreboding mingled with the sweetness of the season: 'Today was a beautiful day, the sky was a brilliant / Blue for the first time for weeks and weeks / But posters flapping on the railings tell the fluttered / World that Hitler speaks, that Hitler speaks'.

Though the war is coming and the leaves are falling, the sap is rising. Connolly (what a debt we owe to our Anglo-Irish writers!) again expertly sums up: 'The creative moment of a writer comes with the autumn. The winter is the time for reading, revision, preparation of the soil; the spring for the thawing back to life; the summer is for the open air, for satiating the body with health and action, but from October to Christmas for the release of mental energy, the hard crown of the year.'

In the English country the trees put on a showbiz bezazz for us which only the North American fall can match: a dazzling spectrum from the terracotta of September through the gold and crimson of October to the deep purple of November. In these deep-freeze days, preparations for Yuletide pud and pies quicken. It is time for that weird English rite, the toasted crumpet*, made if possible on that indestructible English oddity, the open fire. It is the time for piss-ups and teach-ins, for launching new books and films on a generally uncaring world, for advertising bonanzas and winning football pools. It is a good moment for party conferences and a bad one for trade union militants as the chap on the shop floor begins to count the cost of Christmas.

It is the moment when the well-thumped football, tracing its sweet parabola in the rinsed sky, mirrors the soaring spirits of the young, and stirs the lees of forgotten delights in those who have hung up their boots. English air in autumn is ichor, and the buttered light, filtered through mist, gives the English that gift for allusion and ambiguity which their enemies call imprecision and deviousness. Autumn in England is not an incident. It is the quiddity of Englishness.

Baked Beans   Though they now seem as English as HP sauce* they are a totally American invention, based on a traditional New England recipe, and were slow to catch on over here. Indeed they began life in England as a delicacy sold by Fortnum and Mason*. At first they were far too expensive for the working man: in 1911 a 16 oz. can cost nine old pence or about three per cent of the average wage then. Gradually as their cost came down (to five old pence a pound in 1939) baked beans became a staple of English working-class life. The piece of pork which used to flavour each tin was left out because it was hard to come by in the last war, but in their vegetarian guise baked beans still prevail and today the Englishman packs away more of the flatulent fodder than any other race on earth (no less that 13 lb. per person each year). Like so many grand old English institutions, baked beans have recently found a potent new source of respectability: as a staple of the internationally famed high fibre 'F-Plan' diet.

Balls   In the sense of rubbish the word has been recorded for only a hundred years, while its logical concomitant, the 'balls-up', can be traced no further back than 1939, and 'balls-aching,' in the sense of boring, has not yet been dignified with an *OED* definition. In medieval English 'ball' was, among many other meanings, short for eyeball, with the result that generations of English schoolboys have been unable to take with the respect they deserve any lines of Shakespeare in which the ardent suitor rapturously claims that the image of his lady love is riding on his balls. In their straightforward slang sense of testicles one would have thought the word now had almost universal currency; it was not always so, and a BBC recording of a children's programme in which the young listeners are urged to throw their balls in the air is one of the most treasured in the entire archive. We must, however, grant to our American cousins the most memorable confusion over the handy monosyllable. Marilyn Monroe, after having been served matzo balls for Friday-night dinner for the third time at the house of her parents-in-law when married to Arthur Miller, inquired plaintively if there was not some other part of the matzo one could eat.

Bangers   'Give us a bash of the bangers and mash me muvver used to make' sang Peter Sellers famously if ungratefully to Sophia Loren. He was tired of the constant diet of canelloni and macaroni on which she was feeding him in the song, just as in reality English secretaries in New York grow weary of a steady diet of frankfurters and hamburgers and implore visitors from home to include in their luggage a pound of good old British sausages*. It is an English predilection, dating certainly from Roman times (the *salsicia,* which came fresh, dry, or smoked), and much fortified by the house of Hanover's residual weakness for the *Wurst* of their original homeland. Queen Victoria herself ordained that the royal banger was to be chopped, not minced, and that the sausage skins should be filled by hand through a funnel. George V always included well-grilled sausages in his breakfasts and his granddaughter's subjects currently put away six billion a year.

Bank of England   For over three hundred years now – it opened its doors on 1 August 1694 – it has played a central part in the life of the country and the imagination of its inhabitants. To be as safe as the Bank of England was the ultimate index of total, copper-bottomed, unassailable reliability. The passage of the centuries and the attrition of the politicians may have worn the phrase a touch thin; but the Old Lady of Threadneedle Street (as she has been known since the cartoonist James Gillroy depicted her thus in 1797) can still show her wiles. Her life-saving operation to rescue Slater-Walker, for example, drew unqualified admiration from, *inter alia,* the Deutsche Bundesbank, whose bureau-cratic regulations would not have permitted such a dashing rescue.

The Bank's independence was formally ended when the Labour party nationalised it in 1946. The effect was not immediate; but over the next four decades the Bank has subtly lost its erstwhile sway over the nation's finances. Nevertheless, more than one post-war government has had reason to be grateful to the Bank for whistling up billions of foreign currency to shore up the pound during the series of sterling crises which cropped up monotonously for the first thirty years after the Second World War. At one such crisis, the then governor, Lord Cromer, jotted down the list of those he would call on for support round the world on the back of an old envelope. By such casual, even seemingly amateurish modes the Bank of England still commands wide respect in the world market-place.

The governor, moreover, can still act as a handy balance between warring ministers: most recently intervening in the row between the Prime Minister, Margaret Thatcher, and the Chancellor of the Exchequer, Nigel Lawson. On this occasion he came down on Maggie's side, arguing that the fight against inflation must take precedence over keeping the pound stable abroad. It was a far cry from the time when Britain fought the Second World War for nearly six years on a fixed bank rate of 2 per cent and a fixed exchange rate of 4.02 dollars to the pound: a tribute to the country – and its Bank.

Barmaid   Whereas in America it has traditionally been a man who has been on the receiving end of the drinker's problems ('set 'em up Joe) in England women have served behind bars for centuries. The word barmaid therefore has an immediate connotation for every Englishman. He sees an amply-bosomed lady of uncertain years, her girth increased by many years of pulling pints of bitter; worldly, humorous, cynical and unshockable. Perhaps she is no better than she ought to be; but most of the saucy talk and amorous proposals she received will be as the froth on the pints she pulls.

The greatest barmaid in English fiction is surely Rosie Driffield in Somerset Maugham's* *Cakes and Ale*. Nowhere in his *oeuvre* does the old crosspatch achieve such a marvellously rounded, human, fallible and female character as he does here. Rosie is the first wife of Edward Driffield, for whose portrait Thomas Hardy (see *Wessex*) undoubtedly sat. The narrator (a look-alike for Maugham himself) meets the Driffields by chance as a boy, and falls in love with Rosie. 'Her breasts were straight and firm and they stood out from the chest as though carved in marble. It was a body made for the act of love. In the light of the candle ...' and so on.

This is the English barmaid at her most lovable and endearing. Quite different, but equally recognisable, is the hoity-toity barmaid so marvellously realised by Joyce Carey in Noël Coward's* film *Brief Encounter*, where her decorous dalliance with stationmaster Stanley Holloway forms a hilarious backdrop to the bourgeois agonisings of

Trevor Howard and Celia Johnson. None of the quartet would quite convince nowadays, but the English barmaid lives on. Today, though, she is quite likely to be an Australian 'Sheila' doing her European grand tour and pulling a few pints on the side.

Bath A scoop of pure honey set in a green bowl, Bath was never intended for anything but pleasure, and has indulged its destiny with style. A stunningly cosmopolitan Roman city, it received visitors two thousand years ago from Chartres, Trier, and Metz; we know, because they left their names in the stone. The Romans saw at once the point of the magical hot springs that gush from the volcanic innards of the earth at the steady rate of a quarter of a million gallons a day and a constant temperature of 46.5 degrees. Over this they built a marvellously sophisticated palazzo for urban diversions: swimming pools, saunas, massage rooms, colonnades for gossip, shops and gyms, sculptures, mosaics and paintings. (The central heating system is far more advanced than anything built subsequently until modern times.) Few stories are more exciting than that of how Roman Bath or *Aquae Sulis* was rediscovered, and is still be unearthed.

From the time when the Romans went till the era when Queen Anne came to take the healing waters, more than a thousand dark years intervened. Then three ill-assorted men of genius – showman Richard (Beau) Nash, who drew up the rules for the conduct of polite society, entrepreneur Ralph Allen, who saw the value of the pale freestone despised since the Romans went, and architect John Wood, who used it to create a graceful and airy miracle of Palladian grandeur – combined to make Bath the focus of the age of elegance. Samuel Pepys took the waters here, and Jane Austen bought bonnets for the ballroom; Hester Thrale came here to escape the tyranny of Samuel Johnson*, and in our own era Cyril Connolly* took cover in Bath to escape the rigours of life in London.

It is still a small city, best seen on foot. With its international music festival, its royal agricultural show, its gorgeously refurbished Regency theatre in cobalt, white and gold, its arcades and crescents, it remains a Georgian city built on Roman foundations, still savouring the accreted delights of the slow centuries while folded into a time-warp in the Somerset hills. One last claim to fame: it is the one English city whose name no American can pronounce.

BBC At a casual glance the Englishman might well be forgiven for deciding that he has not had much of a look-in at the British Broadcasting Corporation, dominated as it has been by a succession of Scottish goers (John Reith, Alasdair Milne), Welsh wizards (Wynford Vaughan-Thomas, Huw Wheldon), and Irish leprechauns (Terry Wogan, Frank Delaney). Yet some doughty English names (Dimbleby, Day, Parkinson, Robinson) have surfaced amid all the Celtic fizz. The subject is so vast, the issues so enormous, that a couple of thoughts only in this ambit must suffice. Nobody wanted the BBC to be born; the press was hostile (for self-regarding reasons that proved invalid); people, it was urged, would cease to read and think.

Yet once under way, the titanic power of the medium was quickly seen, and it was a tall (6 feet 6 inches), lean, dour, war-scarred, God-directed, thirty-four-year-old Aberdonian engineer who was given the first chance to aim that great gusher. John Reith had posted his letter of application in his club before looking up the man to whom he was applying (Sir William Noble) in *Who's Who*. Seeing Noble was a fellow Aberdonian, he retrieved his letter from the club post box, opened it, and added a footnote: 'I think you know my people ...' In truth, no other applicant had Reith's Messianic vision, and though his sixteen-year reign could easily be criticised and was (announcers had to wear dinner jackets when giving the news), perhaps in retrospect it was better that the BBC should start bland but not bent.

Reith maintained his precarious independence during the General Strike of 1926 – but only just, and in effect took the government side. Again, with the coming of war there was an obvious clash of principle between telling the truth and needing to win. The BBC got over that huge hurdle bloody but unbowed and showed its independence in the Falklands* affair by having its camera crews and reporters in Buenos Aires throughout the hostilities.

Throughout the swinging sixties it had a necessary dose of liberalism under Hugh Carleton Greene, but fell foul of Harold Wilson who decided to teach it a lesson by moving Charles Hill, formerly the 'Radio Doctor', from being chairman of the ITA to chairman of the BBC. The BBC smiled through its tears.

The coming of independent broadcasting was a huge shot in the arm, giving the BBC a sparring partner after the years of monopolistic torpor, and forcing it to hone its skills till they were clearly world-class. Still, the charge of political bias remains. The right is convinced that the BBC is full of left-wing activists; the left, that it lost the last four elections because of broadcasting's right-wing bias. The problem is unlikely to go away, and the BBC still badly needs minders like Reith and Greene; though preferably not at the same time.

The battle will manifestly be fought first and foremost for the small square screen: what the Australian jokesmith Clive James arrestingly dubbed the crystal bucket. Increasingly it has become clear that whoever controls the cathode ray controls the hearts and minds of the people it purports to serve, but in truth sways. The opportunities offered by the gift of television to mankind are matched only by its dangers. This evident axiom has been firmly grasped by one or two of the principal television tribunes.

'The instinctive reaction of politicians to the dangers of television', wrote Robin Day in 1961, 'is to think in terms of restrictions, controls, limitations, when what is needed is freedom, diversity, and independence ... During the next quarter of a century let us *distribute* the power of television, so that in 1984 it will not be an Orwellian instrument of mass hypnosis, but will have long been built into a broad and open platform of democratic opinion.'

So how has it all worked out? No mass *hypnosis* perhaps; though to the charge of mass *narcosis* there may not be such a ready answer. Manifestly there are pools of excellence in British television and the admirable *Question Time* is one, but even here the eternal vigilance is the customary price of liberty, and recently the team have had to tighten their grip on the selection of studio audiences to prevent the incursion of pressure groups. While anyone eccentric enough to think any other country's television better than British should be locked up in his hotel bedroom in New York, Zurich, Bombay or Tokyo until he sees the error of his ways, the heartbeat of excellence is uncertain.

The Beatles On Thursday, 9 November 1961, a soberly dressed businessman of twenty-seven went to a lunchtime performance at a dank dungeon in Liverpool called the Cavern. Someone had asked for a record the previous Saturday, and it was the policy of his record shop always to supply customers' requests, however obscure. This time, it had been for a new release by a group called The Beatles. What Brian Epstein saw transfixed him. It was not the music that moved him; though he was shrewd enough to see its effect on the audience. He was an opera buff and devotee of the Liverpool Philharmonic. No, what transfixed him were the four slim, leather-clad, sweat-drenched male shapes. He was a homosexual, and they looked uncannily like figures in his private fantasy world. A few days later he was their manager, and a legend was about to be born. Nowadays a Beatles song manuscript, if original, is worth between £3,000 and £10,000. One of their letters fetches £1,000. John Lennon's psychedelic Rolls-Royce was sold at auction by Sotheby's in 1985 for £1,768,000. They wrote 150 songs, often melancholy, always haunting, that are now part of the collective folk memory. Serious music critics added their accolades to all the others. William Mann of *The Times* noted their pandiatonic clusters and flat sub-mediant key switches. Tony Palmer of the *Observer* called them the greatest songwriters since Schubert; and perhaps they were.

Beaverbrook (1879–1964)   To English intellectuals, Max Aitken was evil incarnate: if not the devil himself, then assuredly one of his imps. Mischief was his business, gossip his pabulum, ink the ichor that flowed in his veins. We still know very little about the financial legerdemain that made him a millionaire before he was thirty; it may not stand too close scrutiny. He regarded himself as a political failure, though his part in the downfall of Asquith in 1916 was crucial. He was a trusted henchman of Churchill's in the Second World War, got the planes built, and could wheel and deal with the Russians on level, or rather equally twisting, terms. He fought all his life for imperial preference, not surely an infamous aim so much as an impractical one.

To push this cause, he bought the *Daily Express* from a Bovril tycoon for £17,000, and got the *Evening Standard* for nothing. It was a sweetener from Rothermere for diddling the dying Edward Hulton into thinking it was not Rothermere but Max who was buying his papers. Max proved a wizard at making popular newspapers. In this he was aided by master craftsmen like editors Blumenfeld and Christiansen, left-wing artists like Low and Vicky (who were given total freedom) and leftish writers like Michael Foot, Aneurin Bevan, Alan Taylor and Harold Nicolson, many of whom, against the run of the play, became lifelong buddies. The interaction between Beaverbrook and his acolytes provided Fleet Street with an unending stream of uproarious stories, for the little gnome with the Canadian accent and prayerbook vernacular was incapable of stringing two dull sentences together.

His speech at the great dinner given by Roy Thomson to celebrate his eighty-fifth birthday was an astonishing *tour de force*. He was dying – indeed had only two weeks to live – but got out of bed to make a titanic and cinematic exit. No Hollywood scriptwriter could have done it better. After reviewing his many apprenticeships – as financier, politician, newspaperman – he concluded that he would be starting a new apprenticeship 'some day soon'.

'He's a dear old bugger,' said one editor, puffing a cigar Beaverbrook had just given him, then added ruminatively, 'The accent is on the word bugger.' Now, though, some privately wish the old bugger were back.

Betjeman, Sir John (1906–84) It has been observed of Betjeman's work that it gives you the key to a lost past which you will instantly recognise *even if you were never there*. Few key words in the lumber room of every Englishman's mind (Ovaltine, Sturmey-Archer bicycles, Home and Colonial stores) are not memorably embedded in his work.
His inimitable artifice has transmuted these folk memories into art.
His skill was a rare one: critical acclaim coupled with best-sellerdom. Every line thumpingly clear: there are no tangled nets in Betjeman. Nevertheless the key is by no means always C major: darkness often obtrudes: and sometimes despair itself beats time to his music. There have been many essentially English poets before Betjeman and many who hymned England: none ever caught the charisma of the humdrum quite so expertly. Betjeman sees glints of the eternal in the ordinary. Open him anywhere, and his idiosyncratic magic leaps from the page: 'Oh! Fuller's angel-cake, Robertson's marmalade, / Liberty lampshades, come shine on us all.'

Betjeman is the apostle of childhood: 'Then what sardines in the half-lighted passages! / Locking of fingers in long hide and seek', but also the weed in need of an earth mother: 'You will protect me, my silken Myfanwy / Ringleader, tom-boy, and chum to the weak.' The conde-scending suggestion that Betjeman is a good bad poet is at once refuted by scores of marvellous lines that continue to chime in the mind. 'When Boris used to call in his Sedanca / When Teddy took me down to his estate / When my nose excited passion / When my clothes were in the fashion / When my beaux were never cross if I was late.'

Though Betjeman saw himself as a serious poet (and was right in his perception) the laughter is never too far away: 'At sundown on my tricycle / I tour the Borough's edge / and icy as an icicle / see bicycle on bicycle / stacked waiting in the hedge.' He is, too, a trenchant chronicler of the sensual thrall: 'Oh whip the dogs away my Lord / They make me ill with lust / Bend bare knees down to pray my Lord / Teach sulky lips to say my Lord / That flaxen hair is dust.' Though he can sometimes tremble on the edge of sentiment ('Oh little body do not die') he is more often astringently hard-nosed ('Come friendly bombs and fall on Slough').

He was fortunate in his time (coeval of Auden*, taught by Eliot, protégé of Bowra) and in his destiny. He was champion of the Church of England*, vindicator of Victorian architecture, staunch defender of stations, follies and piers*. He was besides a broadcaster of true class:

funny, gentle, unexpected, and right. His disasters were, *sub specie aeternitatis,* all little ones. 'Fourth generation, John', his father reminded him in a homily on the family business, 'They'll look to you / They're artist craftsmen to their finger-tips ... Go on creating beauty.'

That kind of beauty Betjeman was congenitally unable to conjure. Another kind, though, he could and did: 'Red hair she had and golden skin / her sulky lips were shaped for sin / Her sturdy legs were flannel slack'd / The strongest legs in Pontefract.' A song of songs, which is Betjeman's!

Big Ben   Originally the Great Bell of Westminster; now the bell, clock, and St Stephen's Tower of the Houses of Parliament. No-one seems to know quite how it got its name. One theory holds that it was named after Sir Benjamin Hall, the outsize Commissioner of Works when it was being made; another, that it is named after the celebrated boxer Benjamin Caunt, an eighteen-stone publican who had just fought an epic sixty rounds with Nathaniel Langham. It first tolled the time in 1859, but was found to be cracked after only a few months; a seven hundredweight hammer had been fitted although a four hundredweight maximum had been stipulated. Famed for its accuracy, the great clock was found to be only one and a half seconds out even after the House of Commons was destroyed in an air raid in 1941 and its face shattered. In 1986 it stopped at 3.45 a.m.; the shaft of the fly fan had fractured. Metal fatigue was diagnosed. The nation – indeed the world – mourned. Get well cards poured in from places as distant as Manhattan and Oporto. Happily Big Ben is now restored, and government engineers say it should remain accurate for at least the next two hundred years. It is, however, still slightly out of tune, but that makes it instantly recognisable world wide. While the sonorous chimes of Big Ben still resound, the Englishman instinctively feels that all's right with the world.

Bird   Another of those oscillating, many-faceted words that show the riotous growth of the language most vividly. As slang for a girl it was much in favour in the thirties, then seemed to falter and fail; but something or somebody brought it back into favour and by the sixties it was about as if it had never been away, and is now more worked than ever. Bird is doubly interesting because of the load it carries on one slim line: not only slang for a young female person, but also for a man, particularly a slightly odd one, as in 'queer bird' or 'old bird'; then again a much favoured term for a prison sentence – 'he's doing bird'; then again, imported from America, a term of derision in 'strictly for the birds'. As if these multifarious uses were not enough, it is still used for the thumbs down in the theatre, learnedly derived (though who remembers?) from *The Birds* of Aristophanes. First and foremost, though, it now conveys to any Englishman a piece of crumpet*.

Birmingham   'One has no great hopes from Birmingham. I always say there is something direful in the sound.' So thought Mrs Elton in Jane Austen's *Emma*. Others have found it more inspiring. When William Hutton, later historian of Birmingham, first went there in 1741, he found a vivacity he had never seen before: 'I had been among dreamers, but now I saw men awake.' What he was in fact seeing was the quick forge in which the Industrial Revolution was made. Many people have thrived in Birmingham, rightly dubbed the city of a thousand trades, but it proved especially fertile for a small clutch of men touched with genius: John Baskerville, the printer; Joseph Priestley, discoverer of oxygen; William Murdoch, inventor of gas lighting; James Watt, maker of the double action steam engine, and his partner, the industrialist Matthew Boulton, who provided to the edge of bankruptcy the capital Watt needed and, just as importantly, the moral support to save him from his own self-doubt.

The tone of Birmingham had long been free-thinking or dissenting, and its most famous son, Joseph Chamberlain, was a pillar of the Unitarian church. When he became mayor in 1873 he claimed that 'in twelve months' time, by God's help, the town shall not know itself'. He was as good as his word. By 1890 an American visitor was able to claim without hyperbole that Birmingham was the best governed city in the world. It gave England its first secondary school, its first children's court, its first municipal bank, and its first municipal orchestra. It was also to have the first workers' model village, Bournville, built by the Cadbury Chocolate family, four miles outside town. It was at Birmingham in 1900 that the first performance of *The Dream of Gerontius* by Edward Elgar* was given, and here that J.R.R. Tolkien, creator of the Hobbits, was educated. As befits a city only forty minutes from Stratford, the library houses the largest Shakespeare collection outside America, with 50,000 items in ninety languages.

Birmingham has always been a risk city, and even the very nature of the metal-based products it traditionally made put it most in peril when the great recessions of the seventies and eighties broke. Birmingham has reacted to the challenge with traditional vim. It is no longer over-dependent on cars and engineering, but has diversified into exhibitions, conventions, business tourism, high tech and communications. The National Exhibition Centre, a monument to civic enterprise, now houses some 80 per cent of the nation's exhibitions and an International Convention Centre was opened by the Queen in 1991. Aston Science Park, designed to test the high-tech ideas of budding entrepreneurs and make them marketable, opened in 1983 and goes from strength to strength.

'Next week-end it is likely in the heart's funfair we shall pull / Strong enough on the handle to get back our money; or at any rate it is possible.' So wrote the poet Louis MacNeice*, who taught classics at Birmingham University from 1930 to 1936. At first he found the place a rude culture shock after Oxford; later, he was to make a group of good and gifted friends there: the writer Walter Allen; the poet Henry Reed; the BBC* producer R.D. Smith. MacNeice's early poems contain many lines redolent of his Birmingham years: 'Tonight is so coarse with chocolate / The wind blowing from Bournville.'

Today Cadbury's has had to rationalise the hundreds of chocolate lines it once made; the old BSA motorcycle factory at Small Heath has been bulldozed; the factory where the Austin Seven was made is now a fraction of its former self. New industries like British Telecom have taken their place; and new metals like titanium, zirconium, and niobium. Not for nothing are there now thirty Birminghams; twenty-two of them in America and one out in space – there is even a Birmingham crater on the moon.

Black Pudding To southern eyes, there is something mysterious, even sinister, about the northerner's black pudding. What exactly *is* it, for a start? The answer does little to inspire your average southerner either. For the black pudding is no more than pig's blood, pearl barley, and diced pork fat stuffed into a sausage skin with marjoram, thyme, sage, spices, salt, pepper and onion. It sounds disgusting, but is in truth delicious. It was the traditional staple of Lancashire housewives on Monday washdays and still is. A rich crop of yarns has accreted round the curious artefact: that it was invented by a Lancashire wrestler (false) that its natural colour is white (true – it has to be dyed black); that it is eaten raw (false – it is cooked for two hours before it is sold); that a basket leaves Bury, capital city of the black pudding, for Harley Street where its therapeutic qualities are well understood (just possible). Beyond question, though, the black pudding is gaining ground south of the Wash, particularly at Christmas time, when people have time to contemplate those fried breakfasts of which it forms such a beguiling part. Though one of the oldest dishes in the world, and known throughout Europe (*boudin* in France, *sanguinaccio* in Italy, *palt* in Sweden, *morcilla* in

Spain, *Blutwurst* in Germany), there are still southerners in England who give it up overnight when they learn what's in it.

Blackberries These are the most common of all English fruit and to go blackberrying or brambling has been one of the most universal treats for English children over countless generations. The blackberry is perhaps the best example of a free fruit: delicious ripe and raw in summer, bottled as blackberry and apple jam or just bottled on its own. The time to pick blackberries is between the beginning of the school summer holidays and the end of September: no later, according to the old country superstition, or the devil will spit on them. Nowadays it is not exactly that the devil has done that, but that hedgerows grow daily more scant and regulated and the blackberries in them rarer and rarer. What was once the largesse of the countryside is becoming a scarce resource.

Blackpool The capital of the old working class. No other town in England glories quite so unashamedly in its plebeian pleasures. 'Blackpool,' says the town brochure, 'is fish and chips and football. Hot dogs and hamburgers and hotels. Juke boxes and jokes and jeans. Pubs and pints and piers* and Punch and Judy.' But we have the picture; and it is hard to believe that eighteenth-century Blackpool was an upper-class resort. Gentlemen found on the beach when the ladies were bathing were fined a bottle of wine.

Not any more, though. The coming of the railway in 1846 changed all that, though it is interesting that Blackpool still needed entrepreneurs with vision to pull it out of various tight corners thereafter. Thus when the development plans nearly foundered in the 1840s for lack of capital, the situation was saved by the notion of cheap excursion trains from industrial Lancashire*. Trippers flooded in. They still do. Again in the 1870s the Central Pier was revivified when open-air dancing for the working classes was introduced; the gentry still promenaded on the North Pier in the evenings.

In the 1890s the town got another shot in the arm when a group of businessmen took what many thought a reckless decision and built the Tower in imitation of the Eiffel in Paris. That iron monster still pays fat dividends, containing as it does the gigantic Tower Ballroom, the Circus, Aquarium, and Mighty Wurlitzer. In an audio-visual age, the Illuminations, with their 375,000 electric light bulbs and fifty miles of festoon, might seem unsophisticated fare. Not so: eight million people still come to see them.

The traditional Blackpool landlady, who according to northern mythology used to sleep two shifts of lodgers in the same bed, is giving way to the self-catering flat, and few will grieve. The many thousands of mill girls who used to invade Blackpool for their annual Wakes Week holidays may now be off to the Costa Brava on the backs of their blokes' bikes: but comedians still pack them in at the Grand. That's Entertainment – in Blackpool anyway.

Bloomsbury   The four Stephen children moved to 46 Gordon Square, London WC1 in 1904. Their widowed father, Sir Leslie Stephen, editor of the *Dictionary of National Biography*, had died after a long and distressing illness and they were now orphans. Thoby Stephen, his eldest son, a massive, charming, masculine and humorous hero-figure, died suddenly and tragically of typhoid in 1907, but before he did so had acted as the vital link between his clever Cambridge friends – Lytton Strachey, Leonard Woolf, Clive Bell, Desmond Macarthy, all four to become distinguished writers – and his two beautiful sisters, Virginia and Vanessa. Thoby was 'At Home' each Thursday evening, and people dropped in from ten o'clock till midnight, were regaled with whisky, cocoa, and buns, and often stayed till two or three in the morning. When Vanessa married Clive Bell in 1907, Virginia and Adrian, the younger Stephen brother, moved to Bernard Shaw's old house at 29 Fitzroy Square, and these two addresses were to be the axes of the Bloomsbury Group. Virginia married Leonard on his return from Burma in 1912 ('I've got a confession to make,' she wrote to her friend Violet Dickinson. 'I'm going to marry Leonard Woolf. He's a penniless Jew. I'm more happy than anyone ever said was possible.')

The high summer of Bloomsbury spans the years 1907–1914, though in a sense it continued to spread its unplanned influence till well into the twenties. Stephen Spender*, who knew the Woolfs as a young left-wing poet between the wars, differentiated between the old Bloomsbury and the new; but essentially the properties of each were the same: a respect for truth, however embarassing the consequences; a love of beauty; a passion for ancient Greece; a distaste for material values (but at the same time a practical insistence on enough money to be independent – what Virginia Woolf called £500 a year and a room of one's own); liberal, verging on socialist, politics; agnostic beliefs and pacifist principles; a reverence for France and in particular for French Impressionist painting; a high regard for personal relationships, coupled with a penchant for free love (Michael Holroyd's revelations about the Bloomsbury sexual merry-go-round when he published his two-volume life of Lytton

Strachey in 1967 and 1968 caused a sensation).

Later key Bloomsberries (as they were called) were the novelist E.M. Forster, painters Roger Fry and Duncan Grant, and Maynard Keynes*. Most members of the Bloomsbury Group had been at one or other of two Cambridge colleges, King's and Trinity; many were members of the Apostles, an elite Cambridge secret society; and a number either were or became members of the Strachey and Stephen families. They have been criticised for their clannish aloofness and emotional aridity; but their achievements speak for themselves. They must have been daunting to know. It was their custom never to smile on being introduced; and once when Lytton's mother, Lady Strachey, came to tea with Vanessa at Gordon Square, Hans, the Stephens' dog, made a large mess on the floor. Neither lady mentioned it. The Bloomsbury revolt from Victorian values was not as thorough-going as all that.

The Boat Race   Not the least of the frivolities spawned by the river Thames* the Boat Race, on the face of it the most boring and predictable of races, in the upshot seldom fails to provide some absurd drama. Both crews have sunk during the race, and in the 130th encounter in March 1984 Cambridge were effectively scuppered before the race began when their tiny cox rowed them in practice flat out into a moored German barge under Putney Bridge.

The race was rowed next day, the first of the 134 contests ever to be held on a Sunday. It was, as it turned out, the fastest ever, with both teams beating the fastest previous time and Oxford prevailing. The score now stands at 73 Cambridge wins to 68 for Oxford, with the 1877 race standing as an equivocal 'dead heat to Oxford by five feet'.

Though Africa is no longer as it once was, a country of blacks ruled by blues, the Church of England have long swung together. The first race in 1829 could boast a future bishop of St Andrews, Deans of Lincoln and Repton, and a prebendary of York in the Oxford boat; bishops of New Zealand and Lichfield, a dean of Ely, and a chancellor of the Diocese of Manchester in the Cambridge boat.

Even forty years ago, future bishops of Chichester, Gloucester and Lichfield were all rowing blues. Nowadays, however, your typical young man in the blue boat is more likely to be a scientist with a first degree already behind him in metallurgy or biochemistry. He is also likely to be six feet three and a little under fourteen stone. Again, though roughly a third of all rowing blues have been Etonians, the eighteen young men who took part in the 1984 boat race included seven born abroad: three Canadians, two Americans and two Australians. In 1988

Oxford's president and stroke were again American. Yet even in 1988, one Etonian, R.S.N. Ames, was still gallantly making sure that Cambridge were steady from stroke to bow by rowing at bow himself.

Book Collecting   An archetypally English mania. Needless to say, there are eminent American collectors, and bibliomaniacs span the world from Mexico to Japan and Argentina to Iran. Yet no other nation can produce a book collector on quite the heroic scale of Sir Thomas Phillipps (1792–1872), who in fifty years amassed the greatest private library the world has ever seen, spending on it some £250,000 (add two noughts for inflation). Since 1886 – repeat, 1886 – Sotheby's steadily sold that vast treasure house at auction and completed the task only in 1981.

No other nation can produce a book forger (only a bibliomaniac after all, with his moral machinery out of kilter) on quite such a grand scale as Thomas Wise, who fooled the world of books with his prodigious skills for half a century, was given an honorary degree at Oxford, and died in 1937 without having ever been charged with an offence. Few other nations can produce such dedicated book loonies as the contemporary savant Bernard Levin, who has been advised that should he ever be rash enough to display on shelves the tons of books he has amassed even so far, he would assuredly bring the walls of his London apartment crashing about his ears.

The bibliomaniac is well answered by the English bookseller, since the day when Samuel Johnson's* father Michael set up his stall in Lichfield, a travelling question-and-answer man, prepared to try to help his customers in all sorts of unexpected ways. 'The phrase antiquarian bookseller scares me somewhat as I equate antique with expensive,' wrote Helene Hanff to Marks and Co. on 5 October 1949, so opening a riveting correspondence that was to last twenty years and become the raw material for a best-selling book, then play: *84 Charing Cross Road.* Scared or no, she sent off her first list, no one book to exceed five dollars, and got a letter back three weeks later with two-thirds of her problems solved, the rest being worked on.

It is the idiosyncratic spell of the mania that a collector will be far more concerned about the ache of missing a long-sought book than distressed about its price. Indeed the price is often only of the most academic interest, since the collector has no intention of selling. Occasionally, of course, he will get a glimpse of what his books are worth. A copy of Ian Fleming's first novel *Casino Royale* – signed to his secretary but no more antique than 1953 – was knocked down at Sotheby's for £2,500. On balance, we should reserve our pity not for the bibliomane but for his wife, who must find space to accommodate his ever-swelling plunder and tolerate his irrational forays in quest of new treasure. One of these unfortunate women has confessed to having sat knitting outside every bookshop in Europe.

Bournemouth   'A hundred years ago there was no Bournemouth,' wrote Brian Vesey-Fitzgerald in his 1949 history of Hampshire* (in fact it already had two hotels). Its story, he added, was 'a romance of big business, but it will never be history, unless it be the history of a ruined coast-line'. You would be lucky, he claimed, to hear a Hampshire voice in it, 'though you will hear plenty of Lancashire and Birmingham, for it is the ambition of most businessmen in the Midlands and north to settle here when they have made enough brass ... It can be dismissed from any book about Hampshire.'

In Thomas Hardy's Wessex it is renamed Sandbourne: 'Like a fairy palace,' he says in *Tess of the D'Urbervilles*, 'suddenly created by the stroke of a wand, and allowed to get a little dusty.' He too, though, regrets the coastline on which it is built, with its prehistoric soil and ancient trackways: 'Not a sod having been turned there since the time of the Caesars.'

On the face of it, then, a boring and inimical place, over which hangs one fascinating question: how did it get there? In 1810 it was a tavern and a few cottages at the mouth of the Bourne, a haunt for smugglers and wildfowl hunters; but in that year a landowner called Tregonwell built a villa there. It became the swanky Royal and Imperial Exeter Hotel, patronised by the empress of Austria and other royal nobs. Edward VII built a house for Lily Langtry in Derby Road. The railway arrived in 1870. Birmingham now lay only five comfortable hours' travel away. Seven miles of sand and two thousand acres of pines lent Bournemouth a luxuriant, balmy, feminine torpor: it is, concluded John Betjeman*, one of the few English towns it is safe to call 'she'. Doctors recommended it for convalescence. 'In no other town,' said a 1908 guide book, 'is the now familiar dress of a nurse so frequently seen.'

While the great, gritty cities of Manchester*, Bolton, Blackburn and Wigan declined between 1911 and 1951, languid, genteel towns like Bournemouth doubled their numbers. Nothing much seemed to happen there; though it was from Bournemouth in 1940 that the Labour Party conference sent word that they would back a Churchill government. The place riveted a young writer called Cyril Connolly* who painted a haunting picture of the Branksome Towers Hotel near there in *The Unquiet Grave*: 'Steamy tropical atmosphere ... led by chance to discover the hanging foot bridge over Alum Chine. Walking over the quivering planks I felt rooted, as in a nightmare ... What a place to make away with oneself or some loved one!'

His book was published in 1944. Two years later the sadistic psychopath, Neville Heath, murdered twenty-one-year-old Doreen Marshall. Police discovered her body one hundred yards down the hill from the Branksome Towers Hotel.

Bread   One of the very few foods that was not rationed in the 1939–45 war. It may have been sad stuff, grey, grimy, coarse and bland; but at least you could eat as much of it as you liked to fill yourself up. When therefore bread was rationed in the austere imperatives of postwar Britain, it seemed to the British people the unkindest cut of all. Yet bread has made a dramatic comeback, and today will stand up to the best in the world, whether made as split tin, granary loaf, tin twist, notched brick or wholemeal cob. The Englishman has moreover become fond of a whole range of exotic breads introduced to him by the ethnic minorities who now share his country with him: Polish rye, German pumpernickel, French baguettes, Jewish chola plait, Irish barmbrack and Welsh bara brith. The upshot is that your average Englishman now has a range of breads at his disposal far richer than those on offer to his continental neighbours.

Bread and Butter Letter   A staple of middle-class life, the written thank-you for bed and board is slowly being transmuted to the bread and butter card, especially by the young and particularly if they can find a Victorian postcard. It is usually (but not always) written by female guest to female host and, if thanks for dinner, will praise food, booze, and company, usually in that order and not always quite seriously: 'Henry was not totally sober for two days afterwards'. (See page 10.)

Breakfast   Though the English cannot truthfully be said to have invented breakfast, they certainly gave the world the English breakfast, that noble dish of eggs and bacon which Somerset Maugham* once said should be eaten three times a day when one was in England. The fact is that very few Englishmen – and fewer Englishwomen – have time for the full gubbins on working days, usually settling for the ubiquitous breakfast foods invented in America, and sometimes for no more than a cup of tea or coffee. Still, the memory of vast breakfasts taken from groaning sideboards in country houses haunts the collective subconscious of the English, most of whom have got no nearer to the grilled kidneys than the one-and-nines at an old Ealing* comedy.

Similarly, though few Englishmen have had much to do with kedgeree, faint resonances of the imperial Raj convince him that he has, and he will order it with confidence and indeed nostalgia on holiday and especially afloat. The English will to breakfast well is most graphically expressed by British trains, which persist in serving up a monstrous meal with a garnish of sausages*, tomatoes, mushrooms, potatoes and fried bread added to the basic bacon and eggs at a price which seems to escalate weekly. Though it is manifestly the sort of meal that by rights should lay most folk out for the day, many Englishmen and their memsahibs seem to lash into it on trains and survive without evident dyspepsia.

It is a meal designed for silence, and is properly celebrated in gentlemen's clubs where a stand on the table holds the member's *Times** at the right angle as he meditatively tucks in. The improbable notion that an Englishman could be made to eat his breakfast and watch TV at the same time like an American led to the uncertain start of breakfast television here, but it is now catching on. Is nothing sacred?

Brighton Try as one may to stress the cultural and historical role of the place – the Prince Regent and the Pavilion, Thackeray and the Thrales, Pinky's patch in Graham Greene's great novel *Brighton Rock* – it still conveys one overwhelmingly powerful image to your average Englishman: the dirty weekend. The end of the road for Genevieve in a vastly successful Pinewood comedy, it is a town eminently suited to irregular sexual congress with its sugar-cake hotels, regency terraces, handy racecourse and raffish pier. The place seems positively to thrum with oysters and ozone. There is only one snag in this endearing cameo: the English increasingly fail to see anything improper in a weekend for two people who are not legally married to each other. The town has recently reacted to this new style by promoting the dirty weekend as a tourist attraction. But without the illicit flavouring it will never have quite the same tang.

British Beef *Rosbif,* warns the latest Oxford Hachette French dictionary, means an Englishman but is *injur* or offensive. Not to the average Englishman, who despite all the alarms regards roast beef as his birthright; as a metaphor, indeed, for his Englishness. 'On Sunday we had roast beef' wrote the food writer Arabella Boxer of her 1930s childhood. 'My father was an expert carver, and gave each person a thickish slice of undercut, with one or two thinner slices of sirloin. For the next two or three days we ate cold roast beef, rather rare; this was our favourite food.' Most English families could mirror that experience though their cut may not have been so upmarket nor its cooking so rare. Mad cow disease panic has slashed our beef exports; home sales much less dramatically. Shoppers rushed out to buy bargains as beef prices fell; some English hotels even noticed an increase in sales of roast beef Sunday lunches. And at the height of the crisis in March 1996, sales of farm land actually rose to a bouyant £3,000 an acre. The English will not give up their roast beef as easily as that. See also *Yorkshire pudding*.

The Brontës 'Her business is not half so much with the human heart as with the human eyes, mouth, hands, and feet,' wrote Charlotte Brontë (1816–1855) of Jane Austen*; 'what sees keenly, speaks aptly, moves flexibly, it suits her to study; but what throbs fast and full, though hidden, what the blood rushes through, what is the unseen seat of Life and the sentient target of death – this Miss Austen ignores ... If this is heresy I cannot help it.'

Indeed not, for the difference between reading Jane and Charlotte is like that between taking a small sip of madeira and taking a large slug of brandy. What throbs fast and full is what the Brontës are about; three astonishingly gifted sisters whose father relieved his feelings by firing pistols from the back door, and whose brother Branwell was sacked from his job as a railway clerk because of culpable negligence, took to opium and died of consumption. Anne Brontë (1820–1849) wrote *Agnes Grey* and was well called by George Moore a sort of literary Cinderella; Charlotte Brontë wrote *Jane Eyre* and, said G.K. Chesterton, 'Showed that abysses may exist inside a government and eternities inside a manufacturer'; Emily Brontë (1818–1848) wrote *Wuthering Heights*, which was according to Dante Gabriel Rosetti, 'a fiend of a book, an incredible monster, combining all the stronger female tendencies ... The action is laid in Hell – only it seems places and people have English names there.'

Yet the most striking verdict on the Brontës was made by Muriel Spark. In summing up Branwell she wrote: 'The Brontë son did not fulfil his early promise; his great misfortune was that he was a man. If he had been constrained as were his sisters, by the spirit of the times; if he had been compelled, for want of other outlet, to take up his pen or else burst, he might have been known today as rather more than the profligate brother of the Brontës.'

The three Brontë sisters lived a hundred years before Women's Lib was born and are paradoxically the best of all arguments for and against it. For, in the sense that they showed how a woman can equal in power and passion the mind of any man; against, in the sense that they showed how little the rules need matter to a woman with a mind of her own.

Rupert Brooke (1887–1915) 'He is the handsomest man in England,' remarked W.B. Yeats in 1913, 'and he wears the most beautiful shirts.' Henry James, meeting him for the first time in 1909, inquired if her were a good poet. Told no, he said: 'Thank goodness. If he looked like that and was a good poet too, I don't know what I should do.' Virginia Woolf, on the other hand, thought his verse sounded like a barrel organ, and Cyril Connolly* imitated his Latin beak, Mcnaghten, reciting 'Grantchester': '... and hear the bweeze / Sobbing in ver little twees.' Still, Philip Larkin* printed six of Brooke's poems in his *Oxford Book of 20th Century Verse*, and 300,000 copies of his poems were sold in the first decade after his death. So somebody must like them.

He had to pay nine pounds to get his first poems published. It was dying that made him mythopoeic, and Winston Churchill* who set the ball rolling with his *Times* obituary. Interestingly, it was from Cambridge that the first voices were raised, protesting that this was not the man they knew; and within a month of his death. For his centenary in 1987, his old school, Rugby, decided to raise a fund to build a new statue of him. This was just as well. The nude bronze erected where he died on Skyros was said by Lady Diana Cooper to look like 'some ghastly advertisement in a German bugger journal'. He would have enjoyed that.

What did Brooke live on? He lived in Germany, crossed America, dallied in the South Seas. Yet until he became a Fellow of King's College, Cambridge in 1913, he never had a job. Nor did he exactly grow rich on his fellowship. His dividend – as King's call the money they pay their fellows – was around £68 for 1913, and about £60 for 1914. The answer was, of course, that he had an inherited private income; not a lot, but enough. It was death that put him in the big money.

Bullying One of the least attractive traits in the English character. The Poet Shelley was unmercifully bullied at Eton, the novelist Trollope at Harrow. And they were just two among many thousands. The tortures could take endless forms: roasting (as described in *Tom Brown's Schooldays*) or dowsing in water (as happened at Rugby too). The appalling 'tin gloves' ordeal was peculiar to Winchester, where small boys were made to hold burning brands to toughen their hands for fagging. Did these Victorian practices die out as the new century took over? Not so that you would notice it. John Mills, the actor, was so badly bullied at his school (Norwich) that he contemplated suicide. Happily, a kind friend of his older sister taught him ju-jitsu, and at the next encounter the bully was pinned to the floor in a full nelson and had his face banged to the floor till it bled. He was, moreover, sacked after a headmaster's enquiry. The trouble is, as Charles Lamb pointed out in his *Essays of Elia*, it is a popular fallacy to suppose that a bully is always a coward. The most notorious bully in English fiction, indeed, the same Flashman who was the terror of the fags in *Tom Brown's Schooldays*, has recently been transmuted in a brilliant series of novels by George Macdonald Fraser, to a hero, or at least an anti-hero.

Bumf   Short for bum–fodder, a word with an honourable pedigree stretching back now nearly a century, and meaning, first, lavatory paper, and more generally later any paper on which useless information is printed; nearly always government paper.

Bunter, Billy   In the safe enclosed world of Greyfriars School there are many more admirable characters than Bunter. Harry Wharton is more decent, Hurree Jamset Ram Singh more exotic, Linley more clever, Redwing more deserving, and Vernon-Smith more bent. Yet it is Bunter who has become an institution, with a triumphant entry to himself in the *Supplement* to the *Oxford English Dictionary*. Bunter was fortunate in the artist who created his public image for generations of schoolboys – and schoolgirls. It was the prolific Charles Hamilton (Frank Richards) who gave him his lines ('I say you fellows, I'm expecting a postal order') but it was Leonard Shields who drew the check pattern on Bunter's bags, that ample cross-hatch against which boots were perennially thudding. Socially, Bunter was a snob who liked to claim that he lived at Bunter Towers (like many of his schoolmates who, if they did not have a pater and mater at the Towers, then certainly at the Grange or even Castle). Yet Bunter's people were not all that skint. His dad was a stockbroker, living at Bunter Villa in the lush suburbs, and making enough to support both Billy and his young brother Sammy at Greyfriars, not to mention Bessie at the nearby girls' school. Though a liar, a coward and a sneak, Bunter was an excellent cook, a brilliant ventriloquist, and an essential cog in the Greyfriars mechanism. Hamilton created him from the less attractive character traits of three people he knew; but was told by one editor to whom he took an early Bunter story that he would never catch on. Yet Bunter lives on, immortalised in print, radio and television, and his name and exploits are celebrated wherever the English language is spoken. He is moreover brilliantly discussed by George Orwell* in one of his translucent essays; a distinction that not even Mr Quelch, the learned pedagogue whose misfortune it was to teach Bunter Latin, could rival. The Fat Owl of the Remove, as ever, gets the last laugh.

Burgess, Anthony (1917-93)   He was a hero to the Americans and an enigma to the English, who could not decide where he fitted in. The son of a chief cashier who was a gifted pub pianist, and a noted music hall singer called Beautiful Belle Burgess, he was educated at the Xaverian College, Manchester, and at Manchester University. Despite stints as lecturer, civil servant, schoolmaster, and colonial officer he had seen himself as a composer till he was thirty-eight (his Third Symphony in C has been performed and recorded). When the doctors told him – quite wrongly – that he had a year to live, he wrote five novels in that year to leave his wife some money. He was to spin out thirty works of fiction, as well as film and television scripts, translations, musicals, biographies and criticism. In a matter of weeks he turned out a book naming and assessing the ninety-nine best novels written in English since 1939. Modesty prevented him adding one of his own as a hundredth; but he was not always so modest. He was sacked from his job as a literary critic on the *Yorkshire Post* for reviewing one of his own books, published under his pseudonym Joseph Kell. It was, he wrote, a dirty book in many ways; but he praised its 'gross richness'.

It was the comic spirit which fuelled Burgess, but the Balzacian scale which inspired him, and the giant figures of history that enthralled him: Napoleon, Beethoven, Jesus, Moses, Nero. Yet there is nothing portentous about his prose. 'He said it was artificial respiration,' says a woman in *Inside Mr Enderby*, the novel that got him fired, 'but now I find I am to have his child.' He found world fame when his novel *The Clockwork Orange* was filmed, but would have liked much more to see his projected film of Shakespeare's life become a reality. He invented private languages for his characters, and endlessly baffled readers with new coinings (Orwell's 1984 was a *dystopia*, lightening becomes *levin*).

He remains hypnotically readable. The opening to his enormous novel *Earthly Powers* is written tongue-in-cheek, but is none the worse for that: 'It was the afternoon of my eighty-first birthday, and I was in bed with my catamite when Ali announced that the archbishop had come to see me.' Where should the English place this prodiciously fecund, colour-blind, lapsed Catholic, tax exile, writer-composer? Certainly among the top hundred writers in English since 1939; and some would put him very much higher than that.

Cad One of the most interesting words in the language. In its relatively short life – hardly more than a hundred years – it reversed its meaning and then gently expired for want of use. As first noted by the *OED* it was being used contemptuously of townsmen at Oxford in 1831 and within ten years to denote any vulgar or ill-bred fellow. In Compton Mackenzie's celebrated Edwardian Oxford novel *Sinister Street*, there is a scene in which the hero, Michael Fane, and some of his friends decide to rag the rooms of a fellow undergraduate called Smithers. What has Smithers done? Nothing; but he is a cad: a poor scholar, a carpenter's son with a Cockney accent, and he is to be ragged for his general bearing and plebeian origin.

The irony, of course, lies in the fact that insofar as the word still means anything in England, it is Fane and his friends who are the cads, not Smithers. The word has subtly changed its meaning and certainly in inter-war years conveyed the idea of someone who knows how to behave but fails to do so; a gentleman, in short, who has given up his code.

The golden (or rather chromium) age of the cad was undoubtedly the thirties: epoch of the cocktail shaker, brothel-creeper, and silver cigarette case. The cad's weaknesses are girls, gin, and gee-gees, usually in that order. He often turns out to be rather a good man in a tight corner. Capel Maturin in Michael Arlen's story *The Ace of Cads,* for instance, has won the DSO and Bar, but has been cashiered from the Brigade of Guards for pouring wine in a restaurant over a conductor who persists in playing Mendelssohn's 'Spring Song' after being asked three times to desist.

The most thorough-going rotter in recent English fiction must be

Captain Edward Fox-Ingleby, hero of A.G. Macdonnell's *Autobiography of a Cad*. It is a sustained satire on the English upper class – or more specifically the Tory Party – the hard-faced men who had done well out of the war. Fox-Ingleby's especial hero is F.E. Smith, later Lord Birkenhead. That fits.

English cads, if not celebrated by Armenian writers like Michael Arlen, are best portrayed by Russian actors like George Sanders. As he remarked in his *Memoirs of a Professional Cad*: 'I was beastly but I was never coarse. I was a high class sort of heel.' Not even that could be fairly said of the next wave of fictional heroes like Ian Fleming's* James Bond or Len Deighton's Harry Palmer. They have learned that the Queensberry rules don't work any more, that the glory and the girls go to the man who can best aim a swift kick to the crotch, as his adversaries assuredly will.

Besides, women are so fond of cads. In that immortal exchange in *Pygmalion,* Colonel Pickering gallantly tries to make sure Henry Higgins is a fit person to tutor Eliza Doolittle (see *Accent)*. 'Are you a man of good character where women are concerned? Higgins: 'Have you ever met a man of good character where women are concerned' Precisely: we are all cads nowadays.

Cambridge   The other place is quieter than Oxford*, and to some disinterested eyes more beautiful; it is also a little more serious. Good at economics (Marshall, Pigou, Keynes*) and Eng. Lit. (Leavis, Tillyard, Quiller-Couch) it would nevertheless be hard to imagine Cambridge nurturing a Max Beerbohm, a Lewis Carroll*, an Oscar Wilde, an Evelyn Waugh* or a Kenneth Tynan. Though Cambridge cannot boast one college like Christ Church at Oxford which has the portraits of a dozen sons who became prime minister, it can claim one laboratory, the Cavendish, which has nurtured a string of world-class physicists (Maxwell, Rayleigh, Thompson and Rutherford). Newton gave Cambridge a lead in mathematics it has never lost; and the unravelling of the double helix in Cambridge illustrates the place's pre-eminence in biological science as well. The novels of C.P. Snow, set as they are in the corridors of power, illustrate to perfection the slightly more bony feel of Cambridge life.

On the other hand, it must be said that the Footlights Club since the war has turned out a string of real goers, notably Peter Hall, Trevor Nunn, Jonathan Miller, Peter Cook and Clive James. Oxford, of course, can riposte with Kingsley Amis*, Richard Ingrams, Dudley Moore, Alan Bennett, Rowan Atkinson ... but one can go on like this for ever and prove nothing, except that Oxford and Cambridge are yoked together in an uneasy amalgam called Oxbridge, a matter for concern or celebration depending on you own alma mater*.

The degree of seriousness in the ancient rivalry between the two places may best be judged by Harold Wilson's account of how, as a young don at University College, Oxford, he was involved in the appointment of a new Master. The best man for the job was the distinguished academic lawyer A.L. Goodhart, but there were three possible drawbacks to his election: he was a Jew, an American, and a Cambridge man. 'We found the first point interesting,' Harold remembered, 'and the second amusing. But the third gave us a lot of trouble.' Goodhart, needless to say, was elected.

Carroll, Lewis (1832–98) By modern standards he was a snob (the only trouble with Margate, he remarked, was the commercial class of person one found there) and a prig (he ended his friendship with Ellen Terry when she went to live with a man not her husband). He was a useful mathematician, an original logician, a pioneer photographer and, of course, the author of *Alice's Adventures in Wonderland* and *Through the Looking-glass*. The occasion when the story was first told is precisely known: 4 July 1862, as Charles Lutwidge Dodgson, mathematics tutor at Christ Church, Oxford, and his friend Robinson Duckworth rowed the three little Liddell girls – Alice, Lorina and Edith – up to Godstow under a cloudless blue sky, the river a watery mirror below, the drops tinkling from the oars. Dodgson in the story became the Dodo, Duckworth the Duck, the Prince and Princess of Wales (with whom the three little girls had just been playing croquet on the Deanery Lawn) the King and Queen of Hearts. Was Lewis Carroll in love with Alice? Perhaps, but if he ever declared that love there is no record of it, and he wrote formally to her as Mrs Hargreaves twenty-five years later when raising the question of a facsimile edition of the Alice manuscript. (She sold the original at Sotheby's in 1928 for £15,400.)

Modern critics have read sinister depths into his penchant for little girls; if there were any truth in it, no word of complaint about it has survived. The Alice books were immediate best-sellers, and have remained so ever since. The *Adventures* are more widely quoted than any other book outside the Shakespeare canon and the Bible, and are applicable to virtually every human situation. Seen as the precursor of every modern movement from Surrealism to psychoanalysis, Carroll was in truth the master, not of nonsense, but of uncommon sense, which is not the same thing at all. 'I can't explain *myself*, I'm afraid sir,' said Alice, 'because I'm not myself, you see.' 'I don't see,' said the Caterpillar. But children did – and still do.

Cats   The royal family cannot be doing with cats. There is not even a cat below stairs at Buckingham Palace, though there is no objection in principle to them being kept in the Royal Mews. During the Second World War, Churchill* and Roosevelt were famed cat-lovers, while Hitler and Mussolini were cat-haters, and we can all see what happened to them. In Britain there are some nine million cats, most of them shamelessly spoiled. Some cats have owners like historian A.L. Rowse, who talks to his over the transatlantic telephone. Others, like Marmaduke Ginger Bits, have been the subject of pitched battles about ownership in the courts with lawyers' bills of £10,000 resulting.

The ultimate accolade for the cat fanciers of England has been the preposterous success of the Andrew Lloyd Webber musical *Cats,* based on the T.S. Eliot poems, which at the time of writing has just entered its fifteenth year with no sign of a decline in takings. Investors who put their cash into the unlikely project have already had their money back and returns of more than 100 per cent a year. It is still running in London and has beguiled audiences in New York, Budapest, Vienna, Melbourne, Amsterdam, Hamburg, Oslo, Helsinki and Stockholm.

There is one London woman, known simply as the Cat Lady, who saves 1,000 stray cats a year. Five British cats were left £65,000 by their owner, a retired railway clerk. There was a cat in the ladies' loo at Paddington station who was so fat he could do little but waddle, so much money was put in his saucer at the loo. It cost £15 a week to feed him, and he had fan mail and Christmas cards from all over the world. There is, in short, no lunacy the island race will not encompass when it comes to cats. (See, for a general statement of principle on the whole issue, under *Pets.*)

Champagne   It is a much-loved English tipple. The French ship more bubbly here than to any other country in the world (except, last year, America. The island race put away sixteen million bottles a year; and it is the English taste for *brut* or dry champagne that has put it so firmly on the map. Bubbly was pricey till 1861 when wine-loving William Ewart Gladstone reduced the duty on each bottle to let it sell here at around five shillings a bottle. By 1869 the most popular music-hall song was 'Champagne Charlie'; the epithet lingers on to this day. Prominent Champagne Charlies ranged from the great swindler Horatio Bottomley (Pommery) to the great statesman Winston Churchill* (Pol Roger). On

Winston's death Madame Pol Roger ordained that a black border be put round the edge of their label: it remains to this day. 'Champagne certainly gives one werry gentlemanly ideas,' remarked Mr Jorrocks, 'but for a continuance, I don't know but I should prefer mild hale.' Hilaire Belloc is quoted at each general election with never diminishing effect: 'The accursed power which stands on Privilege (And goes with Women, and Champagne, and Bridge) Broke – and Democracy resumed her reign: (Which goes with Bridge, and Women, and Champagne).'

Channel Four   Was to be, ruled its first chief executive, Jeremy Isaacs, for all of the people some of the time. It has been just that. In the fourteen years since it began, it has carved out an idiosyncratic and attractive niche in English life. Its instruction from Parliament was to cater for tastes and interests not served or under-served on television already; to innovate; and to devote a good slice of its airtime – seven and a half hours a week – to education. This, after a shaky start, it has manifestly done. *Channel Four News* is generally seen now as the best of all television news programmes; *Brookside*, its soap opera, has the most appeal among younger viewers; and its critique of other media is skilfully exercised through programmes like *The Media Show*. Most striking of all its contributions to English life, though, has unquestionably been its role in hugely expanding the number of independent production companies and in creating the conditions for the making of new, offbeat, and highly praised independent films. *A Room with a View* and *My Beautiful Laundrette* are just two among the hundred feature films it has already produced. Isaacs has now left Channel Four to become General Director of the Royal Opera House. He leaves a handsome legacy.

Channel Tunnel   It is nearly 200 years now since the idea that England and France should be joined again as they once had been was floated; mainly, it must be allowed, by Frogs. The Brits usually dragged their heels. It was not till 1955 that the British defence minister said he would no longer oppose the notion on military grounds; and not till 1986 that Margaret Thatcher and Francois Mitterand gave the mighty project the go-ahead in Lille. In November 1994 Eurostar went into service with just two trains a day each way; a year later it had carried just on 3 million passengers while Le Shuttle next door had carried a million cars.

The drawbacks were all too evident; the state of the art technology proved fragile and all too embarrassingly often Eurostar broke down. Gradually, however, the charms of being transported smoothly at 300 kph (the speed on the French side) from the heart of London to the heart of

Paris in just three hours began to prevail; by 1996 the ferry companies were beginning to feel the pinch. Yet at the time of writing Eurostar is losing not far short of a thousand million pounds a year. Perhaps this horrendous sum, on the analogy of Concorde*, should have been expected. All the same, it may one day seem a small price to pay for making England once again, to quote Donne's haunting words, 'a piece of the continent, a part of the main'.

Charters and Caldicott Made their debut in 1938 when a classic Hitchcock thriller called *The Lady Vanishes* was released. They were two absurd, cricket-mad Englishmen hurrying back to England for the Test at Old Trafford when a little local difficulty with some Nazi bounders detains their train. Basil Radford and Naunton Wayne were such a hit as the immortal pair that they appeared as the same chaps in two more films, and a BBC TV series based on their updated doings was written by playwright Keith Waterhouse.

Writer-director Sidney Gilliat, who dreamed up the characters, originally called them Charters and Spanswick – his gardener's name, common in Wiltshire. Edward Black, the producer, in a moment of pure inspiration, changed Spanswick to Caldicott. Gainsborough, the production company, kept 50 per cent of the rights in the characters, Gilliat and his partner Frank Launder the rest.

Like Holmes and Watson, Charters and Caldicott never address each other by their first names. Like Wooster* and Wimsey*, they are not quite so daft as they appear. In an allegorical scene, apt for 1938, Charters goes to apologise to the Nazis ambushing the train and is shot in the hand for his pains. A passenger called Todhunter is for surrender. Caldicott asks him for his gun: 'Pacifist eh? Won't work, old boy. Early Christians tried it and got thrown to the lions. Come on, hand it over.' Needless to say, he turns out to be a crack shot.

As *The Times* remarked in its obituary of Radford, he excelled at playing the Englishman of popular romantic convention, no great shakes as a thinker, but never losing his sense of values and, in the thick of fearful hazards, less dismayed by the likelihood of imminent capture than by the news that England had collapsed in the second innings. All Englishmen will trust that Radford and Wayne are now sitting in the Great Pavilion in the Sky, waiting for the celestial covers to come off as they sip a well-earned gin and nectar.

Chat Show The name given to a conversation between an interviewer and an invited guest or guests in a television studio during which the ludicrous pretence is maintained that there are not ten million eavesdroppers. As, however, nothing of any consequence is ever said during these mindless blethers, no great harm is done; nor good either.

Cheese Even to this day some country shops in England offer just two kinds of cheese: mild or tasty. By this they intend the two great varieties of the most English of all cheeses, Cheddar: hard, clean, delicate and golden and for three centuries the simple, portable lunch of farm-workers, miners, builders and soldiers. It is the centrepiece of the ploughman's, still the most popular snack for the English drinker, and the perfect adjunct for the English apple.

Once made in virtually every county in England, and formerly a product of the farmhouse, English cheese has now effectively narrowed to nine varieties: Cheddar, Caerphilly, Cheshire, Derby, Gloucester, Lancashire, Leicester, Stilton and Wensleydale. Stilton has long been the king of cheeses, and can compete against the world for nobility and richness; however, with affluence and travel your average Englishman has been learning of continental enticements like Camembert and Dolce Latte.

To meet this challenge the English cheese industry has therefore evolved a new soft cheese that looks as if it comes from the Dordogne but in fact hails from Somerset. Mild, creamy and lightly veined, it was christened, in a moment of cloth-eared lunacy, Lymeswold. Given this grisly handicap, Lymeswold never won its way in England. They even charged more for it than for Brie.

Cheltenham Laxative, diuretic and antacid, the waters of Cheltenham Spa are naturally alkaline and in this respect unique in England. The Duke of Wellington found them a natural antidote to liver disease brought on by military service, and so put the place on the map. With its caryatids, window boxes, hanging baskets of marigolds and lobelia, Victorian letter boxes, coloured granite lamp posts honouring Gordon of Khartoum, pharmacy with gilded pestle and mortar, and intricate Regency ironwork, Cheltenham still has much of the feel of a hill station at the height of the Raj. Its three public schools – Cheltenham College, Dean Close and Cheltenham Ladies' College – lend emphasis to the sense of elegant torpor. Festivals of music, literature and cricket seem well sited, and the swarms of dog collars at the Cheltenham Races suggest that the Irish priesthood know a good thing when they see one. However, as usual in England, there are subversive currents running beneath this bland surface. The spa is also the home of the country's worldwide electronic intelligence network, and the scene of a major spy scandal. Here too during the war a schoolboy at the college named Lindsay Anderson, son of a major general, was already reacting against the system into which he had been born, and was to make a string of films and plays (most notably *If ...*) which were the living and articulate antithesis of everything Cheltenham stands for.

Christmas   This festival does not find the island race at its best. It has become the apotheosis of materialism. It focuses the minds of children not on what they can give but on what they can get. It is the moment no longer for the accomplishment of grace but the acquisition of gew-gaws. It is the time for the laying up of precisely those treasures on earth that the proponent of treasures in heaven so eloquently despised.

It is the high season for dyspepsia and cirrhosis. It throws together in confined spaces generations of diametrically opposed interests. It is the moment of the year for a torrent of fatalities and dismemberment on the roads. It is a trough of inanition some six weeks across in which no sensible decisions can be expected from anyone. It is the time for the proliferation on the television screen of the very worst that the human intellect can devise: an unending diet of pap and tripe, of tuneless tunes, and plotless plots, all whipped into a bland and saccharine cake mix of spurious goodwill. It is also the time for the Queen's annual broadcast, one of the low points in the royal year.

No other nation has made such a hash of the iridescent simplicities spun out by the revolutionary rabbi from Nazareth. What would the man who told the parable of the rich man and the eye of the needle say to Fortnums* in Christmas week? For the sickly maw of sentiment in which their celebration of the winter solstice wallows the English must thank Prince Albert, who brought the Christmas tree with him from Saxe Coburg-Gotha, and Charles Dickens* who wrapped it in tinsel.

Chuffed   One of the curious English words which means two opposite things; here, pleased and displeased. Writers are still using it in both senses, but the first seems to be getting the better of the argument.

Church of England   It has affected the destiny of the nation only once in recent times. Edward VIII abdicated in 1936 because there was no way the Church of England, of which he was head, could condone his marriage with Mrs Simpson, who had two divorced husbands still living. The issue was of no importance to his hundreds of millions of Hindu and Moslem subjects; it was not even a crucial matter to the Church of

Scotland, which permitted divorce. It was an issue solely for the Established Church which at that time had some three million regular worshippers in England.

Twenty years later there was a faint but far less important reverberation of the same issue, when Princess Margaret wished to marry Group Captain Peter Townsend. It was left to a divorced prime minister, Anthony Eden, to tell her that she could not marry the divorced Townsend and maintain her royal prerogatives. Only in this role may the Church of England still be the Tory Party at prayer; otherwise its influence is fragmentary and inconclusive.

Indeed the sporting connection may be one of its strongest remaining traditions. We have already noted the powerful connection between the Boat Race* and the Bench of Bishops; and J.B. Priestley* remarked that it was difficult to know where the Church of England ended and the MCC began.

Churchill, Winston (1874–1965) He was a small (5 feet 6½ inch), pink-faced, sandy-haired bounder. When Clementine Hozier, his future wife, was introduced to him at a ball, her partner asked why she had been talking to 'that frightful fellow'. The Tories hated him because he had crossed the floor of the House and joined the Liberals; the working class hated him because he put in troops to break strikes.

When he entered the Commons as Prime Minister for the first time on 13 May 1940, he was cheered – but only by the Labour benches. His conduct of the war was bold, eccentric, and vigorous. Ellen Wilkinson noted that when Attlee took the Cabinet in Winston's absence, the work was expeditiously done in three hours. When Winston took it, the agenda was not even reached and the Cabinet went on till midnight: but everyone there knew they had been in the presence of history.

He made himself Minister of Defence and effectively ran the war with his chiefs of staff single-handed, heckling and harrying them unmercifully. His closest friends – Beaverbrook*, Bracken and Birkenhead – were known to his wife as the three terrible Bs. All were self-made men: adventurers and *arrivistes*. He badly misjudged the mood of the country in 1945 and could never understand why he had been thrown unceremoniously from office. None of this matters tuppence.

He was perfectly cast for his role in history and the fates saw to it that his exits and entrances were meticulously timed. The scope and sweep of his life were on a heroic scale. He held almost every great office of state open to a commoner. He not only led his nation to a triumphant victory in the Second World War; but also wrote a magisterial six-volume history of it. He took part in the last great charge of the British cavalry (Omdurman, 1898) and lived to congratulate President Kennedy on sending man into space.

When all the reservations are made, the final balance sheet is clear: the little bounder became the greatest Englishman of his time. Any Englishman who can recall the war at all will get the authentic frisson at hearing again a record of Winston delivering any of his magnificent wartime speeches: 'We shall fight on the beaches, we shall fight on the landing grounds, we shall fight in the fields and in the streets, we shall fight in the hills; we shall never surrender.'

He will remember too, with wry pleasure, that as Winston sat down to an ovation he is said to have turned to his neighbour and added: 'And if they do come we shall have to hit them over the head with bottles, because we have nothing else.'

Clanger To *drop a clanger* is to made a *faux pas*; but note again the superior strength of the Anglo-Saxon. Though so far traced back only to 1948 by the *Oxford English Dictionary*, it was certainly service slang in the 1939–45 war, and probably had its origin when some fitter or artificer dropped some tackle on the floor with a resounding crash. The onomatopoeia helps too.

Claret Originally from the French *clairet* and meaning any clear or light wine as opposed to a dark one, claret imperceptibly came to mean first red wine and then red wines of Bordeaux. The trend is natural enough; the English ruled Bordeaux for three hundred years. One English king is buried there and two more who ruled it lie in French soil. Many of the great estates of Bordeaux are English-owned today, including Latour, Léoville-Barton and, as one might have suspected, Smith-Haut-Lafitte.

Claret is for boys, said Samuel Johnson, and perhaps then it was: but as it has grown in complexity and authority it has become increasingly celebrated in England as the thinking man's tipple and a staple of Oxbridge novels (eg, C.P. Snow's *The Masters*). In English politics claret is indissolubly associated with Roy Jenkins, co-founder of the Social Democratic Party; so much so that Sir Geoffrey Howe, when Chancellor of the Exchequer, had only to mention a change in the claret duty during a budget speech to get the next laugh even before the inevitable sally about Roy's fancy followed.

When the alliance was forged between the SDP and the Liberals an ingenious sobriquet was soon coined to exemplify their balancing act between previously disparate forces in English politics: they are the party of *claret and chips*.

It must be faced, however, that there are formidable claret bores. There is a well-authenticated story of a celebrated wine correspondent whose merest footfall could scatter the drinkers from the bar at the old Press Club. He never bought anyone a drink but bored everyone to distraction with his unending tales of great vintages and *premiers crus*. One day he announced to the cringing assembly: 'And tomorrow I am going to Bordeaux.' From the other end of the bar came the only possible response: 'Who's Doe?'

Class   The English pox. But just as the incidence of pox in England has fallen virtually to zero, so has the prevalence of class. Indeed, we may say of class as we do of money and sex that it really matters very little unless one has too little or too much of it. Yet some Englishmen have seen England as soaked in class. Certainly Orwell*, who placed himself very precisely in the lower-upper middle class, saw it that way; but the world has moved on in the half century since he wrote his great political moralities and what he saw as distinctions in class are now being imperceptibly elided into varieties of style.

The first reason for this is economic. A miner now earns three and a half times more in real terms than before the war. A factory worker earns more than twice as much and now makes substantially more than an executive officer in the civil service.

Dress has also become almost, if not entirely, classless among the young. While the Sloane Ranger may still affect certain class indicators like Huskies and pearls, track-suits are the universal garb of the new chic professions – green goddesses, photographers, advertising men and record managers.

The old working class has dramatically shrunk. Whereas before the war some three quarters of the working population did unskilled or semi-skilled manual jobs, the proportion is now much nearer a quarter, and sinking fast. With the rise of the combine harvester the fields are empty of farmworkers and the car plants will soon be innocent of human inhabitants except for the technicians who service the automated robots.

Even in the forties Orwell believed he could see the emergence of a new class: 'The technicians and the higher paid skilled workers, the airmen and the mechanics, the radio experts, film producers, popular journalists and industrial chemists. They are the indeterminate strata at which the older class distinctions are beginning to break down ...'

It was this new class which surely helped fill the ranks of the

Democrats in politics, that curious amalgam of old fashioned Liberals and new-style Social Democrats which at first made heavy inroads into the traditional Labour vote. But New Labour may prove their natural home.

It is technically possible to slice up the English middle class into a dozen disparate layers if we use a carving knife as thin as Orwell's. For all practical purposes however it remains a simple three-tiered structure. The lower middle class, which as George Mikes once remarked is the only one in England nobody is proud of belonging to, still provides the country with the bulk of its talent and its genius (Dickens, Wells, Lloyd George, Asquith). The middle of the middle class is the hardest layer to identify but was neatly caught by Jilly Cooper when she labelled them the Weybridges, for that is the sort of town round which they typically cluster: the minor entrepreneurs, the solicitors, the engineers, architects and doctors.

The upper middle class is immediately identifiable: a small but enormously powerful group of civil service mandarins, large-scale farmers, managing directors and bright, youngish brigadiers. They will shade into the upper class by marriage and back again by divorce; but they are the most assured segment of English society, and noticeably nicer than their French, German or Italian equivalents. The upper class is discussed under *Aristocracy*; here note only their astonishing flair for survival and renewal; a trick worked by constant inter-marriage with brains and money from abroad: Argentinian tin heiresses, New York Jewish princesses, Rhodesian landowners. In the country they still hunt and shoot as if the world had never changed; in towns they tend to melt into the classless cauldron that now seethes in the capital. Here, anything goes: class is out; style is all.

Clerihew When Edmund Clerihew Bentley was a sixteen-year-old schoolboy at St Paul's, he jotted down in class one day these lines: 'Sir Humphrey Davy / Abominated gravy / He lived in the odium / Of having discovered Sodium.' Thus was the first clerihew born: the word is now in the *Oxford English Dictionary*. E.C. Bentley gave the world many delights in his life; his detective story *Trent's Last Case* remains an early classic of the genre. Nothing, however, that he ever did gave more pleasure than his clerihews.

One can argue about the best. Some give the laurels to: 'Sir Christopher Wren / Said, "I'm going to dine with some men / If anybody calls / Say I'm designing St Paul's".' Others prefer: 'The Art of biography / is different from geography / Geography is about maps / but Biography is about chaps.'

Many poets have had a go at the clerihew, not often with success. Auden* got close with: 'William Blake / Found Newton hard to take / And was not enormously taken / With Francis Bacon.' It is a miniscule art form to which anyone can aspire.

The subject matter can be literary: 'If I had been / Albertine / I'd have disparue / Too.' It can be political: 'President Charles de Gaulle / Staked his future on the poll / And having polled more nons that ouis / Went home to Colombey-les-deux-Eglises'.

They can be sporting: 'Sir Donald Bradman / Would have been a very glad man / If his Test average had been .06 more / Than 99.94' – a true summary of a great sporting record. They can also be subversive, as in: 'Mrs Mary Whitehouse / Caught sight of a lighthouse / It did not escape her detection / That erection.'

Clogs For many years the former prime minister Harold Wilson had to try to live down the charge that he had claimed to have gone to school barefoot. In truth he had said that when he was a boy growing up in Yorkshire, many children – though not Harold himself – had not possessed any shoes; they had worn clogs instead. This indeed was the normal working-class footwear in the industrial north till the age of affluence dawned after the last war; the old northern proverb, clogs to clogs in three generations, is self-explanatory. See also *Lancashire*.

Clubs By rights, they should all be gone by now. In an era when men and women, by law at least, have equal rights and chaps now go home to help with the babies and washing the dishes, the notion of a gentleman's club in the West End of London should be an anachronism. Nothing of the sort: the club flourishes; not least, perhaps, because it enshrines and perpetuates the old ways. If a thousand men are prepared to chip in four hundred a year each, with perhaps another three hundred each as entrance money, they can run an elegant town house far beyond their individual means, hire servants that have now vanished from private service, and enjoy the pleasure of each other's company over honest food and decent wine.

So at least runs the theory; in practice clubs differ dramatically in the quality and quantity of what they can offer. The old aristos' clubs still flourish: White's, where Randolph Churchill and Evelyn Waugh* once exchanged purple-faced insults and Aneurin Bevan was kicked in the arse by an enraged member; Pratt's, the private property of the Duke of Devonshire, where only sixteen can sit down at a time and all club servants are still called George; and Boodle's, the country gents' club in St James's where Dominic Medina MP, the arch-rotter in John Buchan's superlative thrillers, had ensconced himself as a member.

Meantime the literary and artistic clubs have met with mixed fortunes. The Garrick is immensely fashionable and with a daunting waiting list, while the equally elegant Savile, catering for very similar interests and tastes, has no waiting list at all. Possibly this has something to do with the Garrick's decision to admit women each night to dine as guests in the coffee room, while the hard core of members on their own sit down the long table in the middle. The struggle that some clubs have had to survive is seen in the amalgamation of four: The East India, founded in 1849 for officers of the East India Company on leave in London, the Devonshire, an old Liberal club whose fortunes seem to have declined with its party's, the Sports, and the Public Schools.

Perhaps membership of a London club does not have quite the cachet it once did, and the truth is that while the black ball still exists, some of those who have been excluded by it have been far more interesting and worthwhile than those who exercised its veto. One has to think no further than Bernard Levin, blackballed at the Garrick for being rude about the Lord Chief Justice, and George Brown, found *non persona grata* at the Savile.

The phenomenon of the club bore still exists in the best-regulated clubs, but the convention of the clubman swapping stories after dinner as a vehicle for the launch of a novel, so beloved of Somerset Maugham*, is mercifully giving way to fresher tricks. Yet the old image of the somnolent clubman asleep in the library still persists, most vividly captured recently by the cartoonist Michael Heath in a scene where one venerable clubman, reading *The Times*, glances up and remarks to his recumbent friend: 'Good Lord, Fenton, I had no idea you were dead!'

Coal Has a quasi-mystical role in English life. The country stands on a vast foundation of the hard, black carbonaceous rock, made from immense wodges of compressed peat: the fuel that fired the Industrial Revolution. It was to make a small group of landowners in England immeasurably rich (the idea that you owned the mineral rights *under* your land was refuted in France and continental Europe) and obliged many millions of Englishmen to live their working lives out of sight and savour of God's good air and light.

This gave the miners (or pitmen as they like to be called) a cachet they have only gradually lost: an aura of glamour, danger, solidarity and bloody-mindedness that marked them out from their workmates and from their countrymen. In the Second World War one young man in ten eligible for national service was directed down the mines: getting the coal was as important as that. Politically the miners have been since early days a bastion of the Labour movement; though Welsh magicians like Aneurin Bevan and Scottish firebrands like Willie Gallacher have not unnaturally seized the imagination, the Durham Miners' Gala each summer remains a pinnacle of the English working-class year. Until the 1980s, no-one mocked the miners with impunity. Men like Joe Gormley and Arthur Scargill, whether loved or loathed, became perforce part of the fabric of English political life.

Edward Heath, by opposing the miners in 1974, ended his own government. Margaret Thatcher, however, beat them decisively in 1984 by changing the legal rules of the game. There are now so few they hardly matter.

No one who has ever been down an old pit is likely to forget its Stygian thrall: the seams so exhausted that sometimes the men worked in spaces only as high as the length of their own boots: the stalls for the ponies with names like Bounce, Bob, Prince and (improbably) Eton; the big drums in which they once kept the first aid for the horrendous accidents; the stretchers that ran along rails carrying injured men; the rivulets of black underground streams.

The gap between pit-owner and pit-worker was always stark and vast and probably best closed by the state taking over. The Sitwells, exquisite products of inherited plenty, could just hear the picks of the miners at work under their ancestral seat on still evenings near Scarborough. One of the greatest cartoons ever drawn by Vicky, lover and hater of English *moeurs*, showed Sir Alec Douglas-Home, professed intimate of the working man, gormlessly bagging grouse on his broad acres while below him, in cut-away relief, the miners hacked away, as ever, at the coal-face.

The central question remains: if mining is indeed one of the most hateful callings in the land, why are miners so keen to keep their jobs? Between the two wars they left the pits in droves to become schoolmasters or milkmen; anything but the pits. Perhaps the answer is encapsulated in the testimony of D.H. Lawrence: 'My father,' he wrote 'loved the pit. He was hurt badly more than once, but he would never stay away. He loved the contact, the intimacy ... the curious dark intimacy of the mines, the naked sort of contact.' The pull of the pit is not totally amenable to rational analysis; but is best not totally ignored either.

Colour Supplement *The Sunday Times* printed its first colour section (as it was then called) on 4 February 1962. It was a spectacular flop. No one seemed to like it, least of all its progenitor, Roy Thomson, owner of *The Sunday Times* who had envisaged something rather like the funnies back home in Canada – course-grained, downmarket colour pages for women and children. What he got was a curious *mélange* of reportage in text and photographs about a new lifestyle. It was so different from what had been published in England before that it seemed almost surreal. Soon it had given birth to a new and prejorative term: colour supplement living. This was held by those who coined it to exemplify all that was worst about modern England: trendiness and gluttony, cynicism and materialism, a kind of glossy heartlessness. The case was most eloquently put by the art critic John Berger on BBC TV when he contrasted the lush colour ads for cars, clothes, food and booze with the photo essays in between of want and war, cruelty and disease.

It was touch and go for the first year whether *The Sunday Times* colour magazine would make it. About a million pounds was lost before the penny dropped. It occurred one day to just one advertising agency that here was a way of reaching three million AB readers, the top socio–economic group, in colour. They began to advertise, so did everybody else, and the drought of ads turned into a torrent. The *Observer* and *Telegraph,* who had been the first to mock the new colour medium, were obliged to follow suit.

The colour magazines, from being a liability, turned into the spearhead of new circulation drives. Series on the great middle-class preoccupations – education, health, houses, money, marriage – could more than offset the downward pull of a price rise. The magazines were mirrors of the swinging sixties, but they were also vehicles for the best photographers, writers and artists in the business. They still flourish, but inside the commercial constraints which again seem to justify John Berger's original strictures. Between the early disasters and the later bonanzas, they may have done their best work.

The colour supplement opened the eyes of the English by showing them new ways of spending their new wealth. Indeed, it showed them how to feel both wealthy and guilty at the same time: an unbeatable formula in England.

It failed by being irrevocably middle class: a term of abuse used by the English for those that made them what they are.

Conan Doyle, Sir Arthur (1859–1930)   We tend to forget all the other things he wrote and did. Sherlock Holmes and Dr Watson tower over the English imagination – and the world's – obscuring a mass of other work.

There are the historical romances: *The Exploits of Brigadier Gerard*, for example; *Micah Clarke*, set during the Monmouth rebellion; *The White Company*, about the exploits of a band of medieval knights errant; *Uncle Bernac*, set during the French Revolution; and *Rodney Stone*, a novel about prize-fighting in Regency England.

There are the science fiction fantasies: *The Lost World*, in which Professor Challenger discovers an Amazon plateau inhabited by pre-historic beasts; *The Poison Belt*, about the coming destruction of human life; and *The Maracot Deep* in which a submarine finds Atlantis flourishing beneath the sea. There are the war reports, written out of a deep sense of patriotism: *The Great Boer War* (he had served in South Africa as a doctor); and his *History of the British Campaign in France and Flanders* in no fewer than six volumes. He also found time to write a polemic against Belgian colonialism (*The Crime of the Congo*) which was to bring him close to Roger Casement (who as a young British consular official had first drawn attention to the horrors), an allegiance which did not desert him when the Irish rebel – as he became – was tried and hanged for treason: Doyle subscribed most of the money for Casement's defence.

He used his detective skills, learned in his days as a medical student from Dr Joseph Bell, his teacher at Edinburgh University, who sat for the portrait of Sherlock Holmes, to fight tow *causes célèbres*: against the unjust convictions of George Edalji for cattle mutilation and of Oscar Slater for murder. Slater walked out of court a free man in 1928, nineteen years after he had been sentenced to death, with an *ex gratia* payment of £6,000.

It is hard to believe that such a shrewd and intelligent man as Conan Doyle could also espouse the cause of spiritualism and seriously claim in *The Strand Magazine* that some photographs, manifest fakes to modern eyes, proved the existence of fairies. Yet the spiritualism arose from a deep need to believe: he had lost his son Kingsley and his brother Innes in the First World War. He understood more about sex than most writers of his generation (he wrote a thesis on syphilis) and told his daughter that while he was not prepared to call himself a socialist, he thought he might well be one. (In fact he stood for parliament twice, unsuccessfully, in the Liberal Unionist cause. It was Roger Casement who subsequently converted him to the necessity of Home Rule.)

He was in every way a big man. He had played rugby for Blackheath (like Doctor Watson) in his youth; he played cricket with A.E.W. Mason, author of *The Four Feathers*, and with the young P.G. Wodehouse* on whom he remained a lasting influence. 'Don't you feel as you age, that the tragedy of life is that your early heroes lose their glamour?' wrote Plum. 'Now with Doyle I don't have this feeling. I still revere his work as much as ever. I used to think it swell, and I still think it swell.' He is not alone.

Concorde   The island race began work on Concorde in 1943, when the war was far from over (just as they had begun work on postwar reconstruction in 1940 when it looked lost). In view of the vast cost, they tried in 1960 to interest three other nations in making a partnership: America, Germany and France. The Americans were working on quite different lines, envisaging a plane that would fly at three times the speed of sound, or 2,250 mph. The British opted for Mach 2.2 or 1,575 mph. Even at that daunting speed, they would have to cope with a temperature range from –45°C to 164°C; Concorde gets very hot as it cleaves through the sky. Mach 3 would have meant absorbing temperatures of up to 350°C. It could be done; but the Brits reckoned the development would take too long.

Besides, there was another clinching point: Mach 2 could dispatch Concorde across the Atlantic in 3 hours 20 minutes; Mach 3 would lop only 20 minutes off that time. So the Americans decided to go it alone. The Germans said they were not ready for such a vaulting venture just yet; but it turned out that the French were thinking on very similar lines to the British. A deal was struck in November 1962; and the improbable partnership began. Most of the Frenchmen on the project, being involved in international aviation, spoke English already. While the Brits generally commanded French at little more than schoolboy level, most learned enough during Concorde's building for technical discussion.

Odd social differences surfaced. At one meeting the British leader suggested to his French counterpart that they should call in Honorine and dictate a summary of what they had just agreed. 'D'accord,' replied the Frenchman, 'mais qui est Honorine? She turned out to be his own secretary, whom he always addressed as Mademoiselle Dupont.

Concorde first flew on 2 March 1969, a shimmering white mirage that after all the high tech had come out looking like some gorgeous prehistoric bird. Then came the long years of proving and marketing. Concorde flew to Alaska and Rio, to Saudi Arabia and Melbourne. It had plenty of enemies. In March 1971 the American Congress refused to vote further funds for their SST project. On 31 January 1973, the last day of their six-month option to buy Concorde, Pan-Am pulled out. TWA followed a few hours later.

In one sense they were right; but once the British government had written off all development costs and made a present of it to British Airways, Concorde proved one of their biggest money-spinners, with up to a hundred passengers paying £4,845 for the return trip to New York. Concorde customers have become a kind of exclusive jet-setter's club; one already has four hundred flights under his belt. Meanwhile the American airlines have been complaining about the unfair competition Concorde is offering them: handsome tribute indeed to the beautiful and improbable white bird the Brits and Frogs made together.

Connolly, Cyril (1903–74) 'Connolly was on the way to have become one of the outstanding day-dreamers of his generation had not a penchant for the visible world involved him in extravagance which could only be redeemed by a lifetime of literary effort for which in 1946 a grateful country rewarded him with the Legion of Honour.

'Arms: a nez purpure, impaled upon a grindstone proper between two duns rampant. Crest: a hack in his element, hobbled. Motto... filez sans payer.'

With this typical burst of comic self-denigration Connolly introduced himself in *Previous Convictions*, a 1963 collection of his work over the previous decade. It was not the first time he had given himself the treatment. 'I have always disliked myself at any given moment,' he wrote in the opening pages of *A Georgian Boyhood*, the coruscating coda to his writer's primer, *Enemies of Promise*, 'the sum of these moments is my life.'

It was published in the week of Munich, when Cyril was thirty-five, and was intended, he said, as a didactic inquiry into the problem of how to write a book which lasts ten years. It did; but roused one critic's censure because Cyril set to work after a now-celebrated lunch of omelette, Vichy water and peaches, though at that time in France where he was writing peaches were cheaper than potatoes.

Only son of upper-middle-class Anglo-Irish parents ('England = Grannie, Lodgings, School, Poverty, Middle Class; Ireland = Aunt Mab, Castles, Holidays, Riches, Upper Class'), scholar of Eton and Balliol, Cyril came to London with the heaviest of artistic burdens: a glittering reputation as wit, dandy, aesthete, iconoclast and, on the reverse of that polished coin, the obligation of promise to fulfil. How did he make out?

He wrote one minor novel, *The Rock Pool*, which he described as the centre part of a triptych on snobbery set by the Mediterranean, his spiritual watering-hole: 'I think I may claim to have created a young man as futile as any ... The bars are closed, the hotel is empty, the nymphs have departed.' That famous elegiac chord recurs again more insistently in *The Condemned Playground,* an exhilarating collection of his critical essays from 1927 to 1944: 'It is closing time in the gardens of the West and from now on an artist will be judged only by the resonance of his solitude or the quality of his despair.'

Was it really closing time though? He was halfway through a decade of editing the literary magazine *Horizon;* on those 121 honourably battered booklets alone many literary men would gladly rest their reputations. He had moreover recently published his flawed masterpiece *The Unquiet Grave*. 'Approaching forty, I am about to heave my carcass of vanity, boredom, guilt, and remorse into another decade ...' But we have had enough of Cyril's luxuriating self-pity. He was a critic of glittering intelligence, a travel-writer of rare quality, a parodist of undisputed dexterity and withal, an enchanting man. Case dismissed.

The Conservatives While the Labour Party was for long an army of brilliant goers led by honest plodders (MacDonald, Attlee, Callaghan) the Conservative Party was long equally an army of honest plodders led by brilliant goers (Disraeli, Macmillan, Thatcher). Few have seen the true nature of Conservatism more deeply than Disraeli, who nevertheless used it so effectively as a springboard to his own advantage.

'Conservatism', he wrote in *Coningsby,* 'discards Prescription, shrinks from Principle, disavows Progress; having rejected all respect for antiquity, it offers no redress for the present, and makes no preparation for the future.' To the twentieth-century Englishman, conservatism is dominated by the romantic vision of Winston Churchill*, the patrician legerdemain of Harold Macmillan, the artful draughtsmanship of Rab Butler, the doomed interregnum of Anthony Eden, the surly logistics of Edward Heath, the steely imperatives of Margaret Thatcher, and, most recently, the bland platitudes of John Major. What comes after that is not at all clear. Kenneth Clarke and Michael Portillo hardly seem to belong to the same party.

There are those, some of them high in the Conservative Party, who would argue that Thatcherite conservatism precisely echoed every charge made by Disraeli in *Coningsby,* and was thus destined to fail. While they applauded her courage, her decision, and her skill, they deplored her inflexibility, her insensitivity, and her arrogance. There is now, for the first time in its long history, a schism contained within the ranks of the parliamentary Conservative party which could even split it in two. It no longer appears inviolate to such unscripted and previously unimaginable threats. It has won four elections in a row but at the time of writing looks distinctly unlikely to win a fifth. However, as Harold Wilson famously observed, a week is a long time in politics – even the Conservative kind.

Cotswolds   The case against the Cotswolds is easily made. It has been swamped by tourists and gentrified by rich Londoners. The indigenous denizens have been priced out of what has become a nightmare region of cottages with ersatz coach lamps and farmhouses with carports, wrought-iron gates and ornamental fountains. There is something in the charge, but just as there are still postmen and bus drivers in Beverly Hills, so there are still plenty of ordinary folk in the Cotswolds. The trouble is that the Cotswolds are so ludicrously beautiful – and now royally patronised – that the inhabitants do tend to take cover. This is not hard; for it is a curiously elusive place.

What exactly are the Cotswolds? It is easier to ask than to answer. Much of Gloucestershire is Cotswolds; some is not. Parts of Oxfordshire and even Berkshire are essentially part of that same magical blend of honey-coloured stone. Technically, there is a forty mile-long escarpment running from just north of Chipping Campden to a point southwest of Stroud. To the west, the land drops away steeply, yielding stunning views of the Severn valley and deep into Wales; eastward, the land slopes gently away through a tangle of small rivers to the Thames valley and Berkshire Downs. There are no big towns here and no industry to speak of till you get to Bristol in the south or Birmingham* in the north; but there is a whole treasure house of small towns whose names suggest enchantment and do not disappoint: Stow-on-the-Wold, Moreton in Marsh and Bourton on the Water. The Cotswolds are a thousand square miles of rolling hills and deep valleys, chuckling rivers, noble trees and – above all – exquisite houses.

The stone from which they are fashioned is a variety of limestone called oolite. It is composed of small, round grains of calcium like the roe of a fish. When the sun strikes it the stone looks golden; in other kinds of light it seems brown or cream or grey. It is used in the Cotswolds not just for the walls but also for the roofs, so that, clustered together, softened by moss or lichen, they blur into the landscape in a way seen nowhere else in the world. It is a piece of earth that has a fair claim to call itself the heart of England.

Cottage   Like so many other things, the cottage has worked its way right through English society: from the hovel for the starving to the hideaway for the lovesick: from the tied cottage for the farmworker to the weekend cottage for the advertising copywriter. While many have been ruined by additions quite out of keeping with their age, many have been lovingly restored, their inglenooks unblocked and their timber beams exposed again.

The charms of the English cottage are clear enough: made perforce from materials at hand, it followed the contours imposed by timber and stone and thus always looks beguilingly artless and resolutely rooted: there are ugly cottages in England but they are not many; and some, though tarted up, have a dream-like beauty unequalled anywhere in the world.

Besides, the remote chance of finding a cottage going for a song impels the affluent bourgeois still; and even now you can find people who will claim casually that they bought their place from an obliging farmer for a mere £500 a mere twelve years ago. Add two noughts for any cottage within a day's drive of London and you will be nearer the mark.

The central heating now thrums under many a thatch; but it is not all gain. Connoisseurs of the old English cottage will recall the yellow pool of light thrown by the oil lamp, the hiss of the logs in the fire, the voluptuous comfort of the feather bed, the draughty dash to the outside privy, and the creamy feel of the rainwater gathered in the water butt by the back door.

Council House The heyday of the council house lasted some sixty years: from 1923, when the term is first noted by the *OED*, to 1983, when it became an issue at the general election. Inside that era the council house was the bastion and the symbol of the English working class. To the old, it was a sanctuary from the workhouse which might otherwise have been their fate; to the young, a springboard from which to escape to the semi-detached suburbs or indeed beyond.

Despite canards to the contrary, the council house was nearly always well kept by its tenants; the case against it was that it belonged to Big Brother and was administered by him. The Tories saw that selling council houses to tenants could be a huge vote-catcher: it turned the council estate into a new province of the property-owning democracy so beloved of Tory Central Office. The Labour Party did not see the danger till it was too late, and though this was by no means the only issue in 1983, it was a mighty powerful one.

If you want to see the case for the old council house, redbrick, raw-boned, repetitive and regulated though it may have been, take a look at a Victorian photograph of the inner-city slums where the homeless lived. If the sight of Rovers and Jaguars parked in council estates still causes a red mist to swim before some bourgeois eyes (Minis and Escorts are all right), a quick antidote is to consider countries like Cambodia, where power changed hands suddenly and the professors were put to work in the paddy fields. The council house has in truth been a staging post on the long road to peaceable change.

Countryside   Even today, some 82 per cent of England is used for agriculture; a further 5 per cent for forestry. Thus England from the air still seems – and in some ways is – a green and pleasant land. On the other hand four English people in every five now live in a town. The countryside has thus been emptied of human habitation; but the umbilical cord is strong. Three English people in every four make at least one trip to the countryside every year. A third of all such trips are made to some specific place like a stately home; a further fifth to the coast; one in ten to a particular village; but one in four are making for nowhere particular at all. The random thrall of the English countryside draws them back.

Ironically, the traditional roles have been reversed; post-war controls have thwarted urban pollution while the cavalier use of agrochemicals has fouled the rural landscape. As landscape consultant Chris Baines graphically put it: 'Kingfishers and water-spiders thrive in Black Country canals. The once common frog has been evicted from the farming countryside and owes its survival almost entirely to the gnome-fringed garden pond.'

So far, some good; but the real threat to the English countryside must come from its gradual erosion by houses, factories, roads, quarries. This toll is currently running at the rate of 30,000 acres a year and will never be reversed. On the other hand, the number of English people actively concerned for the conservation of their countryside escalates with heartening speed: overnight stays in youth hostels quintupled in the seventies, and one acre in ten of England and Wales is now in a national park.

What may be lost for ever is the *unregulated* English countryside; the kind Rupert Brooke* went to look for with his brother during the weekend of 2 August 1914, last Sunday of the old world at peace: 'I know the *heart* of England. It has a hedgy, warm, bountiful, dimpled air. Baby fields run up and down the little hills, and all the roads wiggle with pleasure. There's a spirit of rare homeliness about the houses and the countryside, earthy, uneccentric yet elusive, fresh, meadowy, gaily gentle. It is perpetually June in Warwickshire and always six o'clock of a warm afternoon ...'

Covent Garden   When the flower, fruit and vegetable market finally left WC2 for its new home south of the Thames, it left behind the piazza designed by Inigo Jones and the large, airy, elegant Georgian building in which the market had been housed. Various proposals were made for its future: helicopter landing pad, atomic shelter, giant ice rink. In the end the GLC decided to develop it into a new shopping centre, and allocated £4 million for the task.

It reopened in 1980 with forty-five shops, a pub, a wine bar, three restaurants and a patisserie. The question of what kind of shops had been hotly debated. Some wanted them just to cater for the local residents and workforce (3,000 and 37,000 people respectively) but Covent Garden has 300,000 people living or working within ten to fifteen minutes' walk and it was this much larger catchment area which became the planners' target.

Goods on sale in the new shops ranged from hand-made dolls to candle-holders, from rare newspapers to glass mirrors, from herbs and spices to pottery and ceramics. Some critics said the shops were too up-market; others too down. At any rate there was a mixture: if the fashion trade had had their way, they would have taken every shop.

Whether or not you like the new Covent Garden will much depend on whether you like instant oldness. However, there is one large slice of customers who clearly do like what they now find there. It already ranks as London's third most popular tourist shopping area – before King's Road.

Most English people, however, will not quickly forget the old Covent Garden, where debs were bought flowers and strawberries by their boyfriends after dancing the night away; even if they were not there themselves. They will not quickly forget Eliza Doolittle, arguably Covent Garden's most celebrated denizen, who was harmlessly selling flowers outside the Opera House when she first came to the attention of Professor Higgins in Bernard Shaw's* enchanted fable, *Pygmallion.*

Though none of them will remember the old theatre's disasters (Charles Macklin, aged eighty-nine, was led off in 1789 after forgetting his lines as Shylock; Edmund Kean was carried off after a stroke during *Othello* in 1833), it would be a dull Englishman who knew nothing of its triumphs: premières for Benjamin Britten (*Billy Budd, Gloriana, A Midsummer Night's Dream*); for William Walton (*Troilus and Cressida*), and Michael Tippett (*The Midsummer Marriage*). Only Sheridan Morley struck a jarring note when he said that the people in dinner jackets at Covent Garden made him feel he had strayed into a convention of head waiters.

Coward, Sir Noël (1899–1973)   'Forty years ago', wrote Kenneth Tynan, 'he was Slightly in *Peter Pan*, and you might say he has been wholly in *Peter Pan* ever since.' Yet the truth is that Tynan got somewhere nearer the mark when he noted that he had a face like an old boot – but an unmistakably hand-made boot. For though Coward had, by his own precise assessment, a talent to amuse, he was also as tough as old boots. He had to be. After the heady triumphs of his youth (he went on the stage at ten and had four plays on together in London at twenty-six) he had to face the doldrums in the forties and early fifties when the world found his work outmoded, irrelevant and precious.

It was the inspired idea of an American impresario to book him for a cabaret season at Las Vegas, of all places. He was paid £40,000 a week ('For that money,' he remarked, 'they can throw bottles at me if they so choose.') He was a *succès fou*, and never looked back. By the sixties he was being revived at the National Theatre in London and in theatres worldwide. He lived to see *Cowardy Custard*, his life story in words and music, at the Mermaid, and to be knighted just before he died in his sleep at his house on a Jamaican hill. It had been a happy life.

He had been the friend of Somerset Maugham*, Louis Mountbatten and the Queen Mum. Winston Churchill* and Franklin D. Roosevelt had sung his *Mad Dogs and Englishmen* after one of their great wartime parleys. ('Hindus and Argentines sleep firmly from twelve to one / But Englishmen detest a / Siesta'). He was manifestly homosexual, but totally discreet. He like women, but had few illusions about them; some, he asserted, should be struck regularly – 'like gongs'.

He once wrote to Lawrence of Arabia, who at the time was rather ostentatiously disguising himself as Aircraftsman Ross, service number 338171: 'Dear 338171, May I call you 338?' He remarked during the war that if an Englishman told you he was a spy, it was a lie; if an American told you he was a spy it was true. He was indeed as English as the puddings he adored.

Cowboy   One of those elusive slang words that is shifting its ground. To the *OED Supplement* he is simply a wild or boisterous young man; in American black idiom he is a rebel or activist; in Northern Ireland he is anyone who gets involved in a sectarian gang; but perhaps most commonly now he is someone who hustles or loudmouths himself into a position for which he is not really suited. It is thus often used for builders who lack skill, care and experience. This usage no doubt derives from yet another American source; the word is used over there for a rate-buster who ignores the pace set by other piece-workers (usually slower than necessary) and who works sufficiently hard to make more money than they do. Whichever, he is an unattractive outsider or loner; perhaps too a downmarket yuppie*.

Cricket Groucho Marx, taken by an English host to see his first cricket match, sat in rapt attention for half an hour. Finally his host turned and asked how he was enjoying himself. 'Fine,' said Groucho, 'when does it start?' Never, for the non-English-speaking world; for though the island race effortlessly exported soccer and rugger to more than a hundred countries, and even taught the Swiss to slalom, they have never persuaded any country outside the old perimeters of empire to take up cricket. French cricket of course exists, but a French cricketer would be an absurdity. What foreigner would be prepared to wait five days for a result which even then may never come? It is not so much a game as a code; not so much a contest as a dialogue; and was well called chess on grass.

'Capital game – smart sport – fine exercise – very,' says Mr Jingle in *The Pickwick Papers*. Dickens wrote beautifully about the game; but then so did Hazlitt and Meredith, Conan Doyle* (who once actually took the wicket of W.G. Grace) and H.G. Wells (whose father, Joseph Wells, playing for Kent on 26 June 1862, took four Sussex wickets with four successive balls). No sport can remotely approach cricket in the profusion and excellence of its literature. It can boast one Nobel prizewinner (Samuel Beckett – who once turned out for Ireland) and, among contemporary writers, Harold Pinter and Tim Rice (both of whom have their own elevens). It can claim one of the best-known (if banal) of English poems ("There's a breathless hush in the Close tonight / Ten to make and the match to win') as well as one of the most beautiful ('For the field is full of shades as I near the shadowy coast / And a ghostly batsman plays to the bowling of a ghost / And I look through my tears on a soundless-clapping host / As the run-stealers flicker to and fro, to and fro ....').

The game is not what it was; but then it never was. Politics – particularly the politics of race and colour – obtrude; but then half a century ago the political ties between Britain and Australia were tried to breaking point by the bodyline controversy. A TUC eleven recently defeated a CBI eleven at the height of an industrial dispute. Unlike soccer and rugger, hunting and shooting, cricket has no class connotation: every Englishman has played it at some time. Besides, it is in its essence a great leveller. 'Lord Frederick had royal blood in 'en, so 'twere said', as Francis Brett Young tells us, 'For his granmer were Nelly Gwynn, King Charles's fancy / But when Billy and him walked out to the pitch, side by side / You couldn't tell which were the farmer and which the gentleman / The pair on 'em looked that majestic...' A postwar prime minister (Alec Home) was president of the MCC, while his arch-enemy Harold Wilson, when President of the Board of Trade, turned out for the British delegation against the British Embassy during a lull in the trade talks with Russia (and was accused by the local press of indulging in lakeside orgies and pirouettes). Floodlit cricket, one-day cricket, and the advent of the helmet and visor (and hence the bouncer) have deprived cricket of its innate grace but have probably done it no inner harm. Despite all the *longueurs,* incidents, rows, feuds and threats, great cricket still suddenly flowers like a benison: Shane Warne, for example, will bowl a series of beguiling overs so lethal in their menace as to be virtually unplayable; or a young player like Tendulkar will hit a maiden Test century at Lords. Besides, cricket flourishes at village level, the real heart of the game. 'It has been said of the unseen army of the dead,' wrote James Barrie, 'on their everlasting march, that when they are passing a rural cricket ground, the Englishman falls out of the ranks for a moment to look over the gate and smile.'

Croquet   The intelligent game, as it has been dubbed, has been played in England since about 1851. It probably came from Ireland. The received opinion of croquet – that it was a diversion for curates and spinsters in crinolines on rectory lawns – endured for more than a century. It is indeed only in recent times that the game has been perceived as requiring a unique blend of intellectual and physical skills – a cross between snooker and chess played on grass. A croquet break can last as long as half an hour, and some close fought games last three hours. The governing body of English – indeed world – croquet is the Croquet Association, run by one man from an office inside the Hurlingham Club on the Thames near Putney Bridge. The sport is booming and there are some ten thousand playing it in Britain – four thousand competitively. It needs forward planning, accuracy, skill and mental ability. It remains one of the few truly sportsmanlike and genuinely amateur games.

Crumpet   In England the word now means two separate, though perhaps occasionally related, things. It is a soft, round cake with holes in the top, made from a yeast batter and if at all possible toasted in front of an open fire. In this context it is an indispensable part of the English autumn, or at least the Englishman's idealised perception of it. Sir John

Masterman, Vice-Chancellor of Oxford University from 1957 to 1960, for example, memorably transfixed the crumpet experience in his autobiography *On the Chariot Wheel.*

Writing of his days as an undergraduate before the First World War (he went up to Worcester College in 1909) he recalled: 'The height of luxury was reached in the winter afternoons. There were no bathrooms, so we fetched boiling water in large tin cans from a tap by the kitchen and filled our tin baths which we put in front of our sitting-room fire. Lying in a tin bath, in front of a coal fire, drinking tea and eating well-buttered crumpets is an experience which few can have today.'

Few indeed. Eighty-five years on, crumpet to most young Englishmen is a collective form for young available female talent and sometimes for female pudenda as well, as in the celebrated rugby song. 'One night in gay Paree / I paid five francs to see / a much-tattooed lady...' and so on till the denouement of the entertainment; 'And on her crumpet, on her crumpet, / Louis Armstrong played his trumpet.' We have thus come a long way from the crumpet in front the fire: or any rate what Sir John meant by it.

The crumpet has a near cousin in the more homely muffin. Though it still flourishes in America as the English muffin, it has been usurped by its sin-laden relation in the land of its birth. Hard to make at home, as even Mrs Beeton noted, it is no longer carried from door to door by the muffin man of Dickensian England.

Custard 'Food, glorious food, cold jelly and custard,' sing the hungry boys in Lionel Bart's musical *Oliver.* This is fair reporting, for most English children seem to like custard as much as some of them dislike rice pudding. Ironically, the word is a corruption of the French *croustade*, which means a dish prepared with crusts and bearing little relation indeed to what the English now mean by custard. Strictly, and certainly in the world of Mrs Beeton, a custard is a mixture of beaten eggs and milk sweetened and then baked.

For over a century and a half now, however, most English people have in truth been happy instead with the cornflour-based custard powder devised by the Victorian chemist Alfred Bird because his wife had a delicate stomach and could not take egg-based dishes. 'From 1837 to this very day,' pronounced Bird's in the *Daily Mail* on the coronation of King George V in 1911, 'Bird's Custard has reigned supreme as the national family dish.' It was 'as welcome at every table as King George himself would be: it crowns every meal with success!'

The craze for custard with every pud is not one that the Brits have exported with any success; middle Europeans starting their restaurants in postwar England were mystified to be asked for custard with their lovingly presented *Apfel-strudel*. As the island race gradually grows more travelled and worldly, the national penchant for custard is giving way to a preference for cream, ice cream, yoghurt, or nothing at all with puds.

Still, custard remains a firm favourite with children, northerners, old-age pensioners and people who eat in caffs. Confusingly, custard powder is now sold in sachets to the French, who rather like it and call it *le pudding*.

Darts Though there have been attempts to trace darts back to archery, all we can say for sure is that the modern game began around the turn of the century. At first it was faced with a legal hurdle: in 1908 a Yorkshire landlord was hauled before the Leeds magistrates accused of running a game of chance in his pub. With a sense of histrionics worthy of Perry Mason, he rigged up a board in the courtroom and threw three darts into the double top – then did it again to show it was no fluke. The case was dismissed.

With the superseding of the old wooden barrel by the new aerodynamic tungsten body, darts began to attract sponsorship money and is now big business. It is a cheap, convenient game requiring both mental and physical skills, appealing to both sexes and all ages. It transcends social barriers, but is obviously played best in a pub* with a pint*. Indeed the dimensions of some of the world's best players, now displayed regularly on television, illustrate vividly how closely the two pleasures relate.

There are now some six and half million players in Britain, and that makes darts the most popular of all English games. One of the top players in the world is the Englishman Bob Anderson of Swindon, known in the business as The Limestone Cowboy.

D-Day Most Englishmen heard of it first on the 8 o'clock news that heady morning of June 6 fifty-two years ago; ironically the BBC then was merely relaying a German announcement; John Snagge's cool voice did not give the official British version till 9.32 a.m. It was probably the best single moment of the war; VE day was a blurred delight that in a sense stretched a week from the 1st of May, when the world heard that Hitler had killed himself, till May 8, when the European war untidily ended.

The south of England had been in effect a no-go area since February but no one knew exactly when the invasion would happen; not even Eisenhower knew himself till the day before; but when he said 'let's go' he was playing a gigantic hunch that worked. The weather to come would have prevented an invasion for the next fortnight, and might have scuppered it. All the clichés applied; and General Montgomery, commanding 21 Army Group, used them unsparingly. 'The time has come to deal the enemy a terrific blow,' he told his troops. 'Let us pray that the Lord Mighty in Battle go forth with our armies ... Good luck to each one of you. And good hunting on the mainland of Europe.' Winston Churchill went to the House of Commons at noon to give them the momentous news looking, wrote Harold Nicolson, then a National Labour MP, 'as white as a sheet'. Did he have some dreadful tidings for them? No; but he deliberately spun out the tension by dealing first with the fall of Rome.

Over the retrospect of the half century two things become plain: the Germans, many marinated on the eastern front, had much the better of the fighting when on anything like level terms; but the Brits brilliantly won the battle of intelligence. They bamboozled the Germans so thoroughly into thinking the invasion would come much further east, in the Pas de Calais, that for weeks after the Normandy landings they continued to believe the real blow was still to fall up there and locked up their armour far from the real battle. Indeed it is now known that the entire German espionage system in Britain had been turned round and, for most of the war, was working a double-cross against its former masters. Perfidious Albion!

Few who took part in D-Day, the greatest armada ever mounted, and came away unscathed, had any regrets. For once the grandiose exhortation of Henry V sounded apt: '...and gentlemen in England now abed / Shall think themselves accurs'd they were not here.' One or two English gentlemen did, however, have other things on their mind that great morning. Evelyn Waugh*, on extended leave from his army duties (his superiors were frankly relieved to be rid of him) was finishing *Brideshead Revisited*. 'This morning at breakfast the waiter told me the Second Front had opened,' he noted in his diary. 'I sat down early to work and wrote a fine passage of Lord Machmain's death agonies. Carolyn came to tell me the popular front was open. I sent for the priest to give Lord Marchmain the last sacraments ... My only fear is lest the invasion upset my typist at St. Leonard's.'

Debrett   The name by which everybody knows the great guide to the Peerage and Baronetage of England, Ireland, Wales and Scotland, which has been published under various guises for three centuries but was given its stamp of authority and accuracy by John Debrett (1753–1822).

John Debrett first put his name to the book in 1802, but the provenance of the peerage can be traced back to 1769 when a Piccadilly bookseller, John Almon, published *The New Peerage* in three slender volumes. The present editors have a copy of this first edition in their offices in Fulham.

Debrett is designed to include information of every living male descended in the male line from the first peer or baronet, and of all living females being issue of males so descended. It is impossible to say how many thousands of names appear in *Debrett*, but approximately 16,000 proofs are sent out to the various families prior to publication. Until 1970 *Debrett* was an annual publication, but it now appears once every five years.

Derby Day   It is the great English lark; the one day of the year when the class structure dissolves in a vast kaleidoscopic blur. The royals are there, and so are the gypsies; the rich arrive in helicopters and the trippers in trains; the clubmen charter private buses and the punters commandeer all the taxis. The bookies have a field day and so do the pickpockets. Men will wear anything from grey toppers to knotted hankies, women anything from Balenciaga to bikinis. Bollinger and Bass wash down the lobster and the whelks.

It is a horse race that was started as a bit of fun by some young aristos two centuries ago; it is still just that. It was said of Lord Rosebery that, by being prime minister, marrying a Rothschild and winning the Derby he had proved that you could improve your bank balance, run the country, and still study form. Though the racing can be spectacular, it is simply the pretext for a national rave-up.

Anyone who takes the Derby seriously is breaking the unwritten rule. When the gallant Emily Davison threw herself under the King's horse at the Derby in 1912 for her suffragette faith, she had unwittingly broken the rule: several clergymen declined to give her a Christian burial.

Dickens, Charles (1812–70)   We tend to think of audience ratings as an essentially twentieth-century device. Not so: Charles Dickens knew all about them. All his working life he enjoyed the challenge of the serial form: the rigour of the deadline and the need to pull something fresh out of the hat each week; the kick of swift reader-response and the chastening constraint of sales. He had been probably the fastest shorthand-writer ever to sit in the House of Commons; and he was to be one of the readiest novelists ever to spin out his own human comedy instead of the one he had previously been paid to report. He got the offer to write *Pickwick Papers* on 10 February 1836, accepted on 16 February, began writing on 18 February, and saw the first number published on 31 March. Understandably it took a few weeks for him to settle down; but once he did, he established a magical rapport with his audience he was never to lose. He did it by filling his books with a huge cast of people so real that they leap off the page at the reader; so real to Dickens himself that he was once found lurching about his study in alarming distress: he was writing a scene for the evil dwarf, Quilp. Characters and readers were thus equally alive to Dickens; and when he picked up his pen he switched on the current between them.

He had hankered after his own weekly magazine as early as 1845 ('price three halfpence, if possible, partly original, partly select, notices of books, notices of theatres … cheerful views, sharp anatomisation of humbug, jolly good temper'). Five years later he became editor of *Household Words*, and remained the active editor of a periodical till his death twenty years later (after a quarrel with his publisher he launched his own magazine *All the Year Round* in 1859). As owner, editor, and writer, therefore, Dickens knew on a week-to-week basis exactly how what he had to offer was going down. If one of his writers contributed a weak serial, sales would melt away as relentlessly as a modern TV-rating. When that happened Dickens had both the generosity of mind and titanic vim to step in and pull the serial round. He ran, in effect, an early writers' workshop.

To do that, he had to have an exact and lively idea of what the common reader wanted. That is why there are few longueurs or obscurities in Dickens. 'He was successful,' concluded Leslie Stephen, 'Beyond any English novelist, probably beyond any novelist that has ever lived, in exactly hitting off the precise tone of thought and feeling that would find favour with grocers.' Queen Victoria concurred 'He had a large loving mind,' she wrote on his death, 'and the strongest sympathy with the poorest classes. He felt sure a better feeling, and much greater union of classes, would take place in time. And I pray earnestly it may.'

Victoria's prayer has been answered, Charles Dickens, pop writer *nonpareil*, must be given a bold credit line.

Dog   Yet another of those common English words which seems to carry far too heavy a load of meanings for its small size. More, this plethora of definitions and contexts leads to all kinds of problems. Why for example should a 'dog's dinner' denote both anything highly ornate *and* a right mess? How can it come to mean both a worthless fellow and a gallant? 'What you dogs,' cried Fr Johnson* from his window, seeing his friends beneath, 'will you have sport?' Nor is it altogether archaic in that sense: 'In the old days with married women's stockings / Twisted round his bedpost he felt himself a gay / Dog but now his liver has begun to groan,' wrote Louis MacNeice* in 'The Libertine'. How do we pick our way among such disparate senses as a showbiz flop (American), feet and, on both sides of the Atlantic, a sausage? Then what about its use as the name of a star, a grappling iron, the tooth of a wheel, or the iron rest for burning wood in a fireplace? All this before we even consider its common-sense use as the name of a domestic animal. When did a 'dogsbody' cease to be a sailor's name for dried pease boiled in a cloth and become the universal English name for a general factotum? Not, according to the *OED*, till D.H. Lawrence used it thus in 1922. The transition is clear. A dogsbody was a junior midshipman; that most lowly of all naval officers. A wretch like this is so often 'in the doghouse' that he must occasionally need 'a hair of the dog' that bit him; after which he's 'like a dog with two tails'.

Perhaps it is just the sheer number of dogs in England which leads to all these meanings. There are some six million in the country, ranging from the lordly champions at Cruft's Dogs Show with exotic names like Grayco Hazlenut and Burtonswood Bossy Boots to the twenty-two thousand anonymous mongrels given refuge each year by the Battersea Dogs Home. Dogs no longer need a licence; but then only half the dogs in England ever had one. This only goes to show that it is as pointless to expect common sense from the English where dogs are concerned as it is with cats*.

Domino   Another multi-purpose word, with new meanings accreting on the ancient ones. It is (a) a monk's habit (b) the keys of a piano (c) a mistake in music (d) the light used to illumine the cyclorama or backdrop of a television studio or (e) most familiarly to English people, a piece of ivory, bone or wood marked with dots and used in a pub game for some two hundred years.

And there is the term *domino effect*, a phrase first coined during the Eisenhower era in the mid-fifties to encapsulate the theory that if any one country in south-east Asia fell to the communists, its neighbours would fall in line.

Of all the varieties of domino games – matadors, sebastopol, bergen, and so on – the best, according to *Hoyle's Games*, is the kind called bingo. Yet bingo is also the exclamation made by somebody winning the desolate game that has now stolen the name of bingo, and is a kind of lotto or, in serviceman's lingo, housey-housey. Do people now cry bingo as they would once have cried domino? The lineage seems insecure, and not for the first time, we must put the echo down to the deep reverberation of coincidence that runs right through the English language.

The Dorchester Hotel   It opened its doors to the public on 20 April 1931. A single room cost thirty-two shillings and sixpence; lunch eight shillings and sixpence; dinner with dancing fifteen shillings and sixpence. The first big night there was the Speed Ball on 9 June 1931, organised by the Air League to celebrate Britain's holding at that point world speed records for land, sea and air. Famed thirties racing drivers Woolf Barnato and Kaye Don were there, air pioneers Sir Alan Cobham and Colonel J.T.C. Moore-Brabazon, later Lord Brabazon – who held the first pilot's licence in Britain; and Sir Malcolm Campbell, who was to hold both land and water speed records.

Later that month the Dorchester was the elegant setting for the Famous Beauties Ball at which the debutante of the previous year, Margaret Whigham, (later Duchess of Argyll, renowned for quite a different sort of fastness) starred. General Eisenhower, finding Claridge's too lush for his taste (to be exact, too like 'a goddam fancy funeral parlour'), moved to the Dorchester during the war. Here his chauffeuse and lady love Kay Summersby did her best to make him feel less funereal. Here too the queen of thirties society hostesses, Lady Sybil Colefax, gave the last of her great Thursday dinner parties. She was by now, relatively speaking, poor; and guests got a discreet little bill some days after each party. But her friends were loyal, kept her secret, and paid up.

In 1976 the McAlpine family, who had built the Dorchester, sold it to an Arab consortium. The Arabs paid £9 million for it and also cleared a debt of £1.5 million. It was a bargain. They then spent another £10 million refurbishing it and, despite some grumbles about alien ownership, have made it one of the most elegant hostelries in the world. But lunch no longer costs eight-and-six.

Dover   Though to most Englishmen the unhappy inspiration for one of the most dire popular songs (Vera Lynn's) and one of the most banal poems (Alice Duer Miller's) the white cliffs of Dover have at least this to recommend them: they are the gateway to Abroad*.

Downing Street   Once the place where James Boswell lodged when first savouring the urban delights of London, and where Tobias Smollett attempted to set up a surgery, Downing Street has become justly celebrated, with No. 10 perhaps the most modest site for a head of government in the civilised world; while the matey proximity of the chancellor of the exchequer at No. 11 only adds to the suburban feel of the arrangement (when he was chancellor, Geoffrey Howe used to refer to the prime minister as Margaret-next-door). No. 10 has not quite recovered from the famous picture of the young Harold Wilson, all of eight and nearly hidden in his flat cap, hopefully posing outside as an earnest of his future plans. He was to occupy No. 10 just forty years on as prime minister himself.

Dunkirk   It is nothing to do with victory or defeat, heroism or cowardice, though all four of course showed their faces there. It is to do with luck, and perhaps with knowing how to play your luck.
   It is also a vivid example of war, not as some ordered gavotte between opposing armies, but what it really is; a dance to the music of chaos. On 23 May 1940 the German army to the south of the British army halted. Why they did so is still not clear. They had been mauled by the British armour. They did not realise the extent of the French collapse. They wanted to regroup for further battles. They probably did not even think Britain would fight on when France had gone. Whatever the reason, they let the British army off the hook.
   Perfect June weather helped 338,226 allied troops get away; a third from the Dunkirk beaches, the rest from Dunkirk harbour. Of these 139,097 were French. Admiral Darlan sent an order to the French forces to let the British withdraw first. Churchill countermanded it: we would go *bras-dessus, bras-dessous*.
   Most of these troops and their officers behaved very well. Some behaved very badly. Churchill told the Commons they should be careful not to assign to this deliverance the attributes of a victory. Wars, he said, are not won by evacuation. But there was a victory inside the deliverance, and it had been won by the Royal Air Force.
   It was nothing like the stunning victory promulgated at the time, indeed it was the usual damn close-run thing. Still, the boys did well.

Dunkirk showed the Brits neither as heroes nor poltroons; but certainly as game-players who know to give luck a chance.

Durham It makes Winchester* and Canterbury seem maelstroms. Perhaps the peninsular foundation on which cathedral and castle stand gives Durham this sense of singular tranquillity; perhaps it is to do with the immense perspective afforded by the enshrinement here of Cuthbert and Bede. Whatever the reason, Durham remains a medieval haven set in some of the most stunning and uncelebrated countryside in the land. It is a curiously tolerant place, able to accommodate both the celebrated Miners' Gala and the Rolls-Royce Car Rally. It can boast the oldest regatta in the country and a cluster of the best castles (Durham itself, Raby, Barnard and Bowes). It has one of the oldest regiments (the Durham Light Infantry) and its university did England a notable service when its inception ended the six-hundred-year monopoly of Oxbridge. Above all, it is a place where you can hear yourself think. The great knocker on the cathedral door symbolised sanctuary for miscreants over the centuries, and still does.

Ealing Studios

Ealing Studios Though films were made in this quiet suburban backwater from the very beginning of the cinema (Will Barker, a pioneer of the industry, bought two houses facing Ealing Green in 1902, and was shooting on his first covered stage by 1907), the apogee of Ealing was the twenty-one-year-period (1938–59) when Sir Michael Balcon was in charge.

From first to last it was an archetypal cottage industry, turning out quiet and honest films about small groups of embattled people at odds with the big battalions. The typical Ealing film would take a sample of widely variegated human beings and follow their fortunes in the grip of some vast extraneous force; *Dunkirk* and *The Cruel Sea* are good examples. It specialised too in polished and urbane comedies like *Kind Hearts and Coronets* or *Passport to Pimlico*.

Sometimes accused of making nothing but comedies and war films, Ealing in fact essayed every genre except the musical (though some may rank *Champagne Charlie* as one) and the Western. The actor most closely associated with Ealing's golden years is Alec Guinness, who turned in performances in films like *The Ladykillers* and *The Lavender Hill Mob* which are masterpieces of understated irony.

Eventually sold to the BBC, Ealing is now used as television studios; a proper destiny for a company that had always excelled with ordinary people doing believable things against realistic backgrounds: what we now call the documentary style of film-making.

The Eighties   Some decades get obvious adjectives; the Swinging Sixties, the Naughty Nineties. What, though, will be the verdict on the eighties? Aching? AIDS-hit? Aimless? It is still hard to know. Clearly, it was a decade when the world swung radically right; Reaganomics dominated America; Thatcherism called the shots in Britain; and though Mitterand had a long run of power in France, it was a troubled one, and hardly another major western power had a government of the left. In Britain the key power struggles were with the miners (who lost decisively) and the print unions (who lost too – and for the first time). Internationally, though the biggest headache was the festering chaos in the Persian Gulf, the most cheerful news for the west was the arrival of Gorbachov as the new leader of the Soviet Union and his dramatic espousal of the new policies of *glasnost,* or openness, and *perestroika,* or new directions. In British terms at least, the media scene was demonstrably gladdened by the safe delivery of Channel Four and a fine new newspaper, *The Independent.* Medically, the onset of the ghastly new affliction of AIDS was terrifying; and perhaps central in inaugurating a new era of sexual orthodoxy. Television serials like *Brideshead Revisited* and *The Jewel in the Crown* did much to enhance the reputation of British television at its best; legal cases like those in which Jeffrey Archer* and Cynthia Payne* starred did much to increase the gaiety of the nation. It was the era of the Big Bang and the Golden Hello. The voice of the yuppie* was heard in the land. It was the heyday of Maxwell and Murdoch and Saatchi and Saatchi. Alternative living was out; making money was in. The SDP was born; the GLC died. The Filofax generation bowed in; the pound note bowed out. As the eighties drew to a close, it dawned on people that they were facing not just a new decade but, soon, a new century, with all the unimaginable challenges that would bring. The twentieth century seemed set to make its exit with a tight fist, a tight belt, and a tight smile.

Elgar, Sir Edward (1857–1934)   When his First Symphony was played for the first time at a Hallé Concert in the Free Trade Hall, Manchester, on 3 December 1908, a nineteen-year-old youth called Neville Cardus was in the enraptured audience. 'No English symphony existed then, at least not big enough to make a show of comparison with a symphony by Beethoven or Brahms', he wrote much later, 'I cannot hope ... to describe the pride taken in Elgar by young English students of that far-away epoch.'
  The audience would not let the symphony proceed after the great slow movement until the composer had come out to acknowledge their

ovation, and at the end of the work the orchestra rose as a man and cheered him to the echo. 'This was not only Elgar's first symphony', wrote his biographer Michael Kennedy, 'it was England's.'

There will be those who prefer the teasing conundrum set in the Enigma Variations, some who are moved by the mystical thrall of The Dream of Gerontius. Others again will opt for the brooding grandeur of the Cello concerto and there will be simpler spirits who still like to hear the stirring melody, albeit worn smooth with use, of the first Pomp and Circumstance March. ('Gosh man, I've got a tune in my head!' he wrote to his friend Jaeger.) Whichever work we choose as our own, Elgar speaks always of England, or more precisely, sets England to music.

Essentially a landscape artist painting in sound, he told his musicians to play the First 'like something you hear down by the river'. Frequently at odds with Edwardian England (he walked out of a Royal Academy dinner because he thought he had not been properly seated and resigned from the Athenaeum when Ramsay MacDonald was elected) he nevertheless caught perfectly its bitter-sweet flavour. When he was born, there was something in the jibe that England was a land without music; by the time he died his own work alone had made nonsense of the charge.

Elms   The notion that elms could be afflicted by disease is not new; the first was noted as long ago as 1838 and was back again by 1927. Yet within ten years the great English elms had shrugged off the epidemic – though not before it had killed at least one in ten; maybe more. Then a new and far more deadly form of Dutch elm disease was identified in the sixties, killing 400,000 trees a year in America and Canada. It reached England before 1970, and by the end of the decade had killed no fewer than eleven million elms.

Nothing is sadder than those great gaunt skeletons straddling the landscape, leaving what had once been the inimitable verdure of the English countryside as bare as a battlefield. To this grievous loss there is no quick answer, but new trees are being planted to replace the dead giants: oak, beech, chestnut, lime, ash, poplar, sycamore, maple and willow. It would be comforting to believe that the most robust elms will in the end grow immune to the beetle that has laid them low; such optimism would be misplaced.

The English Language   Our greatest single national asset. Its capital value is unquantifiable. It is the first language in the world. It is the principal language of business and diplomacy. It has the richest literature and is the greatest treasury of fiction, poetry and drama. It is an exquisitely subtle and endlessly flexible tongue. It is crammed with idiom and slang. It is vastly hospitable to new words and fresh cultures. It is as earthy as it is elegant, as randy as it is fastidious. It is the language of the sea and the air, the international argot of all sea captains and airline pilots. It is the first language of sport and science. It is the language of computer software and hard rock. Any new young English or American writer has an immediate audience of 600 million; a young Armenian or Finn has no such luck. To this vast good fortune in life's lottery your average Englishman is totally impervious. He takes it as a matter of course that the world speaks English: what else would it speak?

Epsom   To Englishmen it means two things: its salts, culled from a local spring and only too effective in moving the bowels, and its racecourse. See also *Derby* Day.

Esquire   Properly a rank between knight and gentleman. Strictly, barristers are esquires; solicitors just gentlemen. Justices of the peace are esquires, but only while they are being JPs. The eldest sons of knights are esquires, and so are their eldest sons. 'The impossibility of knowing who is an esquire and who not,' remarked Sir Ernest Gowers in his updating edition of *Fowler's Modern English Usage*, 'combined with a reluctance to draw invidious distinctions, has deprived *esquire* of all significance.' Just so, and surely the right answer is to drop it altogether. This would at least help the sort of Englishman who has his mail sent to America as John Robinson Esq and never receives it because the hotel desk clerk over there has – not unnaturally – pigeonholed it under the letter E. When we do at last abandon this quaint survival, however, we shall lose certain fine English nuances. One English bank had a handy rule of thumb. Those whose accounts were in credit were always addressed as Esquire; those in the red as Mr. If, however, the account plunged deep enough into the red, they became esquires again. That says a lot about banking – and the English.

Establishment   Earlier contexts can be found, but in precisely the sense now used, one man has the honour of having coined it. In the *Spectator* on 23 September 1955, Henry Fairlie wrote: 'By the Establishment I do not mean only the centres of official power – though they are certainly part of it – but rather the whole matrix of official and social relations within which power is exercised.' It very quickly took on a pejorative colouring it has never lost.

Eton 'I had got in on the first round, being put up by Knebworth but after they had left only the smell of Balkan Sobrani and Honey and Flowers remained to prove it was not a dream.' Thus Cyril Connolly* on his election to Pop, the unlegislated ruling body of Eton. Such was the prestige of Pop Connolly tells us, that some boys who failed to get in never recovered: 'One was rumoured to have procured his sister for the influential members.' In this privileged cocoon the outside world looked bleak, the future empty: 'I dreaded leaving ... early laurels weigh like lead and of many of the boys whom I knew at Eton, I can say that their lives are over.'

In an imaginary dialogue with his old school Connolly is chided for wasting his chances: 'You could have made lasting friendships with people who will govern the country – not flashy people, but those from whose lodges, in a Scotch deer-forest, great decisions are taken. You Bolshies keep on thinking the things we stand for – cricket, shooting, Ascot, Lord's, the Guards, the House of Commons and the Empire – are dead. But you all want to put your sons down for Eton.' How true: then, anyway.

Connolly was at Eton with George Orwell*, Anthony Powell, Henry Green, John Lehmann, Harold Acton and Alec Douglas-Home. Is a contemporary Etonian living among such future goers? Only time will tell. We shall argue under the Old Boy Network* that when Margaret Thatcher's new government took its place on the Front Bench of the Commons in 1983 it contained not a single Etonian. This was true: but only a few months later, one of the grammar school boys (Cecil Parkinson) got a girl into trouble and had to go. Who should take his place? Hey presto, Nicholas Ridley, Old Etonian! Meanwhile in the Lords Eton is always in strength. Yet it is now twenty-four years since the last Etonian was prime minister: how long will it be before the next?

Europe To an Englishman, still the Continent. Thus one of the great political debates of the 1990s turns on whether or not we should go into *Europe;* the fact that we are for all other purposes already in it is ignored. To this day, *we* are in England; *they* are in Europe.

Fag This is one of the portmanteau words that mean different things both on either side of the Atlantic and, in England, to different layers of society. Thus while in America the word is a shortened form of *faggot* and means a homosexual, here it means variously a cigarette, a chore, or a junior boy who works for a senior boy in a public school. In this last sense it has had a good run for its money, surfacing at the opening of the nineteenth century and probably reaching its apogee (if that is the right word) in *Tom Brown's Schooldays*, published in 1857, and drawing a horrendous picture of cruelty practised by older boys on smaller ones.

While fags are no longer (one hopes) roasted on open fires as they were then, at Wellington as late as 1959 fags had to warm the lavatory seats by sitting on them first for their fagmasters. Still, if you must be a fag, it is no doubt better to have a cold bum that a burnt one. The theory of fagging was that however grand your own background, it did you no harm to black somebody else's boots and grill his sausages until you grew big enough to give the orders yourself.

In some schools fagging was even unionised with modest weekly payments to the long-suffering fag for the work he did. Many public schools have now abolished the practice altogether. Yet even in modern England it is possible to meet grown men who have still not got over their old fagging relationship. It may have involved beating, bullying, buggery and perhaps all three; but once you've been through all that with your fagmaster it stays with you for life.

The Falklands Conflict   Does it belong in the annals of glory or the theatre of the absurd? To the average Englishman watching the British fleet majestically sail out of Portsmouth with ensigns fluttering and bands playing there could be only one answer: both. On millions of colour television sets, it looked like a weird signal picked up in a time warp from the world of 1940: perhaps even 1914. It was magnificent, as Maréchal Bosquet had remarked of the charge of the Light Brigade, but it was not war – surely? Certainly no member of the British cabinet who gave the order for the Task Force to sail thought on that day that it would ever be used. Yet, given the dimensions of the dispute and the intransigent personalities of the leading players, it is clear in hindsight that once that mighty engine was set in motion it was inevitable that it should. The moral dilemma was as poignant as it was insoluble: if permanent armed services were to be kept, what were they for if not for this? If Galtieri were not to be confronted, how could the argument for *force majeure* ever be parried? No one saw quite how high the horrendous risks were: if the Argentinians had owned six dozen Exocet missiles instead of a mere six the Falklands could have been a ghastly disaster for British arms instead of a gritty triumph.

It cost one million pounds to free each man, woman and child on the Falklands; and, infinitely more precious, the lives of a thousand young men. The Falklanders got rid of one occupying army; but had to put up with another. The Falklands conflict was a resounding political triumph for Margaret Thatcher, whose fortunes had been wavering before the crisis; and may well have been the main factor that swept her irresistibly back to power in 1983. She told her countrymen to rejoice in the victory; but certainly the men who had fought the gutter war (as their commanding officer called it) eight thousand miles away, the last surely of all Britain's colonial wars, saw little to rejoice about. As the Duke of Wellington had remarked after the Battle of Waterloo when a lady said what a glorious thing a victory must be: 'The greatest tragedy in the world, madam, except a defeat.'

Farming   There have always been three ways to lose money in England, or so they say: gambling, women, and agriculture. The first is the most speedy, the second the most pleasant, and the third the most certain. The coiner of this aphorism was probably a farmer himself, and one who farmed in the inter-war years. Today English farmers, handsomely endowed by the Common Market agricultural policy, highly mechanised and politically sophisticated, are doing very nicely thank you; though they still cry all the way to the bank.

Fields, Gracie (1898–1979) When she underwent major surgery for cancer in 1939, prayers were said for her in English churches, and newspapers and radio carried daily bulletins. She was loved that much. She made a complete recovery; but a few months later was as much the subject of English obloquy as she had been of English adulation. She had agreed to marry, as her second husband (her marriage to Archie Pitt in 1923 when she was twenty-five had been one of convenience on both sides), an Italian film director called Mario Bianchi (otherwise known as Monty Banks). He was an enemy alien; and therefore liable to be interned in England. Archie died in 1940 and she married Mario in the same year. The press at once accused her of deserting England in her hour of need. She was gradually restored to favour; and after Monty died, she married in 1952 as her third husband Boris Alperovici, a Bessarabian radio engineer living in Capri. With him she found real content. From 1931, when she made her first film, till 1945, when she made her last, she fulfilled her true role: in the words of the archivist of cinema, Leslie Halliwell, that of keeping the nation cheerful. Her Rochdale roots gave her instant access to the hearts of English people everywhere, and whether she was singing something serious like 'Ave Maria' or comic like 'The Biggest Aspidistra' she invariably held her audience. Just as Vera Lynn was the Forces' Sweetheart, so she, born twenty years earlier, was always simply Our Gracie. She was the archetypal voice of the factory girl with the heart of gold.

The Fifties The average wage in Britain in 1950 was £6 8s. Petrol was still rationed and food still on points; at one time the fresh meat allocation was eightpence-worth a week, and there was still a five-shilling limit in restaurants. Yet during the fifties the national income roughly doubled. It was, as Harold Macmillan famously remarked, the time when the island race never had it so good.

It was the era of espresso bar and rock'n'roll. The first long-playing record reached England in 1950. It was the decade of the picaresque novel and the shambling, oafish anti-hero, flotsam of the welfare state: Lucky Jim and his first cousin Joe Lampton in *Room at the Top*. Then, in May 1956, the curtain rose at the Royal Court Theatre on an attic flat somewhere in the Midlands* where Alison Porter and her husband Jimmy fought, loved, argued, suffered and made up. Playgoers nourished on the bland pabulum of Binkie Beaumont did not at first know what to make of *Look Back in Anger*, but they could not ignore it. John Osborne had brought a new passion and a new rage into the English theatre.

The coronation of Elizabeth II in 1953 made England rush out and buy television sets by the million; and the coming of a commercial television channel in 1956, run by an Independent Television Authority, gave the BBC a much-needed jolt. Men who put their money in the new commercial television companies took a huge risk and lost initial fortunes. When the corner was turned and the advertising cascaded in many of those who had hung on became millionaires overnight.

Roger Bannister was the first man to run the mile in four minutes (on 6 May 1954); the barrier had evidently been psychological, for it was run inside that magic marker a further fifty times before 1960. England regained the Ashes in 1953 and held them most of the decade. It was the era of great British racing drivers – Hawthorn, Collins and Moss – though only Moss was to survive the decade. It was the era of the great traitors: Pontecorvo, the atomic physicist, defected to Russia; the renegade diplomats, Burgess and Maclean, disappeared in 1951, to resurface in Russia four years later. No one knew then that two more celebrated traitors – Blunt and Philby – still lay undetected in the bosom of the Establishment*.

Twice in the decade the world came close to war: in the Korean conflict of 1950 and again during the complex events of autumn 1956 which culminated in the Suez crisis and the Hungarian revolution. Suez was to divide fathers and sons, husbands and wives, as no issue in England had since the Boer War, and no issue since. Though now seen as an evident folly, a last spasm of the old imperial imperative, then the issue was by no means clear. A million Brits had seen service in and around Suez in the war and had no love of the wogs*; *The Guardian*, which took a strong and clear anti-Suez line, had bricks thrown through its windows for its pains. It had been a turbulent decade: but would the sixties prove any better?

Fish and Chips   Dickens* mentioned a fried-fish warehouse in *Oliver Twist* (1837–9) but in those early days the fish were cooked in open pans at the seller's home and then hawked around the streets with a piece of bread, or later baked potatoes. It was only in 1865 that chipped potatoes (an idea imported from France) began to be sold with fried fish; they were soon to be inseparable, indeed unthinkable apart. The new railways enabled fish from Grimsby, Fleetwood and Hull to be landed one day and on sale anywhere in the country the next. Soon the staple of the working class, fish and chips were the first of all convenience foods: ready cooked, needing no washing-up, eaten standing in the street, delicious, nutritious and cheap. Englishmen of middle years will recall how children could once buy a penn'orth of chips without the fish, shovelled mouth-wateringly from the sizzling fat into a small white bag; and that was when there were 240 pennies to the pound. Properly taken with rock salt and vinegar or HP sauce*, fish and chips should have an outer wrapping of newspaper but this harmless pleasure has now been banned by Brussels. Though they now have to fight for their share of the market with the hamburger boom and the Chinese takeaway, fish and chips endure: they were the first thing the troops called for when they had retaken the Falklands*.

Fishing   Six million Englishmen fish and it is thus the second most popular pastime of the race after darts*. As to why they fish, perhaps only one of the fraternity can explain. One summer day during the last world war the English writer H.E. Bates went fishing and reported: 'There is something mesmeric about it. You can sit sometimes by the water when the wind is rippling it into small rapid waves and watch the float until the waves and the scarlet cap produce a queer feeling of magnetism ...

'You hear people say that fishing is a waste of time. Can time be wasted? ... In a hundred years it will not matter much whether on a June day in 1941 I fished for perch or devoted the same time to acquiring greater learning by studying the works of Aristotle, of which, anyway, I have no copy.

'The day is very hot, and there are thousands of golden-cream roses blooming on the house wall in the sun. Perhaps someone will be glad that I described them, sitting as I am forty miles from the German lines at Calais. Perhaps someone will wonder then at the stoicism, the indifference, the laziness or the sheer lack of conscience of someone who thought roses and fish have at least as much importance as tanks and bombs.' (*The Country Heart*, 1949)

Fleet Street   The Fleet was once a river; today it is a sewer: the symbolism will not be lost on Fleet Street's enemies, and they are legion. As a collective metaphor for the newspaper industry, Fleet Street had a life of precisely a hundred years: from the moment in 1888 when Alfred Harmsworth (1865–1922) founded *Answers* to the moment in 1988 when the last national newspaper pulled out of the Street of Shame, and set up shop in dockland.

Answers gave Harmsworth the platform from which to launch his vastly successful *Daily Mail*, the paper, as Lord Salisbury remarked, written by office boys for office boys. It made Harmsworth rich and gave him power. It made him Lord Northcliffe and ennobled *four* of his brothers.

The Harmsworths were the first bold bad press lords; but there were soon many more: Lords Beaverbrook*, Camrose, Kemsley, Iliffe, Burnham, Bracken and Thomson. They collectively caught and mirrored the aspirations of the newly literate millions; but by a combination of avarice, stupidity and cowardice created a monster riddled with malpractice, inefficiency and over-manning swollen to bursting point. It needed a new generation of ruthless untitled tycoons (Shah, Murdoch, Maxwell) to prick that great bubble. Since the siege of Wapping, the power of the print unions has been smashed. Whether the new generation of computerised, cold metal papers is any improvement is a moot point.

For the last quarter of its uneasy century-long sway, Fleet Street has been hoist by its own petard: mercilessly flayed with ridicule by its incorrigible house journal *Private Eye**, an offset-litho fortnightly begun in 1961 on a capital of £450 and a circulation of three hundred.

Fleming, Ian (1908–64) To Beaverbrook* he was 'The Chocolate Sailor'. To his colleagues on *The Sunday Times* he was Lady Rothermere's Fan (she became his first – and only – wife when he was forty-two). He began to write his first book, *Casino Royale* (1953), at Goldeneye, his house in Jamaica, as an antidote to marriage. It took him seven weeks.

Despite all his disclaimers, there are clear similarities between Ian Fleming and James Bond. Both were worldly womanisers; both were naval officers; both were *aficionados* of food, drink, cards and cars; both knew the seamier sides of the world's great cities from personal patronage. To be fair, flesh-and-blood Fleming was rather less coarse than cinematic Bond, and far more interesting to talk to; he was a noted book collector, for example, and Bond would never have had time.

He became a citizen of the world early, spending all his school holidays, like Richard Hillary*, at *pensions* in Austria, Germany and Switzerland. Though arithmetically successful with women, he shows little sign in his books of understanding them. 'Very poor lover', his old friend Cyril Connolly adjudicated, 'Always used to get up and go home for breakfast.' And when he wrote the Atticus column for a spell on *The Sunday Times*, it was Connolly who dubbed it Attila.

Yet Fleming was never dull, and his faintly arrogant insouciance amused men as it fascinated women. 'Only call God and the King Sir' was one of his early maxims. And how he could write! The first sentence of *Casino Royale* exactly sets the tone for the entire *oeuvre*: 'The scent and smoke and seat of a casino are nauseating at three in the morning.' The world read on.

Flowers 'When daisies pied and violets blue / And lady-smocks all silver-white / And cuckoo-buds of yellow hue / do paint the meadows with delight' wrote Shakespeare, whose work is strewn from end to end with a profusion of country flowers: cowslips, pansies, primroses, thyme, oxlip, eglantine, and marigolds or Mary-buds ('And winking Mary-buds begin / To ope their golden eyes').

This passion for flowers runs right through English writing, and even finds its place among the gritty imperatives of George Orwell*: 'What until twenty years ago was universally called a snapdragon is now called an antirrhinum, a word no-one can spell without consulting a dictionary. Forget-me-nots are coming more and more to be called myosotis. Many other names, Red Hot Poker, Mind Your Own Business, Love Lies Bleeding, London Pride, are disappearing in favour of flavourless Greek names out of botany textbooks ...'

Those botany textbooks, however, have a curious hold over the island race. The Reverend William Keble Martin (1877–1969) was eighty-seven when he published his *Concise British Flora in Colour*, illustrated with his own meticulous and graceful drawings. The book encapsulated a lifetime's love and study of the flowers of England and has sold more than 600,000 copies so far.

Still, the national love affair with flowers is by no means confined to literary men. Benjamin Disraeli adored primroses; Henry Royce was a devoted amateur rose-grower while not designing the world's best car; Joseph Chamberlain loved orchids.

Fog An oddity, since in its most malevolent and man-made manifestation, the pea-souper, it has ceased to be the indispensable prop of the English imagination. There have been mighty and memorable fogs in London since the sixteenth century at least; the pea-souper is an essential accoutrement of many of the greatest Sherlock Holmes* stories as well as of any self-respecting film about Jack the Ripper.

It forms the magnificent opening to *Bleak House* and was well named by Dickens* 'London particular'. In one of his most celebrated images, T.S. Eliot bade fog rub its back upon the window panes, and in one of her most beguiling numbers Ella Fitzgerald sang of a foggy day in London Town that had her blue and had her down. That sort of mock-romantic fog – in truth, no more than a filthy blanket of soot suspended in the freezing air – got its marching orders after the great fog of December 1952, when it was responsible for 4,000 deaths.

A commission of inquiry into the disaster led to the Clean Air Act of 1956. It took a little time to bite – the Lewisham rail disaster a year later was directly due to fog – but since December 1962 London has been without its pea-soupers, to the distress of romantically inclined visiting Holmesians from Manhattan and Moscow, but to the relief of all Londoners.

Football The name for a whole family of games with a common ancestry. At least a dozen kinds of football are still played and six have reached national or international status. They are American, Australian, Gaelic, Rugby League, Rugby Union (or rugger) and Association football (or soccer). When an American says football he means the gigantic war-game played on a grid-iron field with an oval ball, eleven in each team, and all the showbiz bezazz of a presidential election. When an Englishman speaks of football he could mean rugby*; but he probably means soccer.

English football, so defined, is clearly on the up and up. After the Hillsborough disaster there was a massive move to make the game safer, the arrival of Sky TV and the megacash it could inject provided the capital to do it. All major English clubs, for example, are now all-seater, thus dramatically cutting the incidence of crowd violence. The money has also greatly increased the cosmopolitan flavour of football; no fewer than 55 nations provided players for the 1996 English season; England got to the semi-final of the European Cup; players and spectators behaved so well that football became a game you could be happy to be seen at. The gap between the public perception of soccer and rugger closed dramatically. According to the old canard, rugger was a game for ruffians played by gentlemen, soccer a game for gentlemen played by ruffians. There may have been a kernel of truth in the distinction when rugger still clearly showed its public school provenance; but nowadays it is played by all kinds of young Englishmen from policemen to farmers and salesmen to miners. Yet until 1996 there had always been this central difference: in England rugger was played for fun; soccer for money. Now though, the end of amateurism in rugby union and the same avalanche of money from Sky TV that has transformed soccer looks likely to transform rugger too. When money comes in at one door in sport, fun normally soon goes out of the other. Whether it will go out of both codes of English football remains to be seen.

The Forties 'Blood, toil, tears, and sweat' was all Winston Churchill* could offer on 13 May 1940; and for the next five years there was to be enough of it for the British people. Paradoxically though, it was a curiously carefree era. People were given jobs and had no choice but to get on with them. 'These are not dark days,' Churchill told the boys at Harrow* in 1941, 'These are great days.'

The man in the street had far more money in real terms than he had in the bleak thirties, and all the statistics show the health of the country dramatically improved from 1942 on. Whether this was because of better medical care, simpler food, or from some psychosomatic root has never been proved. Bombing proved a great leveller. The rich had to do without servants, clothes and travel; the whole nation, as A.J.P. Taylor* noted, lived roughly on the standard of the skilled artisan.

Besides, one day it would all be over and there would be peace. Johnny would go to sleep, as Vera Lynn* crooned, in his own little room again. The atomic bomb, which was to deny all men the taste of true peace for good, was not yet born. The word teenager was not in use. There was no drug epidemic, no drink problem, and no dieting mania. There was no unemployment; the golden handshake was not invented. The dark progeny of affluence lay in the womb of the future. Men in the services went to current affairs lectures and talked of the brave new world they would build. Perhaps, as is sometimes alleged, the Army Bureau of Current Affairs precipitated the Labour landslide of 1945; but it was probably inevitable anyway.

When the new House of Commons assembled the Conservatives and their allies had lost 203 seats, Labour had gained 227, and the Liberal Party was reduced to a bare dozen. In the first three months of 1946 Atlee's government brought in bills to nationalise the mines, set up a national insurance scheme, repeal the Trades Dispute Act, and establish a National Health Service. Independence for India* was to follow next year. 'We are the masters at the moment,' proclaimed the Labour Attorney-General, Sir Hartley Shawcross, in a sentence that was to haunt him and his government for many years, 'and not only for the moment, but for a very long time to come.'

One thing not even the Attlee government could master was the weather. The winter of 1946–7 was the vilest in living memory. Scotland was cut off totally; there was no power at all in the south, midlands and northwest; two million were thrown out of work; parsnips were dug out with pneumatic drills. Domestic power, where it was available, was banned five hours a day; television and the BBC Third Programme were suspended. There was less food than in the war. In one week in 1948, for instance, the average man's allowance was thirteen ounces of meat, one and a half ounces of cheese, six ounces of butter and margarine, one ounce of cooking fat, eight ounces of sugar, two pints of milk and one egg. In desperation, the government imported ten million tins of an unknown fish called snoek. The island race did not take kindly to it.

This was the heyday of the spiv and the wide boy. It took a special kind of heroism in all this compacted misery for the government to plan a Festival of Britain. One wit was to describe the plethora of new design on show in the 1951 south bank exhibition as all Heal let loose. However, eight million went along, and the Festival worked as a kind of natural watershed between the shabby deprivation of the forties and the high, wide, handsome days of the fifties which surely lay in store. Nothing, the English decided, at any rate, could be any worse than what they had been through. But each decade holds its own horrors.

Fortnum and Mason William Fortnum was a footman in the royal household of Queen Anne; Hugh Mason, a small shopkeeper in St James's market, gave him lodgings. Being in royal service then provided useful perks; in William's case, the disposal of all the unlighted candles used by the royal family. Since fresh candles were provided every day, this proved a flourishing sideline, and in 1707 he persuaded his friend Hugh to join him in starting a grocery business – at first no more than a stall in Piccadilly on the site of the present green and gold building.

By the time Charles Fortnum, grandson of William, entered the service of Queen Charlotte in 1761 at the age of twenty-three he could command a wage of £10.5s.3d per quarter; but this was only the beginning of it; for the royal perks now extended to flogging food, coal, linen and wine. By 1788 the shop sold food with a distinctly modern flavour: game in aspic, potted meats, Scotch eggs and mince pies.

Since there was then no NAAFI Fortnum boxes were dispatched to all parts of the British Raj to feed hungry officers in the Zulu war, the Chinese rebellion, the two Boer wars; Sir William Parry took two hundredweight of Fortnums cocoa with him on his expedition to find the North West Passage; Queen Victoria sent two hundred and fifty pounds of concentrated beef tea to the troops in the Crimea.

On Derby Day* the staff would be on duty at 4 a.m. to stock the long line of coaches that queued in Piccadilly for their hampers. To this day Fortnums staff wear morning coats, thus often getting confused on the days of big society weddings with their customers.

But it is not so much homely jam as exotic delicacies with which the name of Fortnums is perennially associated: a small memento from a maharajah to a lady, say, made up of half a dozen bottles of champagne, a ham, a tongue, three tins of sardines, a box of fruits, a box of chocolates and a little basket of Turkish Delight.

The real point of Fortnums is that it still represents the delights of home to thousands of Brits abroad: from India comes an order for *marrons glacés*, from Saudi Arabia another for Christmas pudding, from Zimbabwe a call for chocolate digestive biscuits.

The French 'Frogs', declared Uncle Matthew in Nancy Mitford's *The Pursuit of Love*, 'are slightly better than Huns or Wops, but abroad is unutterably bloody and all foreigners are fiends.' Time may have softened the edges of this judgment a little, but something of it still lingers in the English mind. The trouble is that the French are not merely the *first* foreign people an Englishman normally meets; they are the *most* foreign. The first and most evocative memory of France any Englishman carries in his head is her smell; that inimitable odour of mingled Gauloises and garlic. And how can a race who still make such divine food endure such deplorable plumbing?

Yet the French have many friends in sophisticated England; traditionally intellectuals, writers and the left are francophile, while business, music, and the right instinctively favour Germany. The trouble is that to the English, politically the French remain a pain in the arse. When Edward VII made his triumphal tour of France in 1903, thus paving the way for the *entente cordiale* next year, he was greeted with cries from the street of 'Vive Edouard' but also by counter-cries of 'Vive Jeanne d'Arc'. On the English side of the Channel, the man in the street still regarded France as the corrupt and traditional enemy; so much so that the leaders of the new Liberal government of December 1905 felt justified in concealing from most of the Cabinet, not to mention the Commons and the country, the fact that conversations had begun between the British and French general staffs.

Things were no better by 1940, when most Frenchmen saw, and perhaps still see, the British withdrawal at Dunkirk* as a supreme betrayal. Charles de Gaulle was to prove one of the thorniest allies any country could wish for and it was his systematic hostility which kept Britain out of the Common Market till after his death. Whether it is such a good idea to be in it now, as Britain is flooded with Golden Delicious apples and French farmers sportingly respond by blockading English lorryloads of spring lamb, is something many Englishmen doubt. Their melancholy conclusion tends to be that while you can't live with them, you can't live without them; and so in Brussels the interminable wrangles with these intolerable and indispensable neighbours roll ever on. *Entente*, maybe; *cordiale*, no.

Gardens   If class is the English pox, then gardens are the English passion. It runs right through the race. There is a long dull street in San Francisco which was suddenly lit one spring by a pyrotechnic display of colours: great tubs of crocuses, hyacinths and daffodils. The neighbours thought it must be a new funeral parlour; but later learned that an Englishwoman had come to live there.

England can claim not only a rich roll call of the finest professional gardeners – John Tradescant, father and son, Joseph Banks, Lancelot (Capability) Brown, Humphrey Repton, Joseph Paxton, and Gertrude Jekyll – but also some of the most celebrated amateurs. No one in this group is more remarkable than the writer Vita Sackville-West who, when she bought Sissinghurst with her husband Harold Nicolson in 1930, found a rubbish dump with a few old apple trees and in a decade had turned it into one of the most celebrated gardens in England.

There are plenty of prose poems to the glory of the garden in English literature from the grace of Francis Bacon to the guff of Compton Mackenzie; but Rudyard Kipling got closest to the truth: 'Oh Adam was a gardener, and God who made him sees / That half a proper gardener's work is done upon his knees.'

Harold Nicolson concurred. In his diary for 20 March 1932 he wrote '... we weed the delphinium bed ... It is very odd. I do not like weeding in any case. I have a cold coming on. I cannot get a job and am deeply in debt. I foresee no exit from our financial worries. Yet Vita and I are as happy as larks together.' He spoke for every English couple who have ever made a garden.

Gazumping   So it has settled down, though the *Supplement* to the *OED* traces it back to 1928 when it was spelt *gazoomph* and meant swindling; but the specific practice of charging more for a house after you had closed with a buyer at a lower figure dates specifically from 1971, when an unhealthy boom in property prices was precipitated by the lax budgets of the Tory chancellor at that time, Anthony Barber. Clearly the word has settled down to the simple and vivid form of spelling it now enjoys; but the actual practice disappeared with the great recession that has filled much of the last decade, and has only just begun to be heard of again. It is yet another example of the edge brought to new idiom by the last letter of the alphabet (see also *Zizz* and *Zonked*).

Gentleman   He has had a long innings: roughly from the moment when Chaucer's verray parfit gentil knight makes his debut (1387) till the moment when a very gallant gentleman called Captain Oates makes his exit (1912). The First World War saw the notion of the temporary gentleman born, but by then the old idealised romantic figure was already beginning to sound a touch apologetic if not downright comic. Thus Daisy Ashford gave us the magnificent Mr Salteena ('I am not quite a gentleman but you would hardly notice it'). Lord Curzon contributed to posterity the absurd if endearing observation that no gentleman eats soup at luncheon. Bernard Shaw* introduced us to the millionaire cannon king Undershaft, who offers his future son-in-law Adolphus Cousins half what he has asked to work in the factory. Cousins: 'You call yourself a gentleman and you offer me half? Undershaft: 'I do not call myself a gentleman but I do offer you half.'

Just as in cricket the separate pavilions which, within living memory, served gentlemen and players have now been amalgamated, so in the great pavilion of life gentlemen and players now rough it together and are hard to distinguish. If there are any gentleman farmers left they are too busy driving the combine harvesters to mention it. The word lingers on in unexpected places; in saleroom catalogues, for example, where a consignment of wine will be gnomically labelled 'the property of a gentleman'. It probably survives best in the imperial Raj, where much of a lost England is enshrined. Thus, in the Second World War, Nehru, released from prison to see his wife, was asked to sign a paper saying he would not try to escape. He found this demeaning. After hours of debate, the perfect formula was found: he would make a gentleman's agreement not to cut and run, shook hands with his captors, and kept his word. Happy, vanished Days!

In England now though, it is used (if at all) with increasing desperation, and often in a contrary sense; the gentlemen of the press, for instance, are manifestly nothing of the sort. We might still just speak of one of nature's gentlemen, but the word is too covered with custard to be used alone and straight.

So we shorten it and tacitly apologise for it: 'He's a real gent.' By the same token, gents' is now the most handy shorthand for the male loo and tends to be spelled out only in contexts like the famous British Rail appeal (or do they intend it as an assertion?) 'Gentlemen lift the seat'. Gentlemen adventurers like Richard Hannay have given place to right bastards like James Bond. A gentleman never willingly gives pain, said Cardinal Newman. Tell that to 007.

The Germans   The English, despite two world wars, have never been able to work up any lasting antipathy towards the Germans. To this general principle there will of course be exceptions; notably among the 176,000 people now living in Britain who were born in Germany. Many, though not all, were refugees from Nazism; many, though not all, have the best of reasons to retain a bitterness to all things German for the rest of their lives.

Yet the Englishman finds the Germans rather more like him in his language, his religion, and even his national drink than any Frenchman. In the First World War there were the celebrated meetings between English and German soldiers in No Man's Land on Christmas Day. There was a strong sense that Fritz and Tommy were equally victims of faceless brass-hats back at GHQ. In the Second World War it was Germans themselves, Catholics, trade unionists, socialists, army officers – who were the first casualties of Nazism. Many died heroes' deaths. Besides, simple arithmetic shows that there are Germans now well into their fifties who had not even been born on VE Day; and to have seen any action in the Second World War a German – or Englishman for that matter – will have to be pushing seventy.

Then again, few nations seem to have changed their spots quite so thoroughly. The Germans have given the world some unpleasant words in their time: *Blitzkrieg* (lightning war), *Herrenvolk* (master race) and *Ubermensch* (superman); but since the war have been more noted as proponents of green peace, nuclear disarmament, and economic miracles. While old war movies and newsreels still project the alarming image of disciplined, blond stormtroopers goose-stepping across Europe, modern German youth is reassuringly indistinguishable from our own; scruffy, disorganised, and bolshie. German leaders too give, on the whole, a sympathetic account of themselves now: not only decent men but able to speak fluent English into the bargain. So they must be all right.

Gilbert and Sullivan   It was Lord Robert Cecil who remarked that Gilbert and Sullivan did not like each other as men; not did either want to write operettas. There is an element of hyperbole in the epigram; certainly the two men quarrelled often enough in a collaboration that lasted nearly thirty years; certainly each had another and more serious career already behind him. Gilbert was a successful playwright (he was estimated to have made £40,000 – in Victorian money – from his play *Pygmalion and Galatea* alone) and Sullivan an accomplished composer. When Charles Dickens* went to hear his *Tempest* music at the Crystal Palace in 1862 he said afterwards: 'I don't profess to be a musical critic, but I do know that I have listened to some very remarkable music.' The critics concurred.

W.S. Gilbert (1836–1911) and Arthur Sullivan (1842–1900) were first introduced to one another by John Holingshead, owner of the Gaiety Theatre, in 1871; the fruit of that meeting, *Thespis*, was staged at his theatre without success. Playwright and composer went their separate ways until an enterprising young man called Richard D'Oyly Carte brought them together four years later to write *Trial by Jury*. It opened on 25 March 1875 and ran for 175 performances. This encouraged D'Oyly Carte to commission further pieces from the temperamentally ill-matched but artistically fine-meshed pair. The dramas of their long and turbulent partnership are as vivid as anything they wrote for the stage.

Sullivan wrote the carefree music for *HMS Pinafore* racked with pain from a stone in the kidney. *Pinafore* mania swept America and within months no fewer than fifty unauthorised productions were mounted there. It was performed by all-Catholic and all-black casts, and on a Mississippi paddle-boat. When they decided to give the world première of *The Pirates of Penzance* in New York, Sullivan unpacked his bags after landing and discovered he had left the score of Act One in England. He frantically rewrote it from memory, finishing the overture at 5 a.m. on the day of the opening performance, 31 December 1879. He rehearsed all morning, went to bed at 1.45 p.m. but could not sleep. He dined off a dozen oysters and a glass of champagne before taking up his position in the orchestra pit. 'Fine reception,,' he recorded in his diary. 'Piece went marvellously well. Grand success.'

Five years later though, Gilbert and Sullivan were in the doldrums. D'Oyly Carte called for a work that would revive their fortunes; Sullivan told Gilbert he was fed up with absurd plots. Gilbert, pacing his library in Harrington Gardens, was unable to come up with the answer – till a large Japanese executioner's sword mounted on his wall crashed to the floor before him. Thus was the idea for *The Mikado* born. At one point in 1886 there were 170 separate productions running in America. There was a jazz version in Berlin in 1927; while the Americans have mounted *The Swing Mikado* (1938), *The Hot Mikado* 1939) and *The Black Mikado* (1975). There was even a *Cool Mikado*, made in 1962 and starring Frankie Howerd.

Success did not make the warring collaborators any happier together. 'Another week's rehearsal with WSG and I should have gone raving mad,' declared Sullivan. 'He is like a man who sits on a stove and then complains his backside is burning,' riposted Gilbert. In the end though, their admiration for each other as artists prevailed. 'I must thank you for the magnificent work you have put into the piece,' wrote Gilbert to Sullivan on the morning after *The Gondoliers* opened on 7 December 1889. 'It gives one the chance of shining right through the twentieth century ...' He was right.

Gin   Mother's ruin is its English nickname, and though not so much in use now, reflects the Hogarthian world in which domestic gin, backed by a breathtakingly daft law made by William of Orange to discourage imports, became the favoured tipple of the working classes. Drunk for a penny, reported Smollett, dead drunk for twopence, clean straw free.

With the expansion of empire, angostura bitters were prescribed on all British navy ships as a preventive medicine; soon someone realised that by putting in a little gin an attractive drink could be made and sailors are still renowned takers of pink gin. In the same way, tonic water containing quinine was prescribed against malaria for Brits in India; gin and tonic soon caught on.

From denoting depravity and want, gin came to convey affluence and even decadence, as in 'floating gin palace' for motor cruisers, and 'gin and Jaguar belt' to denote the terrain of stockbroker self-indulgence. What you add to your gin, though, still denotes class and age: gin and orange is thus middle-aged and downmarket; gin and French much smarter than the sweeter gin and Italian vermouth. But the gin base has a mighty pull. Pimm's No. 1, the only one of the six Pimm's drinks to have it, is the only one to survive. Besides, as all the world knows, gin has the devoted patronage of the Queen Mum, and there can be no firmer seal of approval in English eyes than that.

Golf ' "After all, golf is only a game," said Millicent. Women say these things without thinking. It does not mean there is any kink in their character. They simply don't realise what they are saying.' Thus wrote P.G. Wodehouse* in *The Clicking of Cuthbert*, the very first of his books to celebrate a magnificent obsession that was to continue for more than half a century.

It would be agreeable to report that the male chauvinism buried in the amiable observation was a mere whim of the Master, brought on by using a mashie at a moment when a light iron would have been the right answer. The truth is more shameful: for on any given Sunday in England 200,000 people are out playing golf, and of these nearly all are men; for there is hardly an English golf club that allows women to play on that hallowed morning.

It is a sad record for a country that can boast the oldest golf club in the world (the Royal Blackheath – founded 1608) and a god-given profusion of clubs from the heather and gorse-strewn Sunningdale and Wentworth southwest of London, to daunting windswept seaside places like the Royal Birkdale in Lancashire, and the Royal St George's at Sandwich which has the unusual honour of starring in the *oeuvre* of Ian Fleming*.

The Good Food Guide Founded in 1951 by a socialist historian, detective novelist and classical scholar called Raymond Postgate (1896–1971). The combination of leftish politics with gourmet leanings is common enough in France; rare in England. The little guide (as it then was) from the start proved incorruptible, elegantly written and idiosyncratic. Its main drawback was that it relied on amateurs to report on restaurants; and though it is now swollen to glossy prosperity so that proper paid inspectors can be afforded, a small army of anonymous unpaid spies remains the backbone of its workforce.

The consequence is that the *Guide* sometimes seems bafflingly capricious, especially in London; though in fairness it must be conceded that a visit to a restaurant inexplicably dropped often reveals that the *Guide* is just ahead of the game. It is also now dangerously close to self-parody, being couched sometimes in a ludicrous Latin beak's lingo. At the Étoile, for instance, it reported that one ate 'between the Scylla of the spirit lamps and the Charybdis of customers' cigars'. Yet the *GFG* has always fought the good fight and over the years brought incalculable benefit to English cooking. Besides, it is always rivetingly readable.

An entry for the Betjeman* restaurant in the Charing Cross Hotel, for example, was done in a spirited parody of the laureate's own style: Betjemania's in season / At this BTH hotel / Read his verse: admire (with reason)/ Barry's dining room as well.' The middle falters. Betjemen could never have brought himself to rhyme Walewska with Avelsbacher. But the final quatrain is a triumph: 'Vegetables are best forgotten/ Chocolate mousse will not be missed / Coffee's decent. Cloths are cotton / Wine's good value. Pianist.' But you will scour the pages of the 1996 *GFG* for the Betjeman restaurant in vain. Like so many other proud and vaunting hostelries, it has been given the old heave-ho.

The other principal good guy in the long battle for excellence in food is, ironically, a small, dapper, sophisticated Hungarian called Egon Ronay (born 1922). He launched his first restaurant guide in February 1959. It was a modest, pink little book priced at three shillings. His 1997 guide is ten times as thick and alas, a hundred times the price. The space between the two defines the battlefield on which Ronay has fought his good fight against the compacted horrors of postwar English cooking: tinned and frozen foods; melancholy meals in trains and planes; soggy vegetables and murdered meats. Equally he has identified and celebrated the best English food that tables have to offer. Where do you go if you are spending a summer day at Stratford on Avon and are resolved to eat by the river? (The Black Dog.) Where do you head if you have been up on the Marlborough Downs and come down in the morning mist as hungry as a hunter? Ronay will guide you to that little place in the High Street (Polly's) where they lay on those sumptuous Victorian breakfasts* that will set you up or lay you out for the day.

In his early years Ronay was maligned because his English was not as urbane as it might have been and certainly dim little words like 'tasty' and 'cosy' surfaced too often. It was a curmudgeonly charge to lay against a man who came to England in 1946 with very little of its language to his credit. It is also said against him that he accepts sponsorship. Yet the name of the sponsor is in the public domain; it is not a covert influence; and it is precisely this revenue that enables him to hire and train his inspectors to make their independent and anonymous judgements. He thus avoids the trace of amateurism of the rival *Good Food Guide* and the skeletal solemnity of the new *English Michelin*.

'There is still a smirk on the newscaster's face when the subject of good eating comes up', Ronay chides. 'The sauce bottles that were fixtures on a past Prime Minister's table [see under *HP Sauce*] are still regarded as endearing signs of his British homeliness, whereas they would have lost millions of votes for President Mitterrand.' On, Egon, on!

Gooseberry Another good case of a subtle change in meaning; for whereas the *OED* identifies it from 1837 as a chaperon, the word still flourishes in a world where chaperons have long been out-moded. It now means any third person who delays the dalliance of lovers by his or her presence – very often unconsciously.

Gossip It was the thing Guy Burgess, the British diplomat who fled to Russia with Donald Maclean, missed most in his exile from England. It was what brought Somerset Maugham* home from his voluntary exile in the south of France each autumn. It is one of the great uncelebrated English obsessions.

A high-powered American woman television commentator recently returned to New York complaining that no Englishman would talk to her at dinner parties about mutually phased strategic weapons limitation. She took it as an inclination to sexism: in fact it was a preference for gossip. It is the pabulum that nourishes the House of Commons and the Inns of Court; the tack that feeds Showbiz and the City. It finds its logical if ephemeral enshrinement in the gossip-column, that much denounced and much devoured department of most newspapers. Sixty years ago, in an essay on English snobbery, Aldous Huxley propounded that nowhere else in Europe was gossip writing such a highly paid and creditable profession. Today it may or may not be highly paid; creditable it is not.

The watershed for the gossip-columnist came in 1959 when the playwright John Osborne, goaded to rage by the attentions paid to his own personal life, wrote *The World of Paul Slickey*, an excoriating onslaught on the hacks of Grub Street. He dedicated the play 'To the liars and self-deceivers; to those who daily deal out treachery; to those who handle their professions as instruments of debasement; to those who, for a salary cheque and less, successfully betray my country, and those who will do it for no inducement at all.'

These are fighting words, and there is much to back them: but the average Englishman is dimly aware of some rough balance which ensures that though some deplorable men and women may sometimes waste their words on the innocent and guileless, the cynical operations of the gossip-columnist are used as often to throw a corrective shaft of clear light into dark places. Such certainly would be the general verdict on 'Grovel' of *Private Eye**, whose closely monitored column can sometimes bring down a minister, as indeed it brought down Cecil Parkinson, Secretary of State at the Department of Trade and Industry, because of his love affair with his secretary.

Should such private passions besmirch the public print? The debate is endless; the reality clear. Gossip-columnists in England look set to stay.

As Paul Slickey sang: 'Don't think you can fool a guy like me / The best things in life are never free ... We have professional ways and means / Of getting in behind the scenes.'

Grammar School   While there are those who argue that Eton* is no more than a grammar school (which in strict academic terms is the simple truth) the Englishman is not deceived. To him, 'grammar school' conjures up the image of a Tudor building with Victorian and probably thirties annexes where the abler children of local townspeople went daily to be taught an academic syllabus with a view to going on to university or into one of the professions.

The charge against the grammar school made by the left was that it was socially divisive and unjust, leaving all those children who could not jump the eleven-plus hurdle with a lifelong sense of failure, and gentrifying the clever working-class children who could jump it. It therefore became the policy of the left (and moderate right) to turn these grammar schools into comprehensives where all children, regardless of class, means or ability, could be educated together. The intention was good, but the snag was that the grammar schools fiercely resisted this submersion of their identities, and many simply opted out of the state system altogether, becoming independent if not boarding, and charging the true cost of their teaching to parents, or privately raised funds.

Thus an even greater divide has been driven between the two systems, and the left now accept that only legislation can close it again – legislation, that is, which will forcibly close the public schools. A government of the left with the votes and will to do this seems at present a long way off. If the grammar schools had been allowed to supersede the public schools naturally, as they might well have done, the comprehensive principle could have been quietly introduced later. As it is, English education is in an even worse shambles than usual.

Greenwich Mean Time   Though the meridian is of central import-ance to navigators, it is just as vital to astronomers. They need it to create a fixed line in the sky by which to measure a star's position. As each successive astronomer royal at Greenwich installed a better telescope, he moved his meridian to a fresh site slightly westwards.

Sir George Biddell Airy (1801–92) who became astronomer royal at the age of thirty-four, installed his celebrated transit circle, which defines the meridian, in 1851. A piece of cobweb in the lens fixed the exact spot. It had wandered just sixteen yards since the time of the first astronomer royal, John Flamsteed (1646–1719).

Since most navigational charts already used the Greenwich meridian, it seemed logical to make it the base line of longitude for the world at the international conference called to settle the matter at Washington in 1884. Still, logic is not always the prime mover at world parleys, and in the end Greenwich is said to have won only because the American railroad companies were already working from its time and lobbied their government to do the same.

No Englishman will be surprised to learn that the Irish* refused to recognise it altogether, while the French* accepted in only obliquely: as a line so many degrees to the west of Paris. *Plus ça change.*

Grockle Useful word, not yet in the *OED*, to describe any dim and undesirable outsider, particularly a tourist. Thus a Londoner will speak of coaches decanting loads of unsuspecting grockles at certain pubs or clubs that are well-known clip-joints.

Hampshire   Two English writers of genius were neighbours in eighteenth-century Hampshire. Gilbert White was curate of Selborne most of his life, refusing all offers of preferment so that he could live and die in the place where he was born, writing, without knowing it, an enduring masterpiece in his *Natural History of Selborne.* Twelve miles away the pretty daughter of the rector of Steventon was already penning the early drafts of novels that were to be read and loved two hundred years later: *Pride and Prejudice, Sense and Sensibility, Northanger Abbey.* Did they ever meet? Jane Austen* was rising eighteen when Gilbert White died; since both were clerical families it would be surprising if they did not; but we have no record of it.

White was educated at Basingstoke Grammar School; so, two centuries later, was the late John Arlott, wine writer and cricket commentator. The slow, inimitable burr of his native Hampshire became famous wherever cricket was played. Fifteen miles to the west of Basingstoke another local boy with an incomparable Hampshire accent, Alfred Denning, was educated at Andover grammar school to such effect that he went on to take a double first in mathematics at Magdalen College, Oxford before getting another in jurisprudence and becoming England's favourite judge.

If you subtract from Hampshire the great urban conglomerates of Southampton and Portsmouth, Winchester* and Aldershot* you are left with just on a million acres of still predominantly agricultural land and rivers like the Test and Meon where the trout-fishing is world famous. It is still possible to walk on top of the Hampshire downs all day without seeing a soul. The poet Edmund Spenser, we are assured by John Aubrey, went to live in Hampshire for its 'delicate, sweet air'. Four hundred years on, people still do.

Hardy, Thomas (1840–1928)   'Even in my life I have seen writers who made much stir in the world than ever I have sink into oblivion. When I was young George Meredith and Thomas Hardy seemed certain of survival. They have ceased to mean very much to the youth of today.' So thought Somerset Maugham* in *The Summing Up* (1938). Whatever we may think of Meredith (and there are two views about him too), it is an astonishing misjudgment of Hardy, all the more surprising in coming from Maugham, who had painted such a marvellous portrait of the older Hardy in his novel *Cakes and Ale* (1930). Even if Hardy were not read today (and he is) he would have found vast new audiences by being filmed (*Far from the Madding Crowd* and *Tess of the D'Urbervilles*) and televised (*The Mayor of Casterbridge* and *The Woodlanders*).

It is true that Hardy succeeds almost in spite of himself. He spent a great deal of time and trouble trying to prove he was of gentle birth; while what enthralls his readers is his minute and knowing recall of simple country folk. Thus in *Under the Greenwood Tree*, William Dewy 'was now about seventy; yet an ardent vitality still preserved a warm and roughened bloom upon his face, which reminded gardeners of the sunny side of a ripe ribstone-pippin; though a narrow strip of forehead, that was protected from the weather by lying above the line of his hat-brim, seemed to belong to some town man, so gentlemany was its whiteness.'

Hardy's desire to rewrite the record before his birth extended equally to what had happened after it: he wrote his own account of his life, or what he cared to tell of it, and got his second wife to copy it page by page so that it would look as if it were hers. The ruse failed, and posterity has puzzled much about the true nature of the inner pain that caused this sombre and secretive man to dissemble so. We know that his first marriage was, or had become unhappy; but that after his first wife's death some inner spring released a great spate of marvellous poetry full of remorse.

'His subjects', wrote the poet Philip Larkin*, 'are men, the life of men, time and the passing of time, love and the fading of love.' In almost every Hardy poem, Larkin finds 'there is a little spinal cord of thought and each has a little tune of its own … your own inner response begins to rock in time with the poem's rhythm and I think that this is quite inimitable.' Larkin thinks that Hardy's poetry is not for young people, and is probably right; but everyone can appreciate the thrall of his fiction. The words with which Hardy ends *The Woodlanders*, for example ('You was a good man, and did good things'), are among the most simple and moving in the language. Oblivion, indeed!

Harrods Henry Charles Harrod, a tea merchant, took over a small grocer's shop in the unfashionable and indeed rough village of Knightsbridge in 1849. He had two assistants and a turnover of £20 a week. His son, Charles Digby Harrod, then aged twenty, bought it in 1861, taking three years to pay his father for it on the never-never. By 1868 turnover was £1,000 a week; two years later he had sixteen assistants, but his total wages bill was still a mere £15 a week. By 1874 there were nearly one hundred staff working from 7 a.m. till 8 p.m. and fines of 1½d were imposed for each quarter of an hour they were late in the morning.

On 6 December 1883 the store and all his Christmas stock were totally destroyed by fire. Charles Harrod wrote to his customers: 'I greatly regret to inform you that, in consequence of the above premises being burnt down, your order will be delayed a day or two. I hope in the course of Tuesday or Wednesday next, to be able to forward it.' He was. The store was rebuilt and reopened by September 1884, and a much impressed clientele flocked back to double the turnover.

The year after that Harrods gave credit for the first time. Lily Langtry and Oscar Wilde were early account customers. In 1898 the first escalator in London was installed; an assistant stood at the top with sal volatile and brandy for nervous passengers. The store's motto, *Omnia, Omnibus, Ubique* (Everything, Everyone, Everywhere) is rigorously fulfilled. Harrods has the last circulating library in London, and supplies all its own water from three underground wells. It has delivered a Persian carpet to Persia and a refrigerator to Finland; a 35p handkerchief by air to Los Angeles and a pound of sausages to a yacht in the Mediterranean.

If it has recently been nicknamed Harabs, this merely reflects the influence of one group of customers who contribute healthily and harmlessly to its half million pounds' worth of sales per day. Lit at night like the Blackpool illuminations by thousands of garish electric light bulbs (powered by its own generator), Harrods is a worldwide symbol; and this was no doubt the reason why the Irish bomb was planted at its door in December 1983 – precisely a century after the great fire. Despite the ghastly cost in life and limb, Harrods reopened for its January sales as always; and again the public flocked to buy as if nothing had happened.

Harrow When the great Victorian headmaster Vaughan came to Harrow in 1844, it had just over sixty pupils. Vaughan very quickly raised its numbers to some two hundred, but left precipitately in 1859 to avoid scandal (see under *Public Schools*). The fact is, Harrow has always struck the average Englishman as being a rather rum place. Admittedly Winston Churchill* was there, but even he was adjudged distinctly unsound for much of his political career, and John Profumo did not do the school much good when the great Christine Keeler scandal engulfed him and England in 1963. However Harrow should take heart. It can number among its old boys the immortal Captain Grimes, anti-hero of Evelyn Waugh's* *Decline and Fall* and one of the most sublime crooks in the whole panoply of English fiction.

Henley Regatta While Wimbledon*, Ascot*, and even Lord's* show signs of having been coarsened by the cash nexus, Henley remains, visually at least, what it always was: an Edwardian time-warp; Pimmsville-on-the-water. Though parties of Arab billionaires have been introduced to the delights of this perennial river-party with one eye on the business that might result, standards are still maintained. No woman is admitted to the Stewards' Enclosure in trousers or mini skirt; no man without collar and tie. Within these simple constraints anything goes, and here at least men can and do work the most shameless peacock effects in their pink caps and rainbow-striped blazers. However, the women look pretty good too and endearingly feminine; after all, it's only a hundred years since they weren't able to attend the regatta at all; it was thought unladylike, so they watched from carriages on the bridge. When the Russians first came to row they could not understand how all the stewards could be English; where was the famous English sense of fair play? It was finally put across to them that Henley stewards are incorruptible; now they race there without a single Russian steward to see fair dos.

Henley has seen many moving sights in its 157 years; none perhaps quite so touching as the sight of the 1914 Harvard crew that won the Grand Challenge Cup rowing over the same course (or part of it anyway) on the Saturday of the regatta exactly fifty years later. Fit, steady and well together, they got an ovation from the crowd: the odds against them all being there – senators, bankers, surgeons – and able to do any such thing – was worked out actuarially at 10,000:1. They gave a new Grand Challenge Cup to the regatta – the old one was so battered it no longer held champagne – as a tribute to the Leander eight they had beaten in that 1914 final: gallant fellows, they said, many of whom were destined to die in the war that began a few weeks later.

Hillary, Richard (1919–43) Ask an Englishman under fifty who Richard Hillary was and he will be unlikely to know. He was killed flying in 1943, and as the war fades, so does his mythopeic role. He was perfectly cast for the part of lost hero: young (twenty-three when he died); good-looking (even after he was scarred in the Battle of Britain); athletic (he rowed in a famous Trinity boat at Oxford); and marvellously articulate.

His reputation as a writer rests on one book, *The Last Enemy*, his autobiographical account of how it felt to be one of the last of the long-haired boys, the student pilots who took to the skies in 1940 to play romantic gladiators *sans peur et sans reproche*. They were motivated not by a spirit of crude jingoism but by a sense of the ineluctability of fate and a grateful recognition that war had solved all their problems.

He had been two years at Oxford when the war came; was two days in the Battle of Britain (see *Spitfire; Hurricane*) with five kills to his credit before he was himself shot down over the North Sea but rescued badly burned. His book has sold 300,000 copies in English and been translated into every European language; it was particularly admired in postwar Germany.

Holmes, Sherlock Three fictional characters are known to readers all over the world, or so it is said: Hamlet, Robinson Crusoe and Holmes. Yet in that august trio Holmes has a further claim to uniqueness: neither Hamlet no Crusoe is normally seen as a real, living, three-dimensional, flesh-and-blood human being. Holmes long ago transcended that shadowy divide. A department in the Abbey National Building Society's headquarters in Baker Street, which stands on the spot where the famed consulting rooms were sited by Conan Doyle*, deals with a daily mail bag from all over the world addressed to Sherlock Holmes and soliciting his help.

A vast and whimsical literature has grown up around the Holmesian *oeuvre*, much of it from distinguished pens. A former city editor of *The Sunday Times*, Norman Crump, once retraced Holmes's steps along the London Underground* in the small hours of the morning, to check a point, and later published his researches under the title 'Inner or Outer Rail?' in the *Sherlock Holmes Journal*. Dorothy L. Sayers published profound research on the knotty conundrum of Holmes's university career, and was later joined in the magnificent obsession by Monsignor Ronald Knox. The best summation of all this learning suggests that Holmes was an undergraduate at Oxford from the autumn of 1872 to the start of the long vacation in 1874; and at Cambridge until 1877.

All English experts are known as Holmesians; American *cognoscenti* as Sherlockians. One noted Sherlockian, Franklin D. Roosevelt (who in his off-duty moments was president of the United States) speculated that Holmes was a foundling. Later, he changed his mind, and decided that Holmes was an American, 'brought up by his father, or foster-father, in the underground world, thus learning all the tricks of the trade in the highly developed American art of crime'.

Be that as it may, Holmes began his practice in July 1877 and met John H. Watson M.D., late of the Army Medical Department, in the chemical lab of St Bartholomew's Hospital in January 1881. Watson, recuperating from a wound sustained in the Afgan war, had bumped into Dr Stamford in the Criterion Bar. Delighted to see a familiar face, Watson took Stamford, who had been a dresser under him at Bart's, out to lunch at the Holborn. Over it, he heard about a fellow who was carrying out experiments in the laboratory. He was, Stamford declared, 'a decent enough fellow, but queer in his ideas'. He was, it seemed, also looking for someone to share digs with him. Watson asked to meet Holmes and there in the lab, beside the blue flickering flame of the Bunsen burner, the historic introduction took place – to the world's delight.

Home Counties   Strictly, they were the four contiguous with the old boundaries of London: Surrey, Kent, Essex and Middlesex. Now, though, Middlesex has been finally swallowed up. Originally the land of the Middle Saxons, it lost much of its territory to the new County of London in 1888; the rest in 1965 to the Greater London Council. Today it exists only as a cricket team, a postal address and the northern station in the Boat Race*. Few Englishmen grieve deeply, for its history has long been London's.

Of the remaining three home counties, Kent probably has the greatest claim to its own identity: for centuries the paths of successive waves of invading armies lay through its smiling orchards; and its cathedral towns of Canterbury and Rochester, its medieval Cinque Ports of Dover*, Hythe, Romney, and Sandwich, its great houses and castles (Penhurst, Knole, Hever, and Leeds) make a rich tapestry. Most Englishmen are dimly aware too of the historic distinction between a Kentish man (born west of the Medway) and a Man of Kent (east). Many, however, have to be reminded that Kent, improbably, had its own deep quarrying coal-miners; though very few need reminding that it has one of the best kept cricket teams and a magnificent tradition of great wicketkeepers.

Essex, on the other hand, to most Englishmen, is a flat and indistinct hinterland to the northeast of London famed for its Colchester oysters, as the *mise en scène* for many notable Constable paintings, and not much else. Frankly it has been largely subsumed by the Great Wen of London; and so has Surrey. Drive south from Hammersmith Bridge, for example, and down the Kingston by-pass, and you are still in London: Surrey now begins at Worcester Park. The distinction is perhaps logical, for the line broadly separates urban sprawl from the beginnings of the stockbroker belt (see *Stock Exchange*). The now-diminished Surrey (Box Hill, Hog's Back, Farnham, Guildford) is still beautiful if over-domesticated. One literary critic described a couple in a recent novel as being happy 'in a Surrey sort of way'. Englishmen knew what he meant.

Homesick 'Take me back to dear old Blighty'; 'God I will pack and take a train'; 'Oh to be in England, now that April's there': the island race know what it is to be homesick, though it can be argued that, being a restless and peripatetic people, they have only themselves to blame.

Just as we now know that almost anything under the sun can remind people of sex, so we now know that almost anything can remind the faraway Englishman of home. It may be the thought of kippers, faggots or liquorice; raspberries, strawberries or blackberries; frogspawn or crested newts; hedgerows, flat, full rivers, pollarded willows or simple rain. It can be draught Guinness or double-decker buses.

One antidote is to build your own simulacrum of England: hence the cricket clubs of California and the English pubs of Paris. Oddly, the sickness can strike even those not born in England: thus the erstwhile GI in Manhattan will buy his fish and chips* wrapped in English newspapers; and the Indian politician will inquire wistfully whether the little bus of his student days still runs across Hampstead Heath to Highgate (it does).

Hooray Henry He is a young man in a city suit, probably a merchant banker or wine merchant by profession, who turns up at jazz clubs with his Sloane Ranger girlfriend and applauds politely after each number, while braying 'hooray'. He knows little or nothing about jazz, but thinks he does, and to the professional jazz-man is a pain in the arse.

Henry has two close cousins. The first is the self-explanatory 'chinless wonder' (no doubt a play on the boneless wonder once heartlessly on show in Barnum's Circus). The second, a striking new coinage, is the 'young fogey'. A fogey was originally a Scottish term for an invalid or garrison soldier; hence, an old fogey was anyone with hidebound or antiquated ideas.

It was a brilliantly simple notion of a newspaper columnist to call Prince Charles a young fogey, for such he evidently is; and the breed prospers in 1990s England under such auspicious patronage. But the nerd – yet another English twit – is coming up on him fast.

Horse 'I know two things about the horse / And one of them is rather coarse', wrote our old friend Anon in *The Weekend Book*. The other thing is no doubt Robert Burton's celebrated remark that England is a paradise for women, and hell for horses. A casual intruder from another planet, picking up a paper or switching on the box, could well be forgiven for thinking that it was the other way round.

Housman, A.E. (1859–1936) George Orwell* used to claim that at seventeen he probably knew all the 63 poems in *A Shropshire Lad* by heart. Dennis Potter used one of the most magical phrases in Housman's slim volume – 'the blue remembered hills' – as the title for a prize-winning TV play. W.H. Auden* said that to his generation, no other English poet seemed so perfectly to express the sensibility of a male adolescent. A copy of the poems in a soldier's breast pocket saved his life when it stopped a bullet in the 1914–18 war. Its lyrical pessimism perhaps spoke to the generation doomed to die in that war most eloquently of all.

Housman claimed that a sore throat had caused the feverish intensity with which many of the poems in the book were written, and perhaps it did. But it was probably the symptom rather than the cause of the continuous excitement that gripped him in the early months of 1895. Many matters may have preyed on his mind – his father's death, money troubles, family problems, scholarly disputes. Yet the message the Marquess of Queensberry pinned up in his club on February 18 that year accusing Oscar Wilde of sodomy, and the two Wilde trials that followed in April, must have released deeper springs.

Housman knew all too poignantly what Wilde meant by 'the love that dare not speak its name'. The bitter knowledge that his own lifelong love for a fellow Oxford undergraduate, Moses Jackson, could never be expressed made him a loner and an oddball; but precipitated poetry that still shimmers in the English mind.

HP Sauce It stood for Houses of Parliament when first marketed by a grocer called Garton in 1896, though in truth there was no firm evidence that it was known at all in the Palace of Westminster till 1964, when a newspaper profile of Harold Wilson quoted his wife Mary as saying that he had only one fault: he would smother everything she cooked in it. HP shares at once rose by half-a-crown on the Stock Exchange*, and were ever afterwards known as Wilson's Gravy.

The much-loved sludge now sells all over the world: in Sweden it is proudly displayed on tables as a sign of breeding while in Saudi Arabia it is thought to have aphrodisiac qualities. The French legend on the label, however, owes more to poetic licence than strict logic, for HP is not a big seller over the channel; nevertheless the familiar incantation '*Cette sauce de haute qualité*' remains the first French (and sometimes the only French) that many Englishmen know. Unhappily the words as originally printed contained an unfortunate double entendre; HP was said to be free from *aucun préservatif;* not any preservative, as HP HQ had intended but, to a Frenchman, any French letter.

The slip has since been rectified, and HP continues its onward march for, with its aromatic *mélange* of malt vinegar, fruit and oriental spices, it is nothing less than the English working-class equivalent to Proust's *madeleine.*

Hurricane   It is a well-nigh universal belief among Englishmen that the Spitfire* won the Battle of Britain. That quick, lovely, and lethal plane needs no defence here. Still, it is a simple arithmetical fact that the Hurricane brought down more enemy aircraft in the Battle of Britain than all the Spitfires, Blenheims, Defiants and ground defences together.

The reason is not far to seek: there were far more Hurricanes then than Spitfires. The Air Ministry ordered one prototype high-speed monoplane from Hawker's in February 1935. It first flew in November 1935. The Hawker board decided to tool up and order material for a thousand Hurricanes in March 1936 without waiting for government support. That followed in June; but the Hawker gamble meant that the Hurricanes were that much ahead when the war in the air started.

The chief reason for the superior performance of the Spitfire was its thin wing. Hawker's had been advised by the National Physical Laboratory – wrongly as it turned out – that no advantage in speed would accrue from it. On the credit side, the thick wing could hold a fat, low-pressure tyre when retracted and this enabled the Hurricane to take off from grass when a fully loaded Spitfire sometimes could not. Moreover, the Hurricane with its tubular airframe was less vulnerable to enemy gunfire and could be repaired more easily: a distinct advantage when resources ran desperately low. In the end 14,500 Hurricanes were built: and every one was precious.

I It was Emile Zola, no less, who noted during his enforced exile in England that, whereas the personal pronoun was expressed in France, Germany, and Italy with a small initial letter (je, ich, io) in this country it requires a capital to make its bow. That is no doubt a linguistic accident (to write it as i would look extremely odd) but there is no question that the English try to hide behind this slim capital letter. The Queen, for example, always speaks on official occasions of 'my husband and I' and off duty of herself as 'one' (thus, when her horse won a race, giving *The Sun** one its most durable headlines: ONE'S WON). *Private Eye** has even devised a way of measuring the egocentricity of the nation's columnists by counting the number of times they use I per column inch. Margaret Thatcher, as so often, got round the problem most regally by announcing to waiting reporters: 'We are a grandmother'. No wonder the Queen and Maggie never saw eye to eye; or should it be I to I?

Idiot   The village idiot of English country lore was not quite so daft as he looked. He would sit on his bench outside the village inn, ready to regale unsuspecting strangers with his rustic simplicities in return for a steady supply of free ale. With the rise of sophisticated psychiatric medicine, it has become impolite to call anyone like that an idiot, unless in the strictly defined clinical sense. Instead, the word has moved inside every living room and been assimilated in the 'idiot box' or television set. Whereas one artful poseur used to do for each village, we are all idiots now.

Inch   Long used in English life as the only way to measure rainfall and waistlines, the inch has punched its weight in proverb – 'give him an inch and he'll take and ell' – and epigram – 'every other inch a gentleman'. We shall miss it when we finally go metric. Yet in this as in all else, England must not fail to millimetre forward.

India   The shadow of the Raj still looms large over England. It was not only the nabobs of the East India Company who did well out of it; unnumbered soldiers and engineers, teachers and lawyers, missionaries and misfits, went east. Some, however, found the noonday sun too much for them and went west. Noël Coward* memorably transfixed the syndrome: 'They had him thrown out of a club in Bombay / For apart from his mess bills exceeding his pay / He took to pig-sticking in *quite* the wrong way / I wonder what happened to him?' What indeed.

Yet the scenes and scents of India, the interplay of culture and creed, the laminations of class and caste, the rhythms of sport and work, the code of skin and mesh of sex, the thrall of politics and the mill of money have proved a potent catalyst indeed to generations of English and Indian writers and artists: to E.M. Forster in *Passage to India*, to Somerset Maugham* in *The Razor's Edge*, to Kipling *passim*.

More recently India has inspired Richard Attenborough's majestic if faintly lead-footed film *Gandhi*; and Paul Scott's intricate, subtle and magisterial *Raj Quartet*, marvellously translated to the television screen by Granada as *The Jewel in the Crown*. Certain images of blood and horror continue to haunt the Anglo-Indian imagination; thus the mindless Amritsar massacre of 1919 is recorded unflinchingly in *Gandhi* and finds reverberations in the *Raj Quartet*. Yet there is a happier side. Though India made many Englishmen rich, England is now making many Indians as rich in return: an ironic and perhaps fitting coda to the long saga of the Raj. For details, see under *Mr Patel*.

Initials   There is a curious snobbery about the use of initials in England. The number of people who still use NQOTD – Not Quite Our Type Dear – is happily fast vanishing. Even when it flourished, the code was self-defeating: those using it were self-evidently NQ all right themselves. FHB (Family Hold Back) has a prewar charm: even NSIT (Not Safe in Taxis) is dying out with the demise of the debutante.

The most celebrated codes of all were penned on the outside of wartime letters. SWALK meant Sealed With a Loving Kiss and ITALY meant I Trust and Love You. The longest in this category is probably HILTHYNBIMA (How I long To Hold Your Naked Body In My Arms) and the most romantic BURMA (Be Undressed Ready My Angel).

The army was a fertile progenitor of initials. RAMC stood variously for Rather a Moderate Corps, Rather A Mixed Crowd or – most popular of all – Rob All My Comrades. Even more intriguing in its echoing intimations of time lost is the code for QAIMNS, properly The Queen Alexandra Imperial Military Nursing Service, but to the irreverent, on what hard evidence it is now difficult to say, Queer Assortment of Individuals Mainly Non Sexual.

The Church, however, supplies us with one of the most subtle shorthands. Candidates for the episcopate sometimes had their applications marked with three potent initials: WHM. These stood not, as many supposed, for Westcott House Man (after the distinguished theological college) but for something far more to the point: Wife Has Means.

Introductions In England they are so bad that in certain clubs men will go thirty years or more without knowing each other's names. When introductions *are* made, names are so slurred that they are nearly always lost. Besides, there is a convention in well-bred English society that no extraneous information may be given which will assist the hearer to come to grips with the person he is meeting. Let us say that Air Vice-Marshal Sir Harold Cracker DSO, DFC, is meeting Lady Georgina Farquhar. Then the only polite mode open to the English hostess is to say: 'Georgie, this is Harry Cracker. Harry, this is Georgie Farquhar.' To give people titles or job descriptions is simply not done. The only recourse open to a hyper-conscientious hostess is to say in advance: 'I so much want you to meet Harry Cracker. He's doing something frightfully important with RAF Strike Command.' Even here, though, precise ranks and definitions will not do. This, by the way, is between equals; if children are being introduced handles can and should be given.

The lacuna is particularly hard on our American cousins who not unnaturally like to get things straight thus: 'Doctor Gunge, I'd like to have you meet Professor Grockle.' Worse, the natural American reaction, 'Pleased to meet you,' still grates on well-bred English ears, though on what logical ground it would be hard to say. *How do you do* is both the only possible greeting and rather absurd response in such circles. With such ramshackle conventions, it is hardly surprising that the English go through agonies of amnesia on meeting chance acquaintances in the street. Gladstone's solution was to raise his hat and open the conversation by saying 'Gladstone,' hoping that the unidentified acquaintance would respond with his own name too. Such a device might well have helped the unfortunate gentleman who, meeting Wellington in the street, raised his hat with the words, 'Mr Jones, I believe?' 'If you can believe that,' said the Iron Duke, 'You can believe anything.'

Ireland The hate-love relationship between Ireland and England is reciprocal. Ireland has given England some of her best generals (Wellington, Alexander, Montgomery), playwrights (Sheridan, Wilde, Shaw*) and broadcasters (Robert Kee, Terry Wogan, Frank Delaney). Yet Ireland has also given her the IRA.

The chasm between the quicksilver of the finest Irish minds and the lacklustre of the rest is neatly explained by Hugh Leonard's epigram: 'Ireland is a country bursting with genius but with absolutely no talent.' Still, the English role in Ireland gives no cause for comfort: from Cromwell's iron fist through the horrors of famine to the bloody Black and Tans. The young Disraeli saw the problem all too clearly: a starving population, an absentee aristocracy, an alien Church, and the weakest executive in the world.

The only answer to the Irish Question is one Ireland; but how that is to be honourably (or even practicably) achieved is a matter that has taxed some of the best minds in England: William Ewart Gladstone, Herbert Henry Asquith, and Margaret Hilda Thatcher, to name but three.

Jaegar   Though the name now stands for a certain kind of classic, natural English outdoor chic, it began as the slightly potty brainchild of a Victorian philanthropist called Lewis Tomalin. He was an accountant who had married a German girl and could speak her language well. In 1880 he came across a book called *Health Culture* written by Dr Gustav Jaeger, professor of zoology at Stuttgart. It put forward the principle that *homo sapiens* would be far better off if he – or of course she – dressed in clothes made entirely from animal hair and, in particular, wool.

So enthralled was Tomalin with this notion that he translated the book himself and published it in England at his own expense. So persuasive was his case that in 1884 *The Times* published a leader supporting the idea. Tomalin had opened the first Jaeger shop in London earlier that year, with a licence from Dr Jaeger to use his name. He intended it merely as a philanthropic hobby, and the legend over the door of that first shop was endearingly dotty: *Dr Jaeger's Sanitary Woollen System.* Soon the idea was taken up by eminent Victorians like Oscar Wilde and Bernard Shaw* (who walked about London in one of the first Jaeger suits, looking, so it was said, like a bifurcated radish).

In five years, it dawned on Tomalin that his private obsession had become a thumping success. He went into the business full-time and by 1900 had twenty Jaeger shops. Today there are 150 in the UK, 100 abroad. Stanley took Jaeger with him when he went in search of Livingstone; Scott took Jaeger with him to the Antarctic. The word entered the language, gradually shifting its stance from its first slightly barmy connotation to the international *réclame* it enjoys today.

Nicholas Tomalin, a great-grandson of the founder, was killed covering the Yom Kippur war for *The Sunday Times* in 1973. He was forty-two, one of the great reporters of his time, and in his humanity, intelligence and eccentricity, a chip off the old block.

Jaguar Bill Lyons nearly went into making gramophones, but fortunately at twenty-one decided instead to join a young Blackpool pal called Bill Walmsley in making side-cars for motorbikes. Lyons senior, who ran a music shop, put in £500, Walmsley senior, a coal merchant, another £500, and that was all the capital the boys ever needed. Soon they were making bodies for cars; Standard, Austin, Morris, Fiat and Wolseley. They were curiously graceful, as indeed was everything Bill Lyons ever built. The Standard connection proved most durable and in 1931 the boys were involved in the launch of the new 16 h.p. Standard SS. It was known even then as a real cad's* car: two short men could shake hands over the top, though the engine tended to boil.

In 1935 the company went public; Bill Walmsley took his money; Bill Lyons became sole boss. He took over the name of an obsolete Armstrong-Siddeley aero-engine which appealed to him: the Jaguar. The first SS Jaguar appeared at the 1935 Motor Show; guests were asked to guess its price. The average answer was around £650; the true price £385. Bill then drafted in a young engineer called Harry Weslake to raise the Standard's power from 90 to 105 b.h.p. enticing him with a cash reward for each b.h.p. he squeezed out.

That still wasn't good enough and in the war, during long nights of fire-watching at the factory, Bill Lyons and his lieutenants dreamed up a totally new engine called the XK. It is still fundamentally the unit which powers all Jaguars today. The XK 120 was the sensation of the 1948 Motor Show and hugely popular with starlets and playboys, especially in America. It was followed by the Mark II, famed for its enormous acceleration and therefore popular with the underworld as a getaway car; the Mark VII, much loved by the rag trade; the E-type, favoured transport of the first highly paid pop-stars and footballers; and lastly the feline, silky, and highly refined XJS, Jaguar's final passport to respectability (the E-type had been dubbed the greatest crumpet-catcher known to man). In 1984, Jaguar was privatised, emerging from British Leyland to become, once again, an independent company. It is now owned by Ford, and has just announced its latest model: the XK8. Bill would approve.

Jam In English usage jam is not just the stuff you spread on your bread and butter, but in a transferred sense, any good fortune, as in Lewis

Carroll's* 'jam yesterday and jam tomorrow, but never jam today'. Thus, 'jammy one' since the First World War has meant the sort of minor wound which would get you out of the trenches but not seriously impair your faculties; and the man who got the jammy one became a 'jammy bastard'.

Meanwhile, the business of jam-making has acquired a highly pejorative status in the language of feminist politics; it stands for the work women have done uncomplainingly and indeed with pleasure in country kitchens for centuries and is therefore held to be a backward step in the onward march of the women's movement.

Still, while English home-made jam – strawberry, raspberry, cherry, rhubarb and ginger, greengage, blackcurrant, redcurrant, blackberry, apricot, quince, and damson – remains as good as it is, clear, pure, sweet and brilliant as stained glass, best bought in a marquee on the day of the village fête, it is unlikely to stop being made. At least, we must devoutly hope so.

Japanese   The English attitude to the Japanese has undergone several radical metamorphoses. Before the war they were a comic race known principally as slavish imitators of British innovative skills. In the war, they took Singapore: probably the biggest single catastrophe to befall British arms, and an even more profound psychological trauma. The Japanese were a joke no longer. Indeed, when British prisoners were used as slave labour to build the Burma railway, the Japanese were seen, with some justification, as sadistic psychopaths.

To a new generation of young English people, however, the Japanese are neither buffoons nor bastards, but a brilliant race who have given them their Sony transistor radios, their Hitachi television sets, their Toshiba microwave ovens, and their Honda motorbikes. A young Englishman may now indeed be working for a Japanese bank or in a Japanese car plant while learning judo or karate in his spare time. Recently the Japanese invoked the law against an English manufacturer who was trying to pass off his product with a Japanese trademark. In just half a century, the wheel has come full circle.

Jeeves   'What would I do without you, Jeeves?' sang Ian Carmichael as Bertie Wooster* in the BBC TV serialisation of the immortal *oeuvre*, 'I'd be in the most awful stew, Jeeves.' He would indeed; but the need is reciprocal. Wooster and Jeeves are two halves of a single whole. One without the other would be like the sound of one hand clapping. Jeeves has quite properly entered the English language with an entry to himself

In the *Supplement* to the *OED*. He is an archetypally English creation: an American Jeeves would be an absurdity, a French Jeeves a nightmare, a Japanese Jeeves a mockery, a German Jeeves a catastrophe. The relationship between the two great Englishmen is marvellously balanced. The proper distance is maintained at all times: Wooster is always sir, Jeeves never Reginald. Though Jeeves defers to Bertie's social rank with the innate gravamen of his class he has no respect for Bertie's intellect: indeed he has been heard to speak of the young master as mentally negligible. Bertie, on the other hand, though he may bridle a bit under his man's iron tutelage, especially when his favourite banjolele or purple socks have to go, never loses his awe at Jeeves's giant brain, which he fondly (though as it happens misguidedly) believes to be fed on a steady diet of fish. He also notes, with a proper sense of wonder, that Jeeves's head sticks out at the back to accommodate the massive cerebellum. The relationship is unsentimental: Jeeves can and will give notice if thwarted or temporarily replaced by one of Bertie's girls; but he always comes back. He must. He is the perfect manservant. He does not enter Bertie's room; he shimmers in. His morning cuppa is perfect (see also *Tea*) and his pick-me-up, though it momentarily lifts Bertie's skull off, quickly restores him to his customary zing.

Though Jeeves has been variously traced back to Sancho Panza and Sam Weller, he is in truth triumphantly *sui generis:* deeply read (Spinoza, Nietzsche, Dostoevsky, Pliny the Younger – but the list of his reading is endless), naturally magisterial (he takes the chair at meetings of the Junior Ganymede, the Dover Street club for gentlemen's gentlemen), perennially discreet. 'In times of domestic crisis,' Bertie reports, 'Jeeves has the gift of creating the illusion that he is not there.'

The reason that he is so triumphantly and palpably there in the English imagination is that he has a Boswell of genius in the improbable person of Bertie Wooster: 'It was the soft cough of Jeeves's which always reminds me of a very old sheep clearing its throat on a distant mountain top.' On the other hand, we have Jeeves's word for it that 'In the presence of the unusual, Mr Wooster is too prone to smile weakly and allow his eyes to protrude.'

Occasionally other fellows have tried to snaffle Jeeves. He was with Gussie Fink-Nottle for a few days. But he always comes homing back to Bertie's bachelor rooms in Berkeley Street, where it is eternally spring, in an England that never really existed; more's the pity.

Jews To be a Jew in England does not seem a bad fate, but it will bring its challenges, as being one does everywhere. A strain of antisemitism has disfigured English writing since Chaucer. Orwell*, writing in 1945, detected it in Wells, Huxley, Shaw*, Eliot and Thackeray (and did not even bother with the notorious antisemites like Chesterton, Belloc, Buchan and Sapper). It clearly reflected the way people thought, but never approached the systematic paranoia of central Europe (in 1907 when the Kaiser visited England his conversation on world politics with Grey could not proceed till he had delivered a lengthy diatribe against the Jews). Still, it is unattractive enough.

Open the most innocuous-seeming book anywhere and the words leap from the page. In *The Fifth Form at St Dominic's,* published in 1881, we have to wait no longer than the second page before Bullinger of the Fifth calls a small boy an avaricious young Jew for whistling at the terms of a £50 scholarship. 'A Jewish boy at a public school,' noted Orwell, 'almost invariably had a bad time.'

He was looking back to the pre-Hitler world, but things were no better for English writer Frederic Raphael, at Charterhouse in the 1940s, when the preacher of an antisemitic sermon in the school chapel apologised to him later, explaining that he would never have made such remarks if he had known a Jew were present. (That shows, *inter alia*, just how numerous Jews were at Charterhouse then.) The incident was translated wellnigh unadorned to Raphael's smash-hit TV serial *The Glittering Prizes.* So were things better after the last war?

As late as the fifties candidates for jobs at the Cambridge University Appointments Board were described as Jews with clammy handshakes; there was a fuss when it came out but nobody was sacked.

Among great English writers, Orwell noted, only Dickens* could be said to be positively pro-Jewish (overlooking George Eliot and *Daniel Deronda*). Since the mid-thirties and the rise of Hitler, however, it has been thought uncivilised for any serious writer to commit antisemitic sentiments to paper. Besides, Jews like Frederic Raphael, Jonathan Miller and Bernard Levin have made an increasingly attractive contribution to English life.

Jonathan Miller, for example, explained in a hilarious sketch from *Beyond The Fringe* that he was not a Jew; only Jew*ish*. What this meant, perhaps, is that Jews become accepted in England the more English they become. Thus Julius Victor in John Buchan's *The Three Hostages*, though one of the richest men in the world, is also 'the whitest Jew since Saint Paul'. He has, in effect, become an Englishman.

In a more down-to-earth context, the good done to the Jewish image by a brilliant business like Marks and Spencer*, pervading every household with its bounty, is incalculable. Paul Johnson has said that intellectual life cannot flourish in any country where the Jews are even slightly uneasy. With Jews starring in Tory cabinets (Lawson and Young; Brittan and Joseph; and now Howard and Rifkind) it could be said that in modern England they are easy enough: time will tell.

Johnson, Samuel (1709–84) We tend to think of him as old: he was, after all, fifty-four, the great dictionary already written, Boswell a callow twenty-three on that celebrated day their paths first crossed in Tom Davies's back parlour. By then, as Boswell noted in his journal (a treasure trove which came to light only in this century) he had 'the most dreadful appearance'. In his youth he had been tall and lanky; by now, Boswell noted, he had grown 'gigantick'. He was, moreover, 'troubled with sore eyes, the palsy, and the King's evil … very slovenly in his dress with a most uncouth voice'. None of this mattered when he began to talk.

Every Johnsonian will have his favourite moment. Some will savour the night when Sam sat down to dine with his *bête noir* Jack Wilkes, radical, rationalist and rake, a meeting engineered by Boswell with dexterous cunning. It could have been a disaster; it was a triumph. True, Wilkes went out of his way to please, plying the old trencherman with fine veal; 'Pray give me leave Sir – it is better here – A little of the stuffing – Some gravy – Let me have the pleasure of giving you some butter …'

It worked. 'Sir, sir I am obliged to you sir,' returns Sam. A mutual taste for jokes against the Scots, and later a shared pleasure in a picture, of the curve in a woman's bosom, set the seal on their unlikely conjunction. Others will relish that carefree evening during the tour of the Hebrides when a pretty married Highland lady sat on Johnson's knee and kissed him: 'Do it again [said he] and let us see who will tire first.'

The sound and feel of the man carry over the two centuries with a clarity and freshness denied us by the flat, glassy technology of the tape recorder and the television camera. It is the most vivid case we have of the warts-and-all portrait. 'I have not wasted my life trifling with literary fools as Johnson did when he should have been shaking England with the thunder of his spirit,' complained Bernard Shaw peevishly. Yet it is precisely the trifling in taverns that laces the vast learning with humanity and makes us all feel we would have enjoyed a jar or two with Johnson: before, that is, he gave up fermented liquors.

Boswell's father, Lord Auchinleck, could not understand what Jamie could see in 'the auld dominie', and we all know Mrs Boswell's epigram: 'I have seen many a bear led by a man: but I never before saw a man led by a bear.' No matter; we can see the point of the old bear now; and must be grateful that Boswell survived the collapse of his legal career, the extinction of his political ambitions, and the onset of his chronic drinking to complete the greatest biography in the English language. He knew he had pulled it off. 'I have Johnsonised the land,' he boasted; and he had.

Jug v Straight Glass   Very broadly, the straight glass or sleeve finds its natural home north of the Wash and in working-class hands; though there are plenty of well-heeled southrons who swear that beer tastes better from a thin straight glass and that you can assess the contents far better than you can if it is in a dimpled jug. On the other hand there are those who claim that the straight glass tends to slip from carefree fingers as the hour advances (though a slight bulge near the top of the sleeve has been introduced to obviate this design fault). The jug is most often found in saloon bars, southern rugger clubs, and air force messes where it is characteristically held with three or four fingers through the handle on the far side and the thumb pressed against the belly. It has even been argued in Scotland that the sleeve is to be preferred in a free-for-all, when the glass can be smashed on the bar and the jagged remnant brought up to the ready in one continuous movement. Here, however, we treat only of England, where such an ungentlemanly deployment of the beer glass is happily rare.

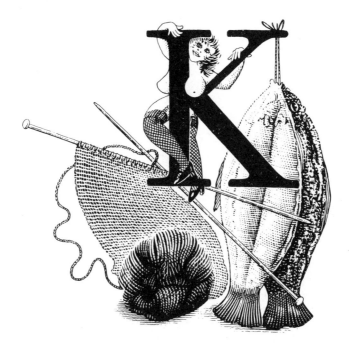

Kew Gardens They have a dream-like quality to the average Englishman, for here he enters a world of sumptuous and extravagant fantasy. With a small dose of laudanum, who knows what new Kubla Khan might not here be spun out by some latter-day Coleridge? For here are the Queen's Beasts, the Campanile, the Pagoda and the Ice-House; the Temples of Aeolus, Bellona and Arethusa; the Ruined Arch, Orangery and Japanese Gateway; within those hot and humid glasshouses where tropical rain forests are re-created, ferns and fronds, palms and pines, loofahs and lotuses, pineapples and paw-paws proliferate. All this exotica was first brought here by the colonising energy of the Victorians. It is the organised plunder of empire; and when he steps into its magical ambit the Englishman, in short, enters his ill-gotten inheritance.

Keynes, John Maynard (1883–1946) He was one of the dozen or so most influential, most original, and most able Englishmen of this century; not to beat about the bush, one of the *greatest* Englishmen. His world fame rests on his seminal book, the *General Theory of Employment Interest and Money* (1936), which did for economics what Einstein's General Theory of Relativity had done for physics twenty years before, that is, stood the subject on its head. There are countless economists today who can explain how Keynes is outmoded or superseded; not one of them could even put his case without the conceptual tools Keynes provided.

Still, another book, published by Keynes in 1919, may have been even more important: for *The Economic Consequences of the Peace*, written in white heat engendered by his anger at the so-called peace at Versailles that year, retails, in prose of glittering beauty, how a more generous and imaginative settlement could have prevented the Second World War. It was precisely because the botched job at Versailles left an appalling moral and material vacuum in Germany that the scum of Europe had the chance to spawn, flourish, and, for a fatal while, prevail.

Quite apart from the grandeur of its theme, *Consequence* teems with unforgettable cameos of the main actors at Versailles. The picture of Lloyd George was at first cut out because Keynes felt it disloyal to print it so soon after working for the Welsh prestidigitator; but it was restored later, and is breathtakingly savage. 'This syren,' Keynes wrote, 'this goat-footed bard, this half-human visitor to our age from the hag-ridden magic and enchanted woods of Celtic antiquity ... is rooted in nothing; he is void and without content ... he is a prism which collects light and distorts it and is most brilliant if the light comes from many quarters at once; a vampire and medium in one.'

It was Keynes's lot to do his most celebrated work for his country at the end of each world war; and if he failed in 1945 to get all the cash Britain wanted from America, he probably did all that was humanly possible; and he was a key figure in the setting up of the International Monetary Fund and the International Bank, both destined to be fundamental in the smooth transition of the world to peace. But the strain on an already weak heart proved too much; and he died in 1946.

Khatmandu The capital of Nepal, an independent country which usually enjoyed friendly relations with the British Raj and generally managed to get away with no more serious occupation than a British Resident. However, British troops were assuredly posted there, none more celebrated than Mad Carew, the hero of a dramatic monologue by J. Milton Hayes, once recited on the music hall with huge effect and perfect solemnity.

The Green Eye of the Little Yellow God is a morality story which celebrates the essential frivolity of womankind, the clash of deeply opposed cultures, and the eneluctable fate which awaits young English-men who flout the *mores* of the foreign soil on which they stand.

'He was known as Mad Carew by the subs [second lieutenants] at Khatmandu,' we are told. 'But for all his foolish pranks he was worshipped in the ranks.' This usually gets the first laugh of the evening nowadays: the ranks no longer worship anyone, and certainly not idiots like Carew.

The real fascination of the ludicrous doggerel lies in the unrecorded moment when it shaded from a perfectly serious, indeed solemn, morality tale into an uproarious comic turn. That moment cannot be accurately pinned down now; almost certainly the laughter began at some time between the two wars, and grew to gale force after India* got her independence and the British rule became a vast subterranean folk memory.

Today's Mad Carews (and the breed miraculously lives on) have to be content with less disputatious dares like walking from the south to the north pole or crossing the Atlantic in a bathtub. Not for nothing did Halvard Lange remark that his countrymen did not see Englishmen as foreigners: 'We look on them only as rather mad Norwegians.' Like Mad Carew.

Kippers Though the Scots have some cause to be proud of their Loch Fyne Kippers, and though they are nowadays often thought of as a quintessentially Scottish dish, there is some evidence that the first kippers were made by a Northumberland fish curer called John Woodger. He knew that salmon had been kippered as long ago as the fourteenth century, and decided to try the same process on herrings. He split them down the backbone, gutted them, and soaked them in brine, then hung them over oak fires to smoke for some twelve hours. He had invented kippers and excellent ones are still made there (as well as in the Isle of Man and around Great Yarmouth). Still a sturdy runner-up on British Rail to the ubiquitous mixed grill as a breakfast dish, kippers have found favour with celebrated Englishmen like George Orwell*, and Laurence Olivier* who made a famous fuss when the kippers were taken off his Brighton–Victoria train. Though the succulent fish have attracted only a small literature, they were commandeered with splendid effect by the Labour politician Eric Heffer. The Conservative Party, he opined, were nothing but a load of kippers: two-faced with no guts.

Knighthoods The honours system in England is a shambles. The man who after the First World War called Birmingham* the City of Dreadful Knights – an enchanting verdict on the sort of people who had been honoured there for making fortunes out of the blood and agony – deserved the accolade far more than those who actually got it. Though Lloyd George's tariff for honours (knighthoods cost £25,000) was notorious, neither Harold Wilson with his resignation honours list nor Harold Macmillan with his cheerfully cynical largesse did the much overhauled system much good.

Certainly, good men are made knights, and some middling men, and some patently deplorable men. The disgrace is the chaos which pervades the honours machinery. Certainly in the imaginative world it is now often more of an honour to be left out. While many truly great writers, whether by accident or design, go unknighted (Wells, Hardy*, Conrad, Eliot, Auden*, Orwell*, Waugh* and Greene) there is no shortage of such accolades for the second-rate: duffers like Henry Newbolt and John Squire.

So laughter may seem the only possible response to the solemn buff envelope. Bernard Shaw* replied that nothing less than a dukedom would do for him.

Knitting   The insidious natter of the knitting needle was once heard only in the purlieu of grannies and maiden aunts. It is now a trendy pursuit among the young, and owes its new rage to an Englishwoman called Patricia Roberts. She took the fashion course at the renowned Leicester College of Art, and knitting, unfashionable then, as her main subsidiary subject. She now has 150 women knitting for her and still runs her business from her shop at Kinnerton Street in London. She has had a galvanic effect on British wool, previously unbelievably awful, now as chic and svelte as her sweaters. Americans, being lousy knitters, are among her best customers.

Knocker   Since about 1940 it has been an idiomatic term for the female breast. The word was most memorably used in recent times by the England rugby scrum half, Steve Smith, who complained that when a well-endowed young woman took it into her head to run across the field topless during the half-time interval at a Twickenham international, it had been impossible for his captain, the great Billy Beaumont, to secure the concentration of his players on tactics for the second half: 'They wouldn't pay attention with those great knockers whistling by.' We may deduce therefore that the colourful phrase is still in lively idiomatic use among young and active Englishmen.

The Knowledge   The compulsory learning of London's streets that any would-be taxi driver must master if he is to be given a licence by the Carriage Office. It is contained in the Blue Book (now confusingly pink) put out by the Metropolitan Police and involves a meticulous grasp of routes through all the streets within a six-mile radius of central London as well as any buildings of interest along them. It takes roughly three years (usually part-time) to learn The Knowledge and, despite the rigour of the series of examinations (known as appearances), there is an eighteen-month waiting list to go on the course. A firm called London Knowledge at 329 Goswell Road, EC1, sell a £30 guide to the basic runs every taxi-driver is required to know and update it with computerised sheets of further expertise every three months at £17.50 each. The consequence is that London's 10,000 taxi-drivers know their city far better than any others do.

Koestler, Arthur (1905–83)   He was part of that unquantifiable credit balance of talent England acquired as a result of fascism, but he was something more: an object lesson in how well English can be written by somebody not born speaking the language. The other two great exemplars are Conrad and Nabokov (though Nabokov learned English in the nursery). For Arthur Koestler it was a third language; he wrote in Hungarian till he was seventeen, in German till he was thirty-five, then in English. Though he grumbled about the alien's uphill fight, taking aboard his hard-won new idiom, only to have to discard it next day as cliché, the truth is that few Englishmen have written better English this century.

Labour Party   'Lunched with Desmond MacCarthy at Gatti's,' wrote Harold Nicolson in his diary for 27 February 1930. 'He tells me a story about Keir Hardie,' (the pioneer labour leader). 'Looking down on the 1905 House of Commons a friend remarked to him how few members there were from the working classes. "Yes, it will take the British working man twenty years to learn to elect his equals to represent him. And it will take him another twenty years not to elect his equals."' Nicolson thought this was true: 'I saw it with Ramsay MacDonald the other day – his longing to get hold of the young university men. His feeling that the *cadets de bonne famille* were the people he wanted.'

Seventeen years later, no longer a *cadet* but indisputably *de bonne famille*, Nicolson joined the Labour Party himself. The decision shocked his family. His son Nigel, Conservative candidate for Leicester, said he was 'struck dumb'. His wife, the writer Vita Sackville-West, wrote to tell him she did not like people who could not speak the King's English. Harold Nicolson later confessed it was the cardinal error of his life: 'the realities, and above all the personalities, of Labour politics really revolted me'.

The melancholy vignette illustrates graphically the headaches men of goodwill have had in trying to come to terms with this ramshackle rag-bag of a party, containing, or trying to contain, within itself intellectuals and trade unionists, Christians and atheists, pacifists and militants, lost liberals and miscast radicals, socialists and communists, Trotskyites and Marxists, pedagogues and demagogues, opportunists and idealists, bullies and ninnies, saints and sinners. It had two short periods of minority government between the wars; three periods of real power in the post-war world, ending when Margaret Thatcher defeated Callaghan in 1979, routed Michael Foot in 1983, and trounced Neil Kinnock in 1987. Now though, re-invented under its faun-like yet streetwise young leader Tony Blair, its ranks slightly more middle-class than the Tories; its constitution at last unshackled by Clause 4, New Labour waits at the time of writing expectantly in the ante-room of true power again. What it will make of that benefaction, if it indeed comes, is anyone's guess.

Lancashire   'In the early morning the mill girls clumping down the cobbled street, all in clogs, making a curiously formidable sound, like an army hurrying into battle. I suppose this is the typical sound of Lancashire.' Thus George Orwell* wrote in his diary on 18 February 1936; the notebook from which *The Road to Wigan Pier* was later to be constructed. 'Clogs are very cheap', he continued. 'They cost about five shillings a pair and need not wear out for years because all they need is new irons underneath costing a few pence.' A vivid picture from a vanished world? The clogs have gone, and so have many of the mills. Yet the unemployment is still there, and relatively at any rate, the poverty. Today the world gets its most vivid picture of Lancashire through the lens of the television camera; twice a week the rest of England peers hypnotised into the alien civilisation portrayed in Granada TV's marathon soap opera *Coronation Street*. Perhaps over the half-century time has softened many of the sharp edges of Lancashire life; the older generation may cling to their cloth caps and hair nets; younger people in the street are indistinguishable from the young anywhere. Yet still the broad vowels and glottal stops of the whippet-fanciers, ale-suppers, and tripe-takers distinguish north from south and in times of recession the gap between them yawns dangerously wide.

There is an agricultural and beautiful Lancashire to the north; but essentially still it is a county of industrial cities: Rochdale and Preston, Wigan and Warrington, Blackburn and Burnley, Nelson and Colne. Ambitious plans and millions of pounds of venture capital are being poured into the great Lancashire cities of Manchester* and Liverpool*, but the heart of Lancashire must be won in these smaller, beleaguered, industrial towns. Disraeli said there were two nations in England, who were as ignorant of each other's habits, thoughts, and feelings as if they were on different planets. Granada TV has reduced the gap from stellar to human distances; but in Lancashire it is still there.

Landscape   Seeing the shimmer and haze of his landscape, insubstantial and dreamlike through the creamy air of any early May morning, the average Englishman tends to think of it as fortuitously given and always there. The truth is that landscapes are made by men just as much as men are made by landscapes; and in England it was the work of the great landscape gardeners – William Kent, Capability Brown, Humphry Repton – which gave England its languorous look.

They did it by a genius for following the artless lie of the land, for the seemingly casual disposition of trees, shrubs and flowers, for the apparently unintended scatter of lake, ha-ha, and folly. Today the landscape architect – as he is more grandly called now – acts not for landed proprietors but for local authorities; his workplace is no longer around the mansion but along the motorway. Even as he faces up to his new challenges, the landscape his forebears left is changing step to the music of time. The intimate patchwork quilt of small fields is disappearing as the immemorial hedgerows of England are swept away; and the land that was once thickly peopled by farmworkers is now innocent of any life except for the solitary technician chuntering by in his combine harvester.

Even the gentle pastel of traditional English crops is now shot through by the saffron blaze of the rape grown for the margarine makers. The electric pylons which caused such a furore when they first marched over the English landscape half a century ago have curiously melted into the picture now; but nothing can be done for a generation about the desolate skeletons of England's eleven million dead elms*.

Larkin, Philip (1922–1985)   If writers had a work-reward unit as engines have a thermal efficiency unit, then Philip Larkin would have rated the maximum score. In his sixty-three years he published two novels: *Jill* (1946) and *A Girl in Winter* (1947); and four very slim volumes of verse. They are: *The North Ship* (1945) which contains thirty-two poems: *The Less Deceived* (1955) with a modest twenty-nine poems; *The Whitsun Weddings* (1964; and thirty-two poems again); and in 1974 *High Windows* (a mere twenty-four poems). In recognition for this exiguous *oeuvre*, he was made a CBE, a C. Lit and a FRSI. He was appointed a Visiting Fellow of All Souls College, Oxford, and a Foreign Honorary Member of the American Academy. He won the Queen's Gold Medal for Poetry and the A.C. Benson Silver Medal. He was given the Loines Award for Poetry and the Shakespeare Prize of the FVS foundation in Hamburg. His home town bestowed the Coventry Award of Merit on its much-medalled son. And no fewer than five universities – Belfast,

Leicester, Warwick, St Andrews and Sussex – gave him honorary doctorates. From this great plethora of palms and prizes we can draw only one of two conclusions. Either the world's honorific machinery had stripped its gears and gone into some kind of ungovernable overdrive; or Larkin's little harvest must have been uncommonly ripe. His poetry was often thought to be pessimistic if not downright melancholy. He thought it was and wasn't. 'A poem,' he once said, 'is a positive and joyful thing: it represents the mastering, even if just for a moment, of the pessimism and the melancholy, and enables you – you the poet, and you, the reader – to go on.'

Lawns   There are eleven million lawns in England. No other nation on earth can boast the lushness and profusion of English grass. In part, this is no doubt the consequence of the wellnigh perfect weather for it: mild, damp and relatively pest-free; but it is also a reflection of the preoccupation the island race has with sport that quite so much grass is grown and tended. In cricket endless hours are devoted to the preparation of the wicket, or more accurately the stretch of turf between the two wickets; in horse racing the punter will want to know how good the going is, in other words, the state of the turf; in the relatively tranquil game of bowls each player must accept the rub of the green; in polo the chief source of social intercourse between chukkas is the quaint habit of treading the divots or restoring the turf cut up by flying hooves.

'Nothing is more pleasant to the Eye,' declared Francis Bacon in 1625, 'than green Grass kept finely shorn,' though the modes of keeping it so – grazing, trampling and scything – were far less precise than those we now have. True, some greenkeepers claimed till recent times that they could cut with a scythe to a smoothness not possible by any other means; but the invention of the lawn mower by Edwin Budding at Stroud in 1830 took much of the sweat out of tending grass; and the arrival of the motor mower around the turn of the century took the rest.

By 1902 the self-propelled forty-two-inch mower with saddle for driver was being used by Cadburys, the Quaker* chocolate firm, at their model village of Bournville, thus providing that broad striped zebra effect now so familiar throughout the land. There is no mistaking the velvet pile of a well-kept English lawn, wrought from fine-bladed bent and fescue grasses mown regularly at carpet height, nor the frequency with which such images recur in English writing. 'Close and slow, summer is ending in Hampshire,' wrote Louis MacNeice* in the great opening to his *Autumn Journal*, 'Ebbing away down ramps of shaven lawn where close-clipped yew / Insulates the live of retired generals and admirals /

And the spyglasses hung in the hall and the prayerbooks ready in the pew.'

Liberty There is an unexpected link between Oscar Wilde and two great London stores: Jaeger* and Liberty. Oscar enthusiastically endorsed the characteristic products of both. Indeed, he can fairly claim to have begun the long love affair between Americans and Liberty, for in his celebrated American lecture tour of 1881–2 he included a talk on house decoration, which turned on the cult of the new 'greenery-yallery' aesthetic school. Gilbert and Sullivan's *Patience* contained the seminal lines: 'A greenery-yallery, Grosvenor Gallery / Foot-in-the grave young man.'

Greenery-yallery, though rather opaque now, made perfect sense then. In 1879 Liberty's had introduced a new cashmere, described at the time by *Queen* magazine: 'There are tints that call to mind French and English mustards, sage-greens, greens that look like curry.'

Liberty's had supplied the fabrics for costumes in Gilbert and Sullivan's *Patience*, and when D'Oyly Carte was working on *The Mikado*, sent special envoys to Japan to bring back exactly the right materials for the clothes. Not surprisingly, Arthur Liberty, founder of the firm, had a box at Gilbert and Sullivan first nights. To give the cult another helpful push forward, *Patience* was running in New York even as Wilde was sweeping America.

The link between Liberty and Japan was not new. Young Arthur Liberty, then a sales assistant at Farmer and Rogers on the west side of Regent Street, had been inspired by the Japanese section of the International Exhibition of 1862. He ran the oriental side of Farmer and Rogers which sold these Japanese exhibits after the show closed; and when they failed to make him a partner in 1875 crossed the road and started on his own.

The fashionable world crossed Regent Street with him. Liberty had a close working friendship with Thomas Wardle, the Leek dyer and printer; together they introduced the new range of delicate pastel tints which had previously been the prerogative of the East and which were to be known worldwide as Liberty colours. To a world accustomed to harsh colours and stiff silks these soft, pretty fabrics were a revelation.

Liberty's customers included William Morris, Alma-Tadema, Burne-Jones and Whistler. Liberty silks make their appearance in Somerset Maugham's great novel *Cakes and Ale*; Liberty curtains are found in a thriller called *The Documents in the Case* by a young writer called Dorothy L. Sayers; a letter from Liberty's features in D.H. Lawrence's *Sons and Lovers*. A penniless Isadora Duncan danced in Liberty fabric bought with a borrowed £10 at her first London party.

Mary Quant used Liberty prints; Yves Saint-Laurent used a whole range when he dropped his skirt length to mid-calf. And while Liberty still scour the East for new ideas, they are now, in a final irony, exporting Liberty fabrics to Japan.

Licensing   For nearly three-quarters of a century it has been impossible to buy a drink at an English pub in the afternoon. The ban on afternoon opening, started in the First World War in case munitions workers were diverted from their work, remained in place till the Home Secretary, Douglas Hurd, recently introduced a bill to allow pubs to remain open on the six weekdays if they wished from eleven in the morning till eleven at night. He told the Commons he failed to see why drinking was perfectly all right in the morning and evening, but not in the afternoon. Logically, he was quite right; but the fact is that afternoon drinking has long had a faintly sinful connotation to Englishmen, and afternoon drinking clubs have long denoted decadence. Still, it was clearly absurd to deny English people the right to drink in the afternoon if they so wished; they have been doing so in Scotland since 1976 with no discernible ill effect. Asked why his new measure did not apply to Sunday too, Hurd replied with manful honesty that he wanted to get the bill through. Drinking on a Sunday afternoon is still something the English seem hardly ready for, although a recent relaxation has made it possible for anyone in England to do even that if they so wished. The new liberty is little understood yet – or used.

Liverpool   When he was Secretary of State for the Environment Michael Heseltine made it his business to pay a visit to Liverpool once a week. As an ambitious minister, he was quite right. Liverpool is a stage on which the contending views on how wealth and power should be distributed in modern England are being dramatically played out. The Toxteth riots, a series of paroxysms of rage or cries for help (depending on one's political colour), had marvellously focussed the attention of the Thatcherite government on the squalor, poverty, and despair which had ignited them. It is a city of infinite extremes and violent contrasts.

Its socialist council barely rescued itself from a collision course with the government and had elected to go bankrupt rather than toe the line about spending cuts. It harbours the Bishop of Liverpool, the Right Rev David Sheppard, who in his 1984 Dimbleby lecture on BBC TV appealed to the conscience of Britain to meet the horrors of unemployment by state intervention. It harbours Professor Patrick Minford of Liverpool University, easily the most ultramontane of all English academic economists in his call for enormous slices of the welfare state to be returned to private hands. There is, in short, nothing temperate or moderate about Liverpool.

It has been a crucible of wealth for some two centuries; and one of the principal ingredients in that vast wealth was the slave trade. It was one corner of the ghastly triangular traffic which carried cotton goods to Africa; exchanged them for black men, women and children, took them across the Atlantic to America; and came home with raw cotton, tobacco and sugar. John Gladstone, father of the great reforming and humanitarian Liberal statesman William Ewart Gladstone, was ironically a Liverpool slave-owner (along with many peers and even some bishops). He defended his moral position vehemently, and when emancipation came in 1833 received £75,000 in compensation for the 1,609 slaves he owned. Thus Liverpool has an old crime lying on its conscience; this has in no whit prevented the city from acquiring a parallel reputation for gaiety, originality, and cosmopolitan fizz. It can boast two of the best twentieth-century cathedrals in England: the Anglican, begun in 1904 and finished seventy-five years later, and the Roman Catholics' ultra-modern Metropolitan Cathedral of Christ the King, completed in 1967 after just four and a half years. Its university can claim (from its university college days) two unexpected and improbable alumni: F.E. Smith and Lytton Strachey. It is celebrated for its racecourse (Aintree); its comedians (Ken Dodd, Tom O'Connor, Freddie Starr); and of course for The Beatles, who made the Liverpool sound world famous. Liverpool has remembered its favourite sons by founding Beatle City, an exhibition centre dedicated to the art of the four fabled Merseyside troubadours, and Cavern Walks, a colourful shopping centre which houses a statue in their honour.

London   But which London? The segments devised for the delivery of the mail break the great wen conveniently for us into a wide spectrum of different villages, each with its own flavour. Thus NW1 or Camden Town is Stringalong territory, though you have to be over a certain age to remember this trendy family created by Mark Boxer and sounding suspiciously like Tomalin in reverse. The Stringalongs stand for trendy, caring, intelligent bourgeois values, often rendered ridiculous in the press of everyday life. They cluster in a few substantial roads just east of Primrose Hill, patronising the same bookshops, restaurants, laundromats, boutiques and delicatessens. You could do worse than join them there; but it will cost you a few bob: NW1 is no longer cheap.

Nor is NW3, melting pot for television directors, senior civil servants, barristers and many other varieties of intelligent high-earners. The flavour of NW3 is leavened by its Jewish flavour and liberal politics. Hampstead (for that is NW3 under another name) is still *sympathique,* but very, very pricey. So what about N1? It's central, and full of interesting, slightly seedy Georgian houses; but other people have had the same idea and for a generation now Islington has been progressively gentrified with aubergine doors and coach lamps taking the place of the broken windows and peeling paint.

We can rule out SW1 or Belgravia; home of American film actors, Arab oil sheiks and, increasingly, Japanese tycoons; while SW3 or Chelsea is now as classy as Hampstead: full of estate agents, stockbrokers, merchant bankers and advertising men. So what about St John's Wood? Again, we are a generation too late: once the favourite nesting ground for mistresses and sculptors, still charming with its Regency verandahs and secret high-walled gardens, it is increasingly the domain of brassy classy foreign money: it has little or no indigenous life left. W1 (Mayfair) is impossible, while W2 (Paddington) still has some interesting enclaves buried between the kebab and tandoori places. W8 or Bayswater may still have some bargains, especially round the Portobello Road*, but Kensington proper (SW7) is now a maze of museums and stuccoed apartments for the well-to-do.

So where should young married people go? Fulham has many adherents, it's ugly but only pricey in patches and not too far from the centre; Hammersmith has possibilities though you will be lucky indeed to find anything by the Thames*. However Hammersmith harbours the increasingly trendy Brackenbury village, handy for BBC TV people and home now to several excellent pubs and restaurants. Perhaps the best bet for those who do not mind going over the river is Clapham, where there are still rows of imposing late eighteenth-century houses facing over wide green spaces.

Much government money has gone into trying to persuade people to move east to dockland and the Isle of Dogs; geographically it's attractive (a City worker can walk to work) but no lemming rush is yet discernible. The Thames east of Tower Bridge is however increasingly in favour, in a move that was led by David Owen, who came to live in Lime Street, and photographer Tony Snowdon, one of the first to have a Thames-side hideaway. Perhaps the smart money should be on Battersea (SW8) – a mere seven minutes by bus from Sloane Square over Chelsea bridge.

Loo A blessing to the English this last half century, for it has at last given the island race a word for 'lavatory' (itself a euphemism) that is neither wincingly genteel like 'toilet', coyly vulgar like 'lav', heartily military like 'lats', arcanely naval like 'heads', coarsely schoolboyish like 'bog', hopelessly archaic like 'closet', or ingratiatingly transatlantic like 'john'. Despite some typically intricate word play by James Joyce, and learned articles which hesitatingly relate it to Waterloo, we should credit Nancy Mitford with first giving 'loo' printed usage, so getting England out of a tight corner.

Lord's Not the House of Lords, of course, though many peers belong, but Thomas Lord's cricket ground, first opened at Dorset Square for the Marylebone Cricket Club in 1787 and moved to its present site in 1814. The headquarters of English cricket, as it now is, intermingles much of the most gratifying and exasperating that country and game have to offer.

The Long Room in the pavilion is one of the most beautiful in the land: but women are not admitted. You can have a drink at Lord's or talk to a girl, or watch the cricket; but the only way to do all three at once is to have tickets for the exclusive Warner Stand or wangle one of the scarce and costly boxes. If you are lucky enough to get one of these latter in the members' draw, it will set you back £5,900 for the first two days of a Test, £2,950 for the third day, and £3,100 for the last two – 25% less if the box is entirely for private (not company) use.

Though the ticker tapes bringing news from far corners of the Empire have long gone, the cavernous men's loo beneath the pavilion still contains discreet in-jokes like the Out and Not Out signs above the swing doors. Ties and jackets are still *de rigeur*, even when the temperature is up in the nineties. The food is schoolboy stuff, mainly of the buns and char variety, but Bollinger have been known to run a champagne tent for racier *aficonados*.

Still, every cricketer worth his salt has dreamed of playing at Lord's, of seeing the massed Charters and Caldicotts* rise to applaud his century for England. The walk back to the pavilion after a duck, on the other hand, the silence in the Long Room, which must be crossed on the way to the dressing rooms, can make it one of the loneliest places in the world.

Yet when the sun is benign and the square a blaze of perfectly kept emerald, a finer setting for the lethal yorkers of the Pakistani bowler Waqar Younis or an elegantly constructed innings from the graceful bat of England skipper Mike Atherton cannot be had in Christendom.

Lottery   There were plenty of voices raised against the notion of a weekly national lottery. It was argued that it would sap the moral fibre of the nation and siphon cash from the poor to the rich: the millions thrown down the drain on scratch cards, for instance, would be funnelled into new opera houses. Something of this has undoubtedly occurred; research revealed in 1996 that welfare claimants were spending £140 million of their state benefits on national lottery tickets every year. The jobless, for example, were spending £2.60 a week on the lottery from their £70 of benefits; challenged, they replied that, like everyone else, they had the right to dream. Yet 238 new millionaires were created in the first 21 months of the lottery. After the government and the organisers had taken their slice of the cake, some two billion pounds were ploughed back to aid the arts, literature, sport, and umpteen good causes, some of them almost perversely obscure. It thus proved a relatively painless new way of funding our heritage and, whether the grousers like it or not, is clearly here to stay.

Love   'Continental people have sex lives,' said that Central European cynic George Mikes, 'the English have hot water bottles.' If you can believe that, you can believe anything. The English are the only people in Europe who habitually address total strangers of the other sex as love, dear or darling. On St Valentine's Day* they go collectively and comprehensively mad in a way not approached anywhere north of the equator. They have a love literature of unparalleled richness and beauty: ranging from the god-given sonnets of Shakespeare* to the wry lines of Larkin* and from the haunting ache of Hardy* to the comic thrall of Betjeman*. Hot water bottles indeed!

Lunch   The word – and the thing itself – cause endless trouble still in England at that join in the class pyramid where it is still called dinner. Any Englishman who does call lunch dinner indicates at once and for sure to any other Englishman that he hails from somewhere below the middle of the middle class. The difficulty is relatively new in the long vista of English history, since the word till quite recently meant a snack between proper meals. There was a time when everyone in England who could afford to do so dined in the afternoon and supped in the evening. Then, with ease and affluence, lunch began its metamorphosis to a meal in its own right: an agreeable pause in the rhythm of the working day for deals and dalliance. It is now a social divider of infinite power. It distances husbands from their wives (he had roast beef in the cafeteria, she had cottage cheese salad in the kitchen). It distances bosses from their workers (grouse and claret in the boardroom, sandwiches and tea on the building site). It separates the employed from the unemployed (steak and kidney in the pub, baked beans by the telly). The proliferation of the expense account has allowed a whole clutch of restaurants to spring up serving meals customers would never dream of eating at home. Whether much business is achieved at these festivals of cholesterol is a moot point: in certain flash callings like showbiz and publishing the point is not so much what you eat but with whom you eat it. Though a socialist government did its best to discourage lunch by making meals no longer tax-deductible it has had little effect. In any event, the left seems as keen to go out to lunch as anyone else. Lunch will cease to be a problem in England when it means the same to every Englishman as *déjeuner* does to every Frenchman.

Lynn, Dame Vera (born 1917) 'What comforts do the men need most? a war correspondent asked an infantry major in France in November 1939. The major did not hesitate: 'The girls they left behind them.' Vera Lynn stood for all those girls. Her plangent voice may have not been great art; but it was consummate talent. She put the poetry of separation to words and sang them clearly, simply and sweetly. She was justly named the Forces' Sweetheart in 1939; though still only twenty-two, she was an old trouper already. She made her public debut as a singer at seven; joined a juvenile troupe at eleven; was running her own dancing school at fifteen. She broadcast first with Joe Loss when she was eighteen, joined Ambrose and his orchestra when she was twenty, and stayed with him three years before going solo in 1940. She had her own radio show, *Sincerely Yours*, from 1941 to 1947; sang to the troops in Burma in 1944 and was rightly given the Burma Star for it in 1945. Yet her career did not end with the war. She made a new career in television, appeared in seven command performances, and earned fourteen gold records. Most significant of all, perhaps, she was the first British artist ever to top the American hit parade. She appealed to the man in the street and to intellectuals too (her many fans included Kingsley Amis*). She was made a Dame of the British Empire in 1975; an award that gave universal pleasure; and when she appears on television, as she still sometimes does, sings in a voice as sweet and true as ever. She still looks pretty good too; and remains an undisputed English heroine.

M

acNeice, Louis (1907–63)   Once the most junior of the thirties poets (see also under *Auden, Spender)* he could end up as the best known and loved. His attributes were a nutcracker brain, a dazzling grasp of technique, and a hard-nosed scepticism about the workaday world. He was leftish but never Marxist; a male animal who liked women and understood them; a Belfast Anglican bishop's son who perceived the English better sometimes than they did themselves; a radio playwright of the first rank.

In MacNeice the ideas may be complex, and the line fastidious; but the sense is always crystal clear. There is none of the encrusted reference that makes Eliot's work so difficult for most readers; nor the rune-like density which sometimes invades Auden even at his most magisterial. None of the other thirties poets quite equals MacNeice's sense of fun: 'It's no go the Yogi-Man, It's no go Blavatsky / All we want is a bank balance and a bit of skirt in a taxi'; and none of them writes such tender love poetry: 'Who has left a scent on my life and left my walls / Dancing over and over with her shadow / Whose hair is twined in all my waterfalls / And all of London littered with remembered kisses.' Each admirer will have his own favourite piece of MacNeice; but the *Autumn Journal,* written in the phony peace between August and Christmas 1938, takes some beating: 'The New Year comes with bombs, it is too late / To dose the dead with honourable intentions: / If you have honour to spare, employ it on the living / The dead are as dead as Nineteen Thirty Eight.' He was in Spain twice, the first time with his Marlborough friend, Anthony Blunt, though never conned by him into treachery; in Iceland memorably with Auden (*Letters from Iceland*). He remained to the end totally without illusions: 'What will happen will happen; the whore and buffoon / Will come off best; no dreamers they cannot lose their dream / And are at least likely to be re-instated in the new regime.' He went much too soon: but his words still haunt the mind.

Madame Tussaud's One of the most intractable puzzles of modern English life is the survival of this weird anachronism. In an audio-visual age, when every public person must live in the glare of the television lights, and can be seen in colour, in sound and in motion, who needs waxworks? Some two and half million people a year, it appears.

Perhaps the chance to gawp at the infamous, departed and mighty without having one's head cut off has something to do with it. Perhaps the macabre pull of the Chamber of Horrors still exercises its malevolent thrall (the Duke of Wellington, a regular habitué, used to ask to be told whenever they had an interesting new exhibit). Perhaps the effigy of the original Madame Tussaud, who lived nine years in the Palace of Versailles, art tutor to Louis XVI, has the strongest attraction of all. She made death masks of many victims of the Terror, some of which can still be seen in her waxworks.

The Tussaud family continued to run the business till 1967 but it is now a public company which has diversified into entertainments as disparate as Chessington Zoo, Warwick Castle and Wookey Hole. Most significant of all, perhaps, is the London Planetarium which adjoins Madame Tussaud's and is owned by the company. Future generations may prefer screen stars to wax stars. However, while there are macabre curiosities on show like the actual blade that cut off the heads in the French Revolution, no doubt there will be those who will still derive some perverse pleasure from becoming, for one brief shining moment, vicarious *tricoteuses*.

Maidenhead Though it is still of course there, the heyday of Maidenhead was indisputably the thirties. At one time during that unpleasant decade there were ninety-seven nightclubs in and around it, ranging from the very plush places like Skindles to shabby drinking dives charging ten shillings entrance at the door. Across the river from Skindles was the even more ritzy Hungaria with its ivy-covered walls, private pools, and lawns running down to the water's edge. Here the Prince of Wales (later Edward VIII) and Prince George (later Duke of Kent) circulated frequently on the celebrated postage-stamp glass dance floor, thus following in the footsteps of their grandfather, Edward VII, who liked to install his medium-term mistresses in the opulent riverside mansions of Maidenhead. Here people used to come on from the Astor house-parties at Cliveden just down the river (see under *Thames* for later shenanigans there). Here Ivor Novello used to drop in from his nearby house with theatrical guests; and here too came thousands of unrecorded merrymakers, speeding down the A4 in their Alvises, Lagonda and MGs (and occasionally indulging in the risky sport of having a drink at every pub on the left- or right-hand side of the road on the way). These affluent young drank beer at 6d a pint and whisky at 9d a shot; it was all right for some. At regatta time in August they took to their punts in droves with picnic baskets, cocktail shakers, cretonne-covered cushions and wind-up gramophones; and flocked at night to hear lewd but classy entertainers like Ronald Frankau. There was a fair bit of canoodling and Maidenhead vied with Brighton* for supremacy in the dirty-weekend stakes. It was all very innocent, this thirties whoopee, compared with the present equivalent, and ephemeral; the war was coming, and after it, Maidenhead would never be quite the same again.

Manchester   Manchester men and Liverpool gentlemen, goes the old Lancashire saying, and there is a kernel of truth in it. Liverpool* retained for too long an unjumpable chasm between rich and poor; in Manchester, the wealth and power founded on cotton were always far more evenly spread. The Manchester School of Cobden and Bright were apostles of free trade while conservative Birmingham remained the citadel of protection; the *Manchester Guardian* became the renowned champion of radical politics, independent ideas, high thinking and plain living (its greatest editor, C.P. Scott, appointed to the chair at twenty-five and dying at eighty-five, cycled to the office till very nearly the end of his life). 'During the 1830s and 1840s', wrote Asa Briggs in his *Social History of England* (1983), 'Manchester was a Mecca for everyone who wished to understand what was happening to society and what would happen to it in the future.' It fascinated Engels, who lived there as a businessman and wrote his *Condition of the Working Class in England* (1887) from a Manchester vantage point. In a new sense it still reflects the condition of England, but now through the lens of the television camera; Granada Television, operating from Manchester, has given the English indelible images of themselves from the sooty saga of *Coronation Street* through the aristocratic annals of *Brideshead Revisited* to its magisterial account of the Raj in *The Jewel in the Crown*.

It was in Manchester that Miss Horniman used a Victorian tea fortune to pioneer the concept of repertory theatre; here that Sir Charles Hallé lived and worked for nearly half a century, bequeathing his name to one of the country's best orchestras. It was in Manchester that the Victorian novelist Mrs Gaskell settled with her husband, minister of Cross Street Unitarian Chapel; here that Charlotte Brontë* visited her and began *Jane Eyre*; here that her friend Charles Dickens* gave some of his greatest public readings. The university could do little for the God-intoxicated, drug-dependent poet Francis Thompson, who failed his medical examinations three times; but under T.F. Tout it acquired a world reputation for history. Manchester Grammar School has long been an intellectual power-house where clever boys could win their way, however poor (and sometimes not so poor: Michael Marks and his brother-in-law Israel Sieff, of Marks and Spencer*, were both there).

'I came to love Manchester as I have known and loved no other city,' wrote the novelist Howard Spring, for sixteen years a *Manchester Guardian* staffer. Manchester is the Dumble of Mrs Gaskell's *Cranford* and the Doomington of Louis Golding's *Magnolia Street*. Neither writer would recognise the modern city with its high-rise office blocks, swanky shopping precincts, and international airport. London is now only two hours thirty minutes away by inter-city express rail: still, we must trust, not near enough to drown out the city's idiosyncratic and independent voice in England's life.

Marks and Spencer 'Don't ask the price, it's a penny' was the slogan with which Michael Marks, a Polish refugee with scant command of English, opened his stall in Leeds market. Today the wonderstore has 285 stores in the UK and 30 throughout the rest of Europe. They help pull in a group pre-tax profit of £993 million. M&S are top of the shops not just for princesses and tourists (some of whom are not as meticulous as they might be in shelling out for what they've bought) but also with housewives and teenagers. They sell a third of all the women's underwear bought in the UK. They are the country's largest fishmongers and sell a million chickens a week. Their Marble Arch store is listed in the *Guinness Book of Records* as having the fastest-moving stock in the world. And so on.

Just one family guided the fortunes of M&S for their first century and one man, Simon Marks, Michael's son, was at the helm for nearly half that century. It was his innate flair that shaped the characteristic M&S strategies: tight control of costs, an insistence on quality, and a formidable control of the merchandise. Cannily, they have never actually owned a factory. Being an M&S manufacturer has never been a bed of roses; but fifty of them have been suppliers for over forty years and have their Rolls-Royces to prove it.

M&S are also renowned for being years ahead of their time as employers. During the thirties, Simon Marks and his brother-in-law Israel Sieff discovered that a salesgirl in one of their stores was working through her lunch break because she couldn't afford a meal. There and then they began subsidised lunches: today they are still heavily subsidised and the chairman of M&S, Sir Richard Greenbury, eats the going lunch at whichever store he is in that day. Indeed, the hungry shopgirl set M&S on the way to becoming a minor welfare state: doctors, dentists and chiropodists visit stores regularly; all female staff are encouraged to have cervical smears and breast screening; hairdos are done in the lunch hour.

M&S was scarcely known on the continent as recently as 1975. Since then, it has opened 17 stores in France, five in Spain, two in Holland, and three in Belgium. Germany is due to have its first M&S in autumn 1996. The learning process works both ways. In the early years there were no changing rooms in the French stores, so customers undressed on the sales floor to try on their clothes. They also bought products intended for cooking, like bacon and jellies, and ate them raw. Never mind, the M&S in the Boulevard Haussman holds the French record for turnover per square metre.

Marmalade   It does not taste right on anything but toast, and at any time but breakfast*. To take it with butter as well is a comparatively modern function of affluence – see A.A. Milne's poem *The King's Breakfast*, Where the dairymaid tells the Alderney cow not to forget the butter for the royal slice of bread and the animal replies sleepily: 'You'd better tell His Majesty / That many people nowadays / Like marmalade instead.' That was in 1924. Marmalade (to be truthful) began its triumphal march in Scotland, where a canny Dundee housewife called Janet Keiller boiled a consignment of bitter Seville oranges from a sheltering ship into orange jam and found it so popular that her husband launched the firm which still bears his name. Within a century two other Scottish houses followed suit: Baxter's of Speyside with their distinctive whisky marmalade; and Robertson's of Paisley with their clear jelly and fine peel which every Englishman knows as Golden Shred. In England it was Sarah Jane Cooper, wife of an Oxford grocer, who first began to make the course, thick, dark marmalade which undergraduates delighted to serve at their gargantuan Victorian brekkers and which were to go with Scott to the Antarctic – as well as to Buckingham Palace in consignments of twenty-four jars. Cooper's also made their marmalade in specially grand pots for VIP passengers on the old British Overseas Airways; an indulgence that has long since gone. All the same, marmalade still conveys the very faint sense of privilege at a price everyone can afford and remains the bitter-sweet début to the English day.

Marques   Originally a licence for piracy bestowed by the sovereign, marque has denoted for much of the twentieth century a make of high-performance motorcar. Any discussion of the great English marques must begin with the fabled prewar Bentleys, victors at the Le Mans twenty-four-hour race in 1927-8-9-30, driven by a small group of wealthy *aficionados* led by Woolf Barnato and known as the Bentley boys. It would also have to include the chain-driven Frazer-Nash, the Alvis Speed 20 with the famous chrome exhaust down the side, the long, elegant Lagonda, the nippy, early MGs (notably the K3 with front blower), the quick, suave Riley, and the pretty little Morgan 4-4. All these grand old marques are now collector's items and command very high prices. At Christie's for example a 1932 MG Midget J-2 type two-seater, which had cost £199 when new, was knocked down for £14,000. As it sparkled from the closed-circuit television in the saleroom, everyone there cheered it to the echo. It had become a work of art. See also *Aston Martin, Jaguar, Rolls-Royce.*

Mate   In the winter of 1972–8 the young George Orwell*, only six years out of Eton* and full of an aching need to expiate the exploitation, as he saw it, practised by his class on the poor, got together with some difficulty a set of ragged clothes and sallied out into the East End to see the working class as they really were. 'Presto!' he wrote later, 'in the twinkling of an eye, so to say, I had become one of them. My frayed and out-of-elbow jacket was the badge and advertisement of my class, which was their class. It made me of like kind, and in place of the fawning and too-respectful attention I had hitherto received, I now shared with them a comradeship. The man in corduroy and dirty neckerchief no longer addressed me as "sir" or "governor". It was "mate" now, and a fine and hearty word, with a tingle to it, and a warmth and gladness which the other term does not possess.'
   The fine and hearty word is still mainly working-class, but is increasingly used by disc jockeys and media people to denote a slightly jokey chum, or even, in the plural, an entire audience. Tacked on to expletives it adds derision, as in 'Up yours, mate' (see under *Up*).

Maugham, Somerset (1874–1965) 'I have noticed that when someone asks for you on the telephone and, finding you out, leaves a message begging you to call him up the moment you come in, as it's important, the matter is more often important to him than to you.' With this enchanting *aperçu* Maugham launches us into the thrall of *Cakes and Ale*, his most delicious and malicious novel. The man on the telephone was the egregious popular novelist Alroy Kear, and the opening twelve pages of the book one of the most sustained exercises in character demolition English writing can offer.

Hugh Walpole, the fashionable thirties novelist, sat up late with an early proof copy of *Cakes and Ale* so transfixed with horror at the mirror image of himself in it that he eventually slid to the floor prostrate with cramp. Maugham denied that he had sat for Kear; but owned up when Walpole was dead. The passage catches Maugham at his most characteristic and effective: the observation is microscopic, the workmanship is scrupulous, the tone is polished, and the invitation to read on irresistible.

It is often observed of Maugham that he won all the glittering prizes except the palm the critics throw, and it is true that some ignored or dismissed him (three key books on the modern novel failed to mention him at all).

Yet he had a lifelong champion in Desmond MacCarthy; Harold Nicolson thought he had been consistently underrated, and Cyril Connolly claimed he was the greatest living short-story writer. The Plays that first brought him fame (he had four running at one time in Edwardian London) are now period pieces and the mystical preoccupation of some novels like *The Razor's Edge* may no longer convince. Perhaps he did fail to push out the boundaries of technique like Joyce or to exploit the nuances of character like James; perhaps his world is dissolving and his position square. None of this matters a jot. The man was a born *storyteller*: ask the readers who bought 64 million copies of his books.

Mews If you want a shorthand account of what has been happening to the kaleidoscope of class in England, take a walk one morning round some of the six hundred mews of London. Originally they were built for servants – specifically, for the coachmen and grooms, their wives, children, and all the tack essential to the servicing of the horses in great London houses as the city sprawled westwards. Since the land in the path of that great drive west lay in the hands of some dozen or so hugely wealthy landowners it was possible for the new squares and crescents to be laid out in coherent blocks, with the rows of mews lying to the rear and below the big houses. Teeming with life and jingling with the sounds of spit and polish, they nevertheless belied their romantic externals by an absence of light, space, drains and water that rendered them pools of pestilence. Because nobody else then wanted them much, many became small workshops or ateliers, thus reinforcing their romantic if un-hygienic charm. As the horse began to give way to the car around the turn of the century, the first garages began to appear in the mews and continue there to this day, though often now converted into extra bedrooms. Then, even before the First World War, as taxes began to bite, the idea of the tarted-up, de-loused mews as a fun place for the well-to-do to have a *pied-à-terre* began to take shape. The inter-war years saw this notion spread until today few of the gallant six hundred retain many of their original inhabitants. Instead, they have become showcases of bourgeois chic; patchworks of window boxes and avocado doors. The charms of the mews are obvious: cobbled streets, little or no passing traffic, access to fashionable London, the chance to own a small house rather than rent a flat, and the sense of slightly raffish fun they purvey. In being gentrified though, they tend to lose the children and artisans who gave them their colour and vivid social mix. Just as the poor have been dispossessed of their cottages in the village*, so they have been eased out of their mews in the city. Nevertheless, the survival of the London mews does provide a warren of secret escapes and vistas of sudden surprise to the perceptive stroller, and helps to make London still the most civilised city in the world.

The Midlands   Sodden and unkind, said Hilaire Belloc, in the only memorable intrusion they make under that name into English poetry. In English prose they are somewhat better served: George Eliot's great novel *Middlemarch* is based on her life at Coventry, much of D.H. Lawrence's fiction is set around Nottingham, where he grew up, and the work of H.E. Bates is firmly rooted in the Nene Valley of Northampton-shire.

All his life the great Samuel Johnson* pronounced 'where' like fear and 'punch' as poonch: he was born at Lichfield, twelve miles from Birmingham*. Anyone who has heard Bernard Miles read Shakespeare as he would have read it himself will remember the frisson at realising that England's greatest poet did not speak like Olivier* or Gielgud but like any other son of Warwickshire: that is, in what is to us now a broad Midland dialect.

Yet the Midlands remain too wide and vague an idea to have any clear identity in the English mind. The *OED* recognises the difficulty by awarding them one of its clumsiest and most long-winded definitions: 'The counties south of the Humber and Mersey and north of the Thames, except Norfolk, Suffolk, Essex, Middlesex, Hertfordshire, Gloucestershire, and the counties bordering on Wales.'

A simpler way to put it might be to say anywhere within commuting distance of Birmingham*. But Birmingham has its own distinct life. Since the Midlands are within such easy reach of London, no separate, modern Midlands school of politics, literature or art is discernible; though there are clusters of good poets from the Potteries (John Wain, Charles Tomlinson, Philip Oakes) they really are part of a separate tradition stemming from the great novels of Arnold Bennet, born at Stoke.

Even the remarkable poetry of Philip Larkin*, a son of Coventry, did not help a discernible Midlands school emerge. But it may yet happen.

Milkman   He is an ambivalent, indeed protean figure in English life, representing as he does probity, enterprise, trust, efficiency but sometimes far more *risqué* values. In the first place, the very sight of milk bottles on English doorsteps still surprises foreign visitors. Not even in great market societies like America is the daily pinta delivered daily to each door. And even if it were, would it not be stolen? And even if not stolen, would it not suggest to thieving eyes that the occupants are away and the house open for the taking? And even if the thieves were baffled by the plethora of pintas, on what trust would the milkman take it that his customers will pay later? Alas, the old verities are crumbling, and in some deprived parts of England milkmen now deliver only in return for milk tokens bought in advance. Yet the milkman remains a shining exemplar of the capitalist system, acting as a mobile retailer and nowadays diversifying into bread, biscuits, tea, coffee, cereals, orange juice, eggs, butter, potatoes and most recently, wine. Still, the very ease and authority of the milkman's penetration into the Englishman's hearth and home does raise certain ribald questions; in the great subterranean folklore of England the milkman typically figures as the rotten sod who put the wife in the family way. While hard logic will suggest that few milkmen would have time for this kind of dalliance on their daily rounds, the sheer numbers of housewives seen each day may have laid temptation at certain doors, as it were. The upshot is that no one treats the English milkman with quite that *gravitas* which is his due.

Money   Any Englishman of middling years has seen a melancholy decline in the pound. It now stands at under a thirtieth of its 1938 value though its decline has slowed. Any Englishman who can remember the thirties can remember when one pound equalled five dollars; and during the 1939–45 war it still equalled four. Then came the trauma of the Stafford Cripps devaluation in 1949 when overnight it was slashed to $2.80. Yet though parity with the dollar was only just round the corner even ten years ago, at the time of writing the pound is fighting back.

At the same time the Englishman has had to adjust to a world where, far from belonging to the richest nation in the world he now ranks in income terms fifteenth, trailing far behind not only the evident giants like the United States, Germany and Japan, but well behind two such comparative monetary tiddlers as Norway and Denmark. The average Englishman, in short, is now just about as well off as the average Italian.

Income in England, however, is more fairly distributed than before the war. A miner is now more than three times as well off in real terms, while GPs have just held their own, and university professors have slipped back.

Yet the English still look wealthy on average in world terms, with each adult owning more than £15,000 in land and buildings, nearly £6,000 in insurance policies, and over £5,000 in bank accounts and cash.

Perhaps unexpectedly, the greatest advance has been in the income of the working woman. Thus in industry her weekly earnings, though still trailing well behind those of men, are dramatically up on 1938. In that year she earned £1.63.

Motorway   Each has its own character. The M1 is a pig of a road: ugly, bad-tempered, treacherous. The M2 is a good-natured road, leading to Dover* and to the delights of abroad. The M3 is a placid, relaxed, under-used road leading to the medieval magic of Winchester* and, for those who can run to it, Southampton and the QE2 (see *The Queens*). The M4, highway to Bath* and Bristol, starts anxiously as its heavy load debouches from Hammersmith, but grows carefree once past London Airport, swinging by the Marlborough Hills into Wales* and (one day) to the Atlantic.

The M5 is a blessing, for it siphons off some of the worst of the Gadarene rush to the west each summer, though not nearly enough; the M6 is too narrow round Birmingham* and overloaded with thundering HGVs, though it grows light-hearted and indeed beautiful as it threads its way through the Lake District. Perhaps the most exhilarating English motorway of all, though, is the M40, slicing dramatically through the Chilterns like the autoroute to the Midi and then swooping down to Oxford* and the Cotswolds*. There will be many more motorways, each establishing its distinctive mood; but the M25 has proved a nightmare and the most eloquent argument for those who believe we should all go by train.

Though motorway melancholia and even motorway madness have been identified, and though motorway cafés are nodal points of modern desolation, it is well to contemplate the alternative. Without motorways, old roads like the A1 and A4 would by now have become infernos. As it is they are, on the whole, pleasant options for the unhurried, restoring some sense of how it must have felt to have motored in uncluttered England before the war.

Mummy   The word used by boys up to about seven and a very few upper-class grown men in England to describe their mothers. It is also the word used by most girls from the middle of the middle class upwards, and here lies a celebrated piece of arcane English social lore; for the words 'Mummy and Daddy' do not mean just what they say but are a class indicator signifying the kind of parents who would drive a Rover, have a cottage in the country, and give dinner parties.

Mummy and Daddy may be dearly loved by their daughters, but not by playwrights like John Osborne, whose Jimmy Porter in *Look Back in Anger* vented all his pent-up social rage against Alison's Mummy, 'an overfed, overprivileged old bitch'; though when Daddy enters the action he turns out to be rather gentle and *sympathique*: 'He likes you,' Alison tells her father, 'because he can feel sorry for you.'

Mummy and Daddy will also not do in the international pop esperanto spoken by all the young, and may therefore be doomed. After all, every Englishman has a Queen Mum; a Queen Mummy would be an excruciating embarrassment. Mama and Papa are the terms used by the royals themselves and by naturalised Englishmen who started life in Central Europe, but sound affected from an indigenous Englishman. Nevertheless, he still feels a bit self-conscious just saying Mum and Dad. Here is another hole in the language (see also *Afters*) that badly needs filling.

Music   *Das Land ohne Musik* was the title of a celebrated German book, branding England: the land without music. That was never true, and today it is evident balderdash. The South Bank alone can offer fourteen concerts during a single weekend; and this before we even consider the Royal Albert Hall, the Wigmore Hall, St John's Smith Square and, now, the Barbican. Nor should we forget the opera on offer not only in Covent Garden, but also at the Coliseum, Sadler's Wells, and now overflowing into the Dominion and Bloomsbury theatres. Then there is music in the cathedrals, the churches, the colleges and the academies – but the argument needs no further pressing; it is a musical cornucopia.

Why will any young foreign musician make London the first place in which to make his bow? Not simply because of the great spectrum of venues we have noted, but also because he is far more likely to be dealing with honest impresarios (it is hard to get a fee out of Madrid), and because he will be assessed by the best music critics in the world. Translate a review by Rodney Milnes or Andrew Porter into French and it will make perfect sense; translate the sort of prose poem that passes for music criticism in *Le Monde* into English and it will read like gibberish. Since a new young artist wants his notices to be immediately intelligible anywhere in the world, he will rather they emanate from England.

It is a sad truth in view of all this excellence that we are so mean as a race to our music. Berlin now supports thirteen classical orchestras; in Cologne it is cheaper to see *The Magic Flute* than to buy a free range chicken in the supermarket. Yet our cathedral music is unsurpassed and our Proms* are the envy of the world: 5,000 to hear a concert, a million to hear the broadcast. Lottery money is coming to the rescue elsewhere; but slowly.

'Extraordinary how potent cheap music is,' wrote Noël Coward* in *Private Lives.* He should have known, for he wrote much of it himself; from the hummable sentiment of 'I'll See You Again' and 'London Pride' to the astringent cynicism of 'Don't Put Your Daughter on the Stage, Mrs Worthington' and 'The Stately Homes of England'. He wrote in a rich vernacular tradition derived from the English music-hall ('Any Old Iron', 'Boiled Beef and Carrots', 'My Old Dutch'); from the vast subterranean musical lore of the services ('Bless 'em All', 'Tipperary'); and from the cognate world of sport ('You'll Never Walk Alone', 'Abide With Me'). This last song started life as a hymn, but the ecclesiastical influence on popular music is now small, and the melodies (if such they be) of the modern young in England are inspired by mega-powered pop groups like Oasis and Blur, and, though they are now becoming part of pop-history, the Rolling Stones ('Brown Sugar', 'Jumping Jack Flash') and the Beatles ('Yesterday', 'Love Me Do'). Nor must we forget that in Andrew Lloyd Webber we have produced a titan of popular music whose work has conquered the world.

Nanny When Sebastian Flyte first takes Charles Ryder to his parents' house at the opening of *Brideshead Revisited* (see also under *Waugh*) it is, he says, to see a friend of his called Hawkins. In the upshot this turns out to be Nanny Hawkins: '... she was fast asleep. Long hours of work in her youth, authority in her middle years, repose and security in her age, had set their stamp on her lined and serene face.'

She has, in effect, become Sebastian's mother; the member of his family he loves most. The scene could be multiplied thousands of times; for the Nanny Hawkinses of England have gone to the ends of the earth to bring up the children of Saudi Arabian shieks, Anglo-Portuguese patriarchs, Indian maharajahs and uncountably rich Texans. To all these exotic settings they brought their traditional virtues: common sense, order, cleanliness, firmness, sweetness and total dependability. A casual glance at *The Times** any morning will immediately show how that accreted, gilt-edged reputation will still earn any proper English nanny a top billet anywhere in the world.

'Other people's babies that's my life; mother to dozens but nobody's wife,' wrote A.P. Herbert. No longer; today's nanny may well wear jeans, drive a mini, have a bloke, and be merely filling in an agreeable few years working in *grand luxe* before marrying, and having her own children. Never mind: while she does her nannying she knows that she belongs to an unassailable elite: for, thanks to the remembered legions of Nanny Hawkinses, for people who must have nannies, nothing but an English nanny will do.

National Trust It does not win all its battles. It lost, for example, its fight to buy Land's End; someone simply bid more. Still, in its first hundred years it has shown a pretty sturdy independence and formidable growth. Despite the 'national' in the title it is a private body, financed entirely by what it can earn, though with special dispensation under two Acts of Parliament to avoid alienation of the enchanted pieces of England, Wales and Northern Ireland it has acquired. (The Scots work separately.)

It began in 1895 when three Victorian conservationists got together to protect the open spaces of England against the incursion of the dark satanic mills. That year it had 100 members; in 1926 still only 1,000; reached 100,000 in 1961, the million in 1981, and 2 million in 1990. Now it is the country's third biggest landowner, ranking only after state and Crown.

There is one snag to such vertiginous success; you can actually have too many people coming round your stately homes: over 11 million visited National Trust properties in 1995–96. As long ago as 1947 it warned that too many visitors would destroy what people had come to see. Some of it had been destroyed already: in a separate campaign, Operation Neptune, the Trust estimated that of our 3,000-mile coastline, some 1,000 miles were already spoilt, another 1,000 of no special value, while the last 1,000 were of the greatest beauty and should be preserved at all cost. Today it owns half of that most precious thousand miles; not to mention more than half a million acres of land, 208 historic houses, 233 gardens, 60 villages, 39 pubs, 51 churches, and 25 windmills and watermills.

So much is beyond debate. However, the National Trust, besides preserving the best of our industrial archaeology, our Roman antiquities and prehistoric sites, does something else: it has devised and perfected a machinery through which the owner of a great English house can go on living in it.

Critics of the system will have to come up with a better one: but the stately home as a museum or mausoleum frankly fails to attract most English people of whatever political persuasion. They would rather see them lived in. Once again the English genius for compromise seems maddeningly to have carried the day.

Navy When the Sultan of Morocco visited the navy's latest battleship a hundred years ago, he was asked what had impressed him most about the ship. Was it the 16-inch turret guns, the 8,000 hp engines, the two torpedo-boats she carried, or perhaps the electric light throughout? The captain's face,' was his reply. Through the long Pax Britannia which stretched from the Napoleonic wars to the beginning of the First World War, though, the navy developed a fatal *hubris*. It was encouraged. When the Americans began to build their own navy in the 1890s, the first of their new armoured ships, the *New York*, even had an admiral's walk at the stern, a quite unnecessary luxury and a direct compliment to the Nelsonic tradition of the Royal Navy.

When the great British fleet began its massive assault on the Dardanelles in March 1915, wrote James Morris in *Farewell the Trumpets*, the Turkish gunners saw 'the towering grey forms of sixteen capital ships. In the van was the splendid *Queen Elizabeth*, the largest warship ever to enter the Mediterranean ... around and behind her sailed a chivalry of warships ...'

But the vaulting plan turned into a nightmare shambles '... and instantly a myth was shattered. The Royal Navy was not omnipotent, and gunboat diplomacy, here carried to its ultimate expression, was no longer sufficient to discipline the natives.'

Next year at the Battle of Jutland Admiral Beatty saw two of his finest ships, the *Indefatigable* and the *Queen Mary*, sent to the bottom of the sea after being blown to pieces by direct hits. 'There seems to be something wrong with our bloody ships this morning, Chatfield,' he remarked to his flag captain. A quarter of a century later the battle cruiser *Hood* blew up after a shell from the *Bismarck* had found exactly the same fault in her construction. 1500 men died; three survived.

Nevertheless, the English have always had a soft spot for their navy. They like its style. As Ludovic Kennedy relates in his memoirs, naval commanders have an uncanny flair for the right words. 'Be pleased to inform their Lordships,' signalled Admiral Sir John Cunningham, 'That the Italian battle fleet now lies at anchor under the guns of the fortress of Malta.' You can't say fairer than that.

Neasden Literally a nose-shaped hill, and until 1876 a hamlet containing three or four large houses, a few cottages and a smithy. In that year houses were built for workers of the new Metropolitan Railway; then two waves of new building followed the extension of the line and the building of the North Circular road respectively. It has thus become an archetypal London suburb, faceless and formless. Perhaps, though, it was the accident of its name which led *Private Eye** to choose it as its example of, not so much suburbia, as what our American cousins would call Nowheresville. Many *Eye* readers who live outside London even now do not credit its undoubted reality. It has one unexpected claim to fame as the birthplace of Twiggy.

Neighbours   To Jesus of Nazareth the term had a universal flavour, connoting all one's breathing, suffering fellow human beings; to Franklin D. Roosevelt a geo-political context, embracing as he did in his celebrated good-neighbor policy all of South America. On an everyday level, the most famous of all neighbours this century have been the Joneses, the notional people we have living next door with whom we feel obliged to keep up. They have been a powerful tool in the hands of the consumer society, compelling Englishmen and Americans to buy the new consumer durables – cars, lawn mowers, washing machines – which are the outward and visible sign that they have not fallen behind in the great race. Yet the word has a derisive undertow: for are the Joneses really worth keeping up with? The Jonesian notion is essentially a function of suburban sprawl, an unloved child of ribbon development; and needs garden fences to flourish properly; flat-dwellers on the whole feel no need to emulate their neighbours whether Joneses or anybody else; while the upper class speak rather grandly of a neighbour when they mean someone who lives in the same county ('our neighbours are coming to dinner' can involve a round trip for them of fifty miles).

Nelson   In darts, according to the indispensable compendium *Hoyle's Games*, the number 111 is known as Lord Nelson. This is 'for a reason that is probably known to most darts players' and, we trust, will be equally clear to worldly readers of this companion who are familiar with his reputation both as sailor and lover.

Nosh   From the Yiddish for a snack, now widely used for any sort of meal, but especially either an informal one or in deprecating description of a formal one. It entered the language suddenly in the fifties and, as with so many Yiddish words, supplanted previous idiom by its innate strength. Similarly with 'nosher' (usually a hearty eater) and 'noshery' for any place selling food, though originally a delicatessen. The Yiddish comes in turn from the German *naschen*, to nibble or eat on the sly, and an element of onomatopoeia probably contributes to the word's comedy and popularity.

Oak 'Heart of oak are our ships, heart of oak are our men.' About the ships, at least, there can be no doubt. With oak from the New Forest they built at Buckler's Hard some of the great ships that fought at Trafalgar: *Illustrious* with its seventy-four guns, *Agamemnon* with forty-four and the smaller *Swiftsure* and *Euryalus*. Long before that they had used the Forest oak for the ships that took on the Armada. Strongest, most durable and long-lived of trees, the oak stands well in the English countryside; and sometimes the sheer vastness of its age leaves the onlooker awestruck.

At Knightwood Oak, for instance, not far from Lyndhurst in the New Forest, stand three giant trees. Each is specially mentioned in the Ordnance Survey map; but the Knightwood Oak itself is by far the most stupendous of the three. It is thought to be among the oldest and largest oaks in England.

'This great tree was here, though no more than a seedling', wrote Brian Vesey-Fitzgerald in his *Hampshire*, 'when Stephen was ruling a troubled kingdom. It was here a mere boy when John was signing the Magna Carta ... It watched its friends fall before the fury of the storm and the cold precision of the axe ... In its old age it heard of Dunkirk and Tobruk ... It has seen kings come and go and dictators rise and fall. It has watched year upon year men make love in just the same way and in much the same words ... And each year in October its leaves come spinning to the ground. They have done so now maybe eight hundred times.' He concluded that it would doubtless still be there long after his own time; in which assumption he was assuredly right.

The OED *The Oxford English Dictionary* was described by Arnold Bennett as the longest sensational serial ever written. It took just on fifty years to compile. Its twelve volumes contained 414,825 words and the type in which they were set if laid end to end would have extended to 178 miles. It is not only the greatest dictionary of English both in scale and content but has few rivals in other languages. There are two American dictionaries but they deal only with the distinctively American branch of the language. American English is, so to speak, a vast dialect of English. However, there is a price to be paid for such daunting labour. One lexicographer employed by the Oxford University Press cut his throat. Another finished up writing an endless epic poem in which Kenneth Sisam, his boss at the OUP, appeared as Anti-Christ.

When the *OED* was finally completed in 1928 it was £375,000 in the red and had of necessity left out all the new words that had entered the language during the half century it was in the making. So a *Supplement* was published in 1933. Another half a century on, and a torrent of further new words spawned in that tumultuous era clamoured for admission. So in 1957 a thirty-four-year-old New Zealander and former Rhodes Scholar called Robert Burchfield was given the task of editing a new *Supplement*. One of his great predecessors at the *OED* had remarked that lexicography is best done on the kitchen table. Burchfield began with not much more: a small room in a modest villa in a shabby Oxford back street, one male assistant, three young women graduates, and a secretary.

He planned to publish in 1967; but gave the world his fourth and final volume in 1986, nineteen years late; not that this matters tuppence in the world of the lexicographer. The last full edition of the two-volume *Shorter OED* appeared in 1944; the *Compact OED*, which is the entire dictionary reduced micrographically to two volumes and read with a magnifying glass, in 1971.

The *Concise OED* is the work of an amazing polymath called John Sykes, a mathematician with a doctorate in astrophysics, who translates textbooks from twenty languages and has won *The Times*/Cutty Sark crossword contest four times in a row, giving away his prize of a holiday for two in Monte Carlo and half a gallon of whisky. Had he been receiving a normal author's royalties instead of a straight salary, his income from the OUP would have been some £250,000 a year. But then fleshly pleasures and the making of great dictionaries do not seem to sit well together.

The Old Boy Network   Not to be confused with the old school tie*, though those who wear the one may well belong to the other. Strictly, it was the name for wartime army radio communications linking squadron, regiment and brigade, and went into action whenever those using it were on close enough terms enough to call one another old boy. Then, the old boy net was used for cutting red tape and getting things done. In peace, however, it has taken on a more sinister connotation: the invisible web of connection between those who have been at the same school or university, used to ensure that those who are part of it get the best jobs.

The left see this network as a lively argument for the abolition of the public schools. Without doubt the old boy network used to work, particularly in arcane and unreconstructed areas of business like the wine trade and the Stock Exchange.* Increasingly though, proponents of the old boy network begin to sound like classic conspiracy theorists; relying as they do on the basic principle that if you are an Etonian you are more likely to give another Etonian a job. Such theorists do not know their Etonians, who must be numbered among the most ruthless and unsentimental products of English society. Network theory also works on the naive assumption that being, say, an old Harrovian will help you get – and keep – the kinds of high-voltage job that matter in modern society: video editor, say, computer programmer, or finance director. It postulates, moreover, that there are plenty of plush jobs nowadays which, once occupied by an Etonian or Harrovian backside, are permanently inviolate to threat or change. Such romantic and primitive theories of modern business take little account of the *Sturm und Drang* to which its denizens must be subjected.

The Old School Tie   Formerly worn as a tribal badge to show where you stood in the complicated hierarchy of the English class structure. Even then, however, it was more of an insider's game than a public display system: how many Englishmen would know an Old Sedberghian from an Old Salopian by his neckwear?

The hard truth is that only certain specialised races like prep-school masters and club porters can recognise many ties beyond the Etonian blue stripe and the MCC egg and tomato, and even these celebrated ties are increasingly worn more in a spirit of larkiness than real camaraderie. Most Old Etonians who sport their school tie look increasingly bogus; most men who wear the MCC tie except on Test days at Lord's* are increasingly suspect.

Perhaps very conservative and elderly men wear the Brigade of Guards tie in the country as a tribal totem; but members of the Garrick who sport the pale salmon and cucumber club stripes do so mainly for fun.

Olivier, Laurence (1907–89)   There will be few Englishmen who carry no image of Laurence Olivier: brimming with brooding power under his pudding-basin haircut in the film of *Hamlet;* the haunted, well-bred quarry of a dead bitch as Max de Winter in Hitchcock's *Rebecca;* paddling the stage with his splayed walk as the Moor in *Othello;* wheedling, nudging, canoodling and camping his way through the seedy title role in John Osborne's *The Entertainer,* upstaging all in sight as the wily, cagey, testy old barrister in John Mortimer's TV play *A Voyage Round My Father.* Hemingway once described courage as grace under pressure. Anyone who saw Olivier in that last role, in his seventy-fifth year, survivor of cancer, thrombosis, pneumonia, piles and gout, but still squeezing the last ounce from his part as if he were twenty-five, will know exactly what Hemingway meant.

Orwell, George (1903–50)   No Englishman can put his hand on his heart and say that no word of Orwell reaches him, or concerns him, or describes him. Orwell saw into the heart of England in a way that no writer had done before or has since.

He achieved this extraordinary vision by moving through the invisible barriers of English life – walls of class, income, lifestyle, time and place. There have been Etonians before who have become doctors or clergymen, politicians or lawyers; jobs that by their nature require and assume some contact with the poor and the disadvantaged. It is hard to think of another who not merely knew the outer perimeters of disease, hunger and want, but also lived right inside them.

Orwell did not deplore poverty; he was poor; he did not simply bewail the fate of the down and out; he was a down and out. Nor was it just the question of a rough weekend in pursuit of copy: he knew what it was not to have enough for a decent meal night after night, week after week, month after month. He knew how the poor died because he had been in a hospital for down and outs and seen them horrendously die; he knew what it meant to earn eight shillings net for picking hops sixty hours a week because he had done it himself.

He had got inside the skin of his suffering brother men as few saints have succeeded in doing, and there is something of the secular saint about his denial of self and messianic vision both of a lost world of innocence and a new world to come in which our destinies will be worked out.

It has been said of Orwell that if he had died half a dozen years earlier he would have been a minor cult figure but no more. If he had died before he had written *Animal Farm*, this would undoubtedly have been true; for it is on the power of this meticulously worked out allegory on the bitter fruit of revolution, and the sombre magnificence of his minatory fable predicating one possible nightmare future, *1984*, that his world fame rests.

Nevertheless, there would remain a whole clutch of vividly etched documents: slightly polemicised reportage which makes a collective testament to the mean and nasty thirties: notably *Down and Out in Paris and London, The Road to Wigan Pier*, and *Homage to Catalonia.*

It is not the least of Orwell's claims that his wincing honesty makes him attractive to many layers of English society; never taken in by the communists, he deeply despised what he called the pansy left: English fellow-travellers who had felt no qualms in making the transition to what he saw as no more than the mirror image of fascism (he once changed places in a restaurant so as not to look at the corrupt face of Kingsley Martin, editor of the *New Statesman*, who was deeply involved in the alliance between communism and socialism).

Yet this stance lent no comfort to the right; Orwell hated too the hidebound minds, instinctive arrogance, easy clichés and braying voices of the English ruling class. He passionately believed in England, but saw it as a family with the wrong people in charge of it. Never an easy man (he drank his tea noisily out of his saucer in the BBC canteen to show his solidarity with the working class), he was self-evidently not one either who could be bent or bought.

He was to make himself adept at a plain, vivid, colloquial style so unobtrusive that it looked artless. In this simple English he wrote books that few Englishmen will be able to open anywhere without a start of recognition; among them two masterpieces that touch men everywhere.

Ovaltine Stood (and stands) for the innocence, comfort, wholesome-ness and safety of English childhood. Originally a drink marketed by a Swiss doctor called George Wander, it was (and is) known as Ovomaltine on the Continent, but the name was shortened when it was first introduced here in 1910. Advertising was always Ovaltine's forte, and the rosy-cheeked dairymaid in the ads with her basket of fresh eggs and sheaf of barley epitomised its spirit of simple purity.

The Ovaltiney Club, founded in 1935 and broadcasting from Radio Luxembourg every Sunday evening from 5.30 to 6 p.m. became a secret society for children, with its own badges, rule books, and inside codes:

by 1939 it had five million members. The programme's signature tune, 'We are the Ovaltineys', became probably the best-known jingle in the world; and was so well embedded in the national subconscious that the company was persuaded to revive it as part of its television commercial in 1975.

Though primarily a children's drink, Ovaltine was supplied to the armed forces in both world wars. Tommies sang 'we are the Ovaltineys' as they marched, in sharp contrast to the German preference for the 'Horst Wessel Song.' It has been an official drink at Olympics since 1932, went up Everest with Sir Edmund Hillary and with Freya Stark to the Arabian desert.

It figures, needless to say, in the Betjeman* *oeuvre*: 'He gives his Ovaltine a stir, and nibbles at a *petit beurre*.' Though still sold simply as a malted food drink, its actual ingredients are somewhat more banal and clinical: barley and malt extract, to be sure, but then dried skimmed milk, sugar, whey powder, glucose syrup, vegetable fat, full cream milk powder, fat reduced cocoa, caseinates, egg powder, emulsifier, stabilisers, flavouring and vitamins. The Ovaltine dairymaid still smiles winsomely out from the goo at us; and her drink still conveys instant childhood.

Oxford   It is the place where the MG was born, and penicillin first given to a patient. It is the place where the first mile was run in under four minutes, and the first six-foot high jump recorded. It is also the seat of an ancient university which has been in the wars now for seven hundred years.

In its earliest centuries a place where poor scholars went to learn Latin and make good in the Church, Oxford gradually changed into a place where young gents went to booze, wench, hunt and roister. It went to sleep in the eighteenth century and woke in the nineteenth. Even in the first decade of the twentieth century it was still, as Bernard Shaw remarked, a place for making a few scholars and a great many gentlemen. Between the world wars, though Auden*, MacNeice* and Spender* had arrived, you could still read for a pass degree or even take no degree at all. The Second World War put an end to all that and Oxford is now a very large incubator for eggheads of both sexes and all classes: Alphaville-on-Thames.

The charge of élitism remains, and will never be dismissed unless some crazed future government does actually, as has been suggested, distribute places there in some kind of mad random lottery. Even this might not be noticed: Oxford is, after all, the place where the story of *Alice in Wonderland* was first told. Television accounts of books like

Brideshead Revisited, though no more in truth than beautifully wrought baloney, do nothing to dispel the sun-dappled myth inside every Englishman's head. Oxford is loved and loathed not simply because it has ancient buildings, priceless libraries, college autonomy and tutorial teaching, but because it is thought to have magic.

Pardon   Its cringing gentility is anathema to middle-class England, and it is the thought of their children being taught to say it (along with 'toilet' and 'pleased to meet you') that still sways some parents to choose the private rather than state sector in education. Certainly one celebrated woman writer of our era told her young son that it was a worse word to use than that other one and she no doubt meant it. It is a vivid example of how certain words, like certain names (Albert, Ada) imperceptibly fall from grace because they have been taken up by the lower middle class and are therefore NQOTD (see *Initials*).

Mr Patel   There are nine pages of Patels in the London telephone directory: not yet as many as the Smiths and Browns; but as many as the Greens. The Patels come from the Gujarati region of northwest India, and have been travellers and traders since Vasco da Gama made landfall there in the fifteenth century.

One in every six London Patels is a shopkeeper*, and there is hardly an urban street corner in England now without a Patel selling papers, sweets, cigarettes or groceries till late at night seven days a week. They thus provide a notable new dimension to the amenities of English life and many have become rich doing so. There are one hundred Gujarati millionaires in London now, most of them called Patel; and they believe there could be a thousand in another decade.

The reasons for their business success are not hard to seek. Many of them were kicked out of Uganda by Amin and have a much keener incentive to succeed that the average English shopkeeper who wants to close so that he can play darts* or watch telly. Then the Patels have a formidable family structure which means any new business is backed by reservoirs of capital and labour at bargain prices from an army of brothers, sisters, uncles, aunts and cousins.

Besides, official policy under Maggie Thatcher, a shopkeeper's daughter, was exceedingly amiable towards small business and there is still a plethora of government schemes to help Mr Patel get started. Then again, small shops do not have to face the might of organised labour. What they do have to face is the might of Sainsburys* and Waitrose, W.H. Smith and Boots; and they may survive only by offering the lure of herculean hours. Meanwhile they make an attractive contribution to English life. Many Patels are qualified well beyond their calling; and it is quite possible now to be sold your eggs by an economist or your milk by a micro-biologist.

Payne, Cynthia (born 1934)   Became a national heroine when she was acquitted of nine charges of controlling prostitutes at her archetypal suburban house in Ambleside Avenue, Streatham. The case greatly cheered the nation, and was often hardly distinguishable from a Whitehall farce, with stories of middle-aged men queuing for the services on offer with their luncheon vouchers, falling backwards into baths when surprised by a police raid, or arriving in wheelchairs to join in the fun. Cynthia has always maintained that her work has done much to cement many marriages, and is probably quite right.

Pets   The code-name given by the English to the animal master-race which has taken them over.

Pevsner, Sir Nikolaus (1902–83)   He came to England penniless from his native Germany in 1935. He was already a distinguished art historian, but had precious little of his new country's langue at his disposal. His first published work over here was therefore stylistically somewhat rough. Yet he was soon the master of a deft and elegant English which led Colin Macinnes to rank him directly after Conrad. His magisterial *Buildings of England* – forty-six volumes written over a twenty-five year span – is full of felicities. He speaks of spare buildings, wilful buildings, playful buildings. He even gets away with naughty buildings. He found England an uncharted territory as compelling as Africa had been to Burton, Livingstone and Speke. In a real sense, he discovered English Architecture.

Pheasant There is one cardinal rule for all English pheasants: stay well away from Sandringham. It has become a tradition among Princes of Wales that each shall try to outdo his predecessor in their slaughter. The record bag there for one day was the 3,114 pheasants shot on 14 November 1896. 'I love shooting more than anything else,' wrote the future Edward VIII to his father George V in 1912.

Next year at the Beaconsfield estate of Lord Burnham, all previous royal records were shattered. As Edward later recalled: 'My left arm ached from lifting my gun, my shoulder from the recoil, and I was deaf and stunned from the banging ... when in the late afternoon the carnage stopped almost 4,000 pheasants had been killed. The bright limp carcasses were laid out in rows of 100; the whole place was littered with feathers and spent cartridges.' That day, however, his father remarked that perhaps they had gone too far.

By modern standards they assuredly had. When newspaper editors were given a stiff wigging by the Palace recently for intruding on royal privacy at Sandringham, the real reason for the Queen's concern was undoubtedly the adverse publicity elicited by the sight of her elder grandson at his first shoot. This bloody slaughter might well precipitate a future rift between the Crown and the English people, most of whom are not amused by it.

Picnics On the face of it, there is something perverse in the English predilection for picnics. If the English summer were half as bad as it is made out, picnics would be a continuing and depressing series of write-offs. That great English cookery writer Jane Grigson has actually suggested that a good English picnic should contain some kind of disaster, and certainly our literature is rich in such lovingly recalled minutiae of discomfort. John Betjeman*, for example: 'Sand in the sandwiches / Wasps in the tea / Sun on our bathing dresses heavy with the wet / Squelch of the bladder-wrack waiting for the sea / Fleas round the tamarisk, an early cigarette.' The English genius is to roll with the punches thrown by the weather and to indulge the national passion with escalating recklessness. There is indeed something very slightly unhinged about the whole exercise. The most famous picnic in English literature (the Mad Hatter's tea party) did not actually take place; and the best loved (*The Teddy Bears' Picnic*), used by the BBC* because of its range to test the sound, is one which every Englishman feels he was at.

Celebrated in England for centuries, picnics have grown distinctly more sophisticated as the years have unrolled. When the three men in a boat of Jerome K. Jerome's immortal masterpiece picnicked by the

Thames*, they did so on such fundamental fare as cold meat, tea, bread, butter and jam. When Lewis Carroll* rowed the three little Liddell girls up the river on that golden day in 1862 and first told them the story of *Alice in Wonderland* they took a picnic of cold chicken, salad, cakes and tea. This may sound well enough, but on the simple side by today's elaborate standards (when crisps and coke, bangers and biscuits would certainly be required; and where were the boiled eggs?). Interestingly, even then William Harcourt, owner of the riverside land at Nuneham, allowed people to land on Tuesdays and Thursdays and use his purpose-built picnic huts, thus foreshadowing today's faceless picnic areas.

Carroll and his friends were sufficiently informal to borrow glasses, plates, knives and forks from cottages by the riverside; compare these casual preparations with the sophisticated hamper provided by that other great river-picnicker, the Water Rat for his friend Mole in *The Wind in the Willows*. "'There's cold chicken inside it," replied the Rat briefly, "coldtonguecoldhamcoldbeefpickledgherkinssaladfrenchrollscress sand-wichespottedmeatgingerbeerlemonadesodawater –" "Oh stop," cried the Mole in ectasies. "This is too much!"'

Today a whole industry provides picnic hampers and fills them with even more elaborte fare than Rat could command: smoked salmon for Glyndebourne*, caviare for Ascot*, strawberries for Wimbledon*, Pimm's for Henley*, and so through the whole scrumptious, lunatic cycle of the English summer*. Yet, with all its elaboration, the English picnic is essentially an informal meal taken sitting on the grass. To eat at a table like a Frenchman might well be more logical and less messy; but it would not be a *picnic*.

Piers   John Betjeman* once described the pleasure of piers as being at sea without the disadvantage of being sick. To Malcolm Muggeridge they were pasteboard Taj Mahals. They have played a key role for 150 years in English life now: graceful, spindly, fretted, domed and turreted pavilions of pleasure that seem at times to float on the waves.

They still symbolise a kind of raffish fun the English understand better than anyone else. It is the world of Max Miller and *The Good Companions,* of flickering autoscope films with saucy titles like *What the Butler Saw* or *Paris Can-Can;* of teeth-breaking rock in psychedelic colours, pierrot shows and palm court orchestras. They stood, and stand, for nostalgia-by-the-sea.

With the great lemming rush of the English to the Cote d'Azur and the Costa Brava since the war, they ought to have sunk into a sad and perhaps terminal decline. Yet every now and then they enjoy an Indian summer. They play bit parts in party conferences or are chosen by some television megastar for a summer season. Their dreamlike grace wins them an unforgettable role in films. Brighton West Pier was an ironic setting for *Oh! What a Lovely War* and Weston-super-Mare Pier an elegant backdrop in *The Remains of the Day*. English piers, the prettiest and jolliest in the world, have seemed down and out time and again, yet always seem to bounce back. For this long lease of life, the lottery* must now take much of the credit. Quite rightly too: we need our follies.

Pint The Englishman has been taking his pint since time immemorial; but the written testimony goes back two and half centuries (Henry Fielding refers to the pleasant practice in 1742). It is not so much a measure of cubic capacity as a definition of ritual – 'I'm just going out for my pint'. Around it have grown such comparatively new diversions as 'poems and pints' (when poems are read between draughts of Ale*). A pint is a curiously satisfying amount of beer, and will not seem quite the same when it becomes .5683 litres.

Plonk Yet another of those handy words that have changed their meaning. Originally rhyming slang for vin *blanc* (plinkety-plonk) it has gradually shifted its load till now it conveys to most English people cheap *red* wine. Recently, though, a new subtlety has crept in. People tend to say 'have some plonk' when what is on offer is, say, fair-to-middling claret; they would not say it if offering some of the really dire red ink on sale at the very bottom of the market. This trend to defensive deprecation runs through the whole language now (see for example under *Gentleman*, which is decreasingly used seriously).

Pong Another of those words which change meaning as they cross the Atlantic; to an American, an electronic game resembling ping-pong, played on a pinball machine or a television screen; to an Englishman, an exceedingly disagreeable smell.

Porn There are three main charges against porn: it demeans women, it incites violence, and it uglifies whatever it touches. Some defence may be mounted against the first two charges; to the third there is no answer. In Orwell's *1984*, porn had replaced religion as the opiate of the masses and was called, contemptuously, prole-feed.

Portobello Road Increasingly it is becoming the true Latin Quarter of London. Its exotic name is a fortunate accident: in 1739 Admiral Vernon captured the Caribbean city of Puerto Bello from the Spanish. A number of English places were named after the victory; one was Portobello Farm and another the lane which led from it down to Notting Hill Gate.

By the early 1870s the first dealers had appeared in Portobello Lane: gypsies buying and selling horses at the nearby Hippodrome and offering herbs as a sideline. By the twenties there was a flourishing market with many of its street vendors recruited from demobilised wartime troops; but it was strictly illegal till 1927 when London County Council gave it a licence.

Today it stretches two miles and is visited by a quarter of a million people a year. Some of the vendors nowadays are actors or actresses; a stall works well with the long periods of enforced rest between roles; but there are also housewives who take a stall simply for Saturday when the street antique market is open (the fruit, vegetable and flower market is open every day of the week, and so is the bric-a-brac which stretches north above that to the Grand Union Canal).

Insiders know that the best time to be at the market is very early, before the tourists have arrived and when the dealers are trading among themselves. Anything goes here: silver, maps, porcelain, linen, lace, maps, books, dolls, glass, medals. Christian's, the delicatessen, puts its stalls outside and sells salt beef sandwiches, croissants, coffee and *Gefilte Fish*.

Here you will find one of the best wine bars in London ("192"), an exhilarating number of art galleries, a proper bookshop (Elgin Books) and, at the southern end of the market, one of the best pubs in London (The Sun in Splendour). Poet Christopher Logue, singer George Melly, playwright Chistopher Hampton and politician Roy Jenkins are all locals; among celebrated former denizens was George Orwell*, thin, ill and angry from his stint as a Burma policeman, who worked on *Down and Out in Paris and London* at 10 Portobello Road.

Post Office   Like all English institutions, it is not what it was. Though a letter now costs nearly forty times what it did when Sir Rowland Hill launched the penny post, no Englishman in his right mind banks on first-class mail arriving next morning. Nor could a master sleuth like Sherlock Holmes*, who used telegrams as a principal tool of his trade, possibly operate with a post office that has given them up.

Still, we must at least grant the post office this: it acted as patron to one English novelist of genius, Anthony Trollope, who kept up a steady output of ten thousand words a week, written while working in its hospitable maw, and to one English poet of genius, W.H. Auden*, who worked for a while with John Grierson in the GPO Film Unit. Here he turned out soundtracks for documentaries which, despite the obvious constraints of the brief, have his inimitable stamp:

'This is the night mail crossing the border / Bringing the cheque and the postal order / Letters for the rich, letters for the poor / The shop at the corner and the girl next door.' The only office space they could find for him was in the corridor with the messenger boys. 'There, on that old Post Office table,' recalled his director, Harry Watt, years later, 'he wrote the most beautiful verse.'

Priestley, J.B. (1894–1984) When someone asked C.P. Snow how a Russian wishing to understand English life at every level should go about it, he suggested reading the complete works of J.B. Priestley. Between his debut in 1922 with *Brief Diversions* through *English Journey* in 1934 to his last book, *English Humour*, in 1976, Priestley chronicled England with enormous and evident scope and relish. He is the ordinary Englishman writ large: outwardly comfortable and complacent; inwardly passionate and romantic.

He is moreover a genuine, old-fashioned man of letters with a huge range: novelist, essayist, playwright, reporter, travel writer and social commentator. His most successful novel, *The Good Companions* (1929), does not reflect him quite so fully as more complex works like *Bright Day* (1946). The solid Yorkshire persona is at odds with the experimental writer of the 'time' plays inspired by the serial universe of J.W. Dunne – *Time and the Conways, I Have Been Here Before* (both 1937) – and the quasi-surrealist morality play *Johnson Over Jordan* (1939). He would be remembered, if for nothing else, for his wartime broadcasts which equalled and perhaps sometimes outdid Winston Churchill's* in formulating the feelings and aspirations of the man in the street.

He was an articulate champion of the unemployed in the thirties and a principal advocate of nuclear disarmament in the fifties. He gave up writing plays too early (in 1963) but could always console himself with the true thought that at any single minute of the twenty-four hours some company somewhere was performing *Dangerous Corner* (1932), his most popular play.

Private Eye Sometimes at smart parties in England you will see a figure who very slightly disturbs the bonhomie of the evening. He may well be wearing a corduroy jacket when all about him are sporting their black ties. He will sip water as the company quaff their wine: not quite in the swim yet by no means out of it either. This is Richard Ingrams, embattled editor, from 1963 to 1986, of *Private Eye*, a puritan publication that has grown uncommonly rich and powerful by playing its hunches and living on its nerves. Intolerant and indispensable, he (and it) were skeletons at any feast during the 23 years of his editorship. He acted out a dangerous destiny: the conscience of England. Whether the new men at the *Eye* have done the same is a moot point.

Prole Short for proletarian. Though widely associated with George Orwell* and *1984*, it was in fact used fifty years earlier by George Bernard Shaw*, and has always been derogatory. However, it now seems to be losing ground, probably due to the rapidly shifting shape and nature of the English working class.

Proms Literally, concerts where the audience could walk about, but now where they stand, if they so choose, to hear good music at bargain prices. Although the first English promenade concerts were held as early as 1838, the word now instantly conveys to every Englishman the image of Sir Henry Wood. His bust is ritually enwreathed by Promenaders on the last night of the Proms each year in the sight of some 200 million television viewers, and rightly so.

He launched and conducted the new series of Proms at the old Queen's Hall in 1895, aided by a gift of £2,000 from a music-lover and throat specialist called George Clark Cathcart, who offered the money on the condition that the existing high pitch, ruinous to singers' voices, should be abandoned in favour of the lower French pitch.

Wood was a tireless champion of modern music, who played the work of Tchaikovsky, Sibelius, Strauss, Scriabin and Debussy to English audiences before they were widely known, conducted the first performances in England of Mahler's First, Fourth, Seventh and Eighth Symphonies, and introduced the music of Jánáček to the English. Every major English composer of his lifetime was performed at the Proms. He was the first conductor to introduce women to an English orchestra (in 1913). In August 1944, though now seventy-five and in failing health, he achieved his ambition of conducting the first night of his fiftieth Prom season; he died later that month.

A worthy laureate then; and if the televised second half of the last night of the Proms may well strike foreign viewers as some kind of mad football celebration scored for orchestra and massed choirs, it might be remembered that this is the culmination of an eight-week feast of music, devoured by the army of Promenaders. By most measures, it is the greatest festival of music in the world, and gives the lie yet again to the old canard that England is a land without music.

Prostitution 'There is something utterly nauseating about a system of society which pays a harlot twenty-five times as much as it pays its prime minister', said Harold Wilson during the Christine Keeler scandal. He was not the first prime minister to take an interest in the subject. William Ewart Gladstone conducted clandestine work among fallen women, no doubt with the loftiest of motives, though now that we have access to his private diaries we can see that he probably derived a vicarious kick from his good deeds.

Victorian England was the heyday of the whore, with 80,000 and perhaps more to serve a London only half the size of the modern city. It took an eminent Victorian surgeon, William Acton, to point out to his hypocritical readers that, contrary to received opinion then, a woman on the game (to use their own time-honoured euphemism) did not invariably end up ruined; her health was often quite as good as that of a working-class mother of the same age who had all the drudgery of a Victorian family to contend with; and very often the prostitute retired and took up respectable life with no one in her new milieu being any the wiser.

Mrs Warren's Profession, the play in which Bernard Shaw put the point with brutal force, was written in 1894, but refused a licence till 1925. It is the story of a woman who, weary of working in the bar of Waterloo Station fourteen hours a day for four shillings a week and someone else's profit, decides to sell herself for her own profit. What else, she asks, are girls in society taught to do but sell themselves to some rich man? It was altogether too near the truth for comfort.

With the rise of the permissive society and the coming of the age of affluence, London no longer needs 80,000 whores; but it has no more eradicated them altogether than any other civilised society has been able to do since the dawn of history. All it has been able to do is to take them off the streets and into service flats for Arabs, clubs for northern businessmen, and the so-called massage parlours for the man in the street.

The theme of the good girl what's been ruined has given rise to much lore and a couple of memorable snatches of verse. First, Thomas Hardy* at his most wry, knowing, and worldly: '"You left us in tatters, without shoes or socks, / Tired of digging potatoes, and spudding up docks: / And now you've gay bracelets and bright feathers three!' – / "Yes: that's how we dress when we're ruined," said she.' Then, a cheery observation from our old friend Anon*: 'When Lady Jane became a tart, / It almost broke her father's heart. / But blood is blood, and race is race, / And so, to mitigate disgrace, / He bought a most expensive beat / From Asprey's up to Oxford Street.'

Public Schools   In America, Scotland* and the colonies, says the *OED*, they are schools provided at public expense and managed by public authority, to provide public and usually free education. Quite so. In England, though, they are a different kettle of fish altogether: 'large boarding schools, drawing from the well-to-do classes pupils who are prepared mainly for the ancient universities or public services'. This common-sense definition probably fits the average Englishman's mental picture nearly enough. It noticeably omits, however, the newer criteria of independence, fee-paying, and selection, none of which totally fits either. Like the OED's famous dictum on the English language, the public school has a well-defined centre but no discernible circumference.

A book entitled *Our Public Schools*, published in 1881, named just seven: Eton*, Harrow*, Winchester*, Rugby, Westminster, Marlborough and Charterhouse. In 1889 the first *Public Schools Year Book* included a list drawn up by 'three Public School men' who were guided by such principles as 'Does the school possess the Public School spirit?'. By such cloudy criteria it extended the list to thirty-eight schools, including Portsmouth Grammar School, and Boston Grammar School in Lincolnshire. Clearly the task of definition was already proving a headache. Ten years later the *Year Book* abandoned its own judgement and simply listed the schools attending the Headmasters' Conference. This rule of thumb is still often used, though it omitted the two grammar schools previously listed and brought in a number of others (King Edward's, Birmingham; Lancaster; Wolverhampton).

In the beginning *all* English schools were religious foundations for clever poor boys training to enter the Church, the clerical establishment who would conduct the nation's business. The secret code for this career was *grammar*, specifically Latin grammar; the teaching of it laid down by *public* statute; herein is the seed of the perennial confusion. For many centuries aristocratic boys were educated at home or *privately*; gradually the increasing prestige of the new grammar schools like Eton encouraged their parents to send them away to be educated *publicly*.

Through a long stretch of Victoria's reign one new public school was founded every year to provide the men who would officer her armies and rule her dominions. Thomas Arnold pioneered the concept of character and the cult of muscular Christianity at Rugby; he was, it was remarked, 'among the first to see that although our Saviour taught us to turn the other cheek He did not mean that we were not to tackle our man low'. Arnold's disciples spread his message throughout Victorian England: Hart at Sedbergh, Butler at Haileybury, Cotton at Marlborough and Vaughan at Harrow. Vaughan, however, came to a sticky end. His impassioned love affair with a boy called Alfred Pretor was leaked to Alfred's friend, J.A. Symonds, who blurted it out eight years later during a reading party to John Conington, Corpus Professor of Latin. Conington advised Symonds to tell his father. He did, and Dr Symonds confronted Vaughan with his infamy. Though Mrs Vaughan threw herself at the good doctor's feet, Vaughan had to go. He finished up as Dean of Llandaff.

Little local difficulties like this did nothing to impair the onward march of the public school, nor the innate confidence of its products. When Stephen Spender* went to Oxford* in the late twenties he found his fellow Etonian undergraduates helpless with mirth at the discovery that the senior scholar of their year was the son of an Eton confectioner. The wheel has not taken too long to come full circle. There are English universities now – though perhaps not Oxford and Cambridge* – where public schoolboys are reticent about their provenance. Even at Oxford they have become the object of caricature.

Pubs In Hampshire there is a pub with no name. You have to bump up an unmarked track to get there, and, apart from having no name, it has no sign to help you find it, though once inside, you will find the barman sports a sweatshirt: The Pub with No Name it proclaims. Here there are log fires and oak settles, ancient drop-leaf tables, fox masks, gazelle heads, farm tools and candle-lit country pictures.

There are some beguiling country wines: cowslip, parsnip, peach, elderberry, damson, wheat and raisin. There are moreover some handsome hand-pumped ales: not least a local brew called (but you've guessed) No Name. If you choose your day, you can buy Jersey cream over the bar ('eat in two days' says the legend on the lid) and pheasants* in season. On summer days there is a mind-smoothing view of the Hampshire Downs. It is an enchanted pub: but it is in effect a secret one.

There are still, on the other hand, rebarbative boozers in inner cities where the beer tastes of disinfectant and the ploughman's lunch of blotting paper, mousetrap cheese and margarine, and it is still a good general rule not to take wine in pubs unless well recommended.

Having said that, there is a scattering of English pubs that are a solace and a delight: riverside pubs like the Dove at Hammersmith, ritzy pubs like the Bells of Peover in Cheshire, medieval pubs like the Fleece near Evesham, alfresco pubs like the Flask at Highgate, sleepy pubs like the Lamb at Burford; smugglers' pubs like the Jolly Sailor at Orford; and beautiful pubs like the Horse and Groom at Charlton, near Malmesbury. Intruders will be treated strictly on their merits.

Pudding 'Ah, what an excellent thing is an English pudding!' exclaimed François Maximilien Misson, a French visitor to England in his memoirs of the journey published in 1698. He noted that the English made puddings 'fifty several ways' and his admiration was absolutely genuine. Slowly things went wrong after that: country people lost the old skills as they migrated into the towns; poverty made them opt for margarine instead of butter and thicken with cornflour rather than eggs; then an influx of premixed puds in packets seemed to spell *finis* to the old sweet glories. Besides, there was the undeniable toll that puds took on teeth and tums.

Now a new generation of English cooks, inspired by the late Jane Grigson, are rediscovering their lost heritage. And what a rich heritage it is! The names alone ring like a great roll of chivalry: flummeries, frumenties, fools and fritters, dumplings and crumbles, junkets, charlottes and tansies, syllabubs and whim-whams. There is the fascination of trying traditional puddings with such come-hither names as Boodle's Orange Fool and Sussex Bailiff's Bliss, Suck Cream and Tipsy Cake, Half Pay Pudding and Bedfordshire Clanger, Clipping Time Pudding and Apricot Brown Betty. So it looks as if the English pud is back to stay. As Misson roundly declared after his English odyssey: 'Blessed be he that invented pudding!' See also *Afters, Custard.*

Pudding Club To join this select body is to be expecting a baby; vernacular destined to survive, like its celebrated synonym, 'having a bun in the oven', if only because it combines mordant humour with tactile homeliness.

Quakers The Religious Society of Friends has a high standing in English life. The record speaks for itself: Quakers led the fight against slavery, pioneered prison reform, have always opposed war, are concerned about mental health, build excellent schools, and did quiet but invaluable work in bringing refugees from fascism to England. There are not many of them here – some twenty thousand arranged in about four hundred meetings – but because of the example they set, their influence is out of all proportion to their numbers.

Queen, HM The (born 1926) Anyone who attacks Elizabeth II will not be hanged, drawn and quartered; but he may well feel that he has been. Such was the experience of Malcolm Muggeridge when he ventured to suggest that the Queen's broadcasting style was ill-suited to the demands of the medium, her voice being far too high and her manner altogether too stiff. There was some truth in the charge, and the Queen did indeed work at the problem with some success. Muggeridge took a drubbing but lived to fight another day. The English people have it firmly in their heads (and here they have some support from the law) that unlike other members of her family the Queen is above the battle. Each year of her reign that passes entrenches this position more surely. She has now been on the throne longer than any English monarch since Victoria; and is already well on the way to equalling that heroic innings. It has not always been as easy as it looked. The monarchy, when she succeeded to the throne, was only fourteen years away from one of its worst nadirs: the abysmal interregnum of Edward VIII. Her father, George VI, had provided a breathing space. He was a thoroughly decent but hardly scintilating man, and by the time Elizabeth succeeded him the monarchy was in much need of a new sense of style and drama; of expansion and distinction. With the aid of Prince Philip, not everyone's cup of tea but no ineffectual cypher either, she has done just this. On top of all the nation's adventures and misadventures (the Suez folly, the Falklands conflict*, innumerable sterling crises, a string of traitors from Pontecorvo and Nunn May through Burgess and Maclean to Philby and Blunt) she has had more than her fair share of family disasters, ranging, be it remembered, from divorce for three of her children and her sister to murder (Mountbatten) and sudden death in the air (Prince William of Gloucester).

Apart from being of necessity at the centre of every national drama, she has met in the last forty-four years far more English people than anybody else; and thus has a unique knowledge of this curious and eccentric race. In short, the Queen's own story would be one of the great publishing coups of all time: but we can rest assured that here is one diary that we shall not see in her lifetime. More's the pity.

The Queens The great Cunard Liners *Queen Mary* and *Queen Elizabeth* were floating encapsulations of England at her most apocryphal. They ferried people between Southampton and New York with a style and luxury that not all of them would have enjoyed on dry land, and did it with seeming effortlessness. The American liners may have been more free and easy, the cooking a shade better on the French boats, but only the Queens conveyed the sense of travelling in a time warp. It took eight hundred staff, including six liftmen and a gardener, to serve the whims of about the same number of passengers. The impression of feudal largesse was begun with the breakfast menu, opening as it did with the chilled cantaloup melon and all the juices and cereals, then casually offering onion sup or Yarmouth bloaters before getting down to the serious business of eggs any way you liked, the three different bacons, American hash and griddle cakes with maple syrup before moving on to the nine kinds of bread and seven distinct coffees. It was as well to choose a smooth crossing. After breakfast the well-disciplined would take a few turns round the deck before settling into their deckchairs to be solicitously wrapped in a blanket by stewards and then served steaming bouillon. There would be time for a drink before lunch and then an afternoon programme of films, music or games before tea and then a swim in the ship's pool before cocktails with the captain, doctor or purser – the invitations came thick and fast. Or perhaps you felt like giving your own party in the cabin. Then Cunard would be happy to supply staff who had not noticed that their pre-war world had ended, drinks duty-free and canapés with their compliments. After dinner, the nightclub would open and the dancing would go on till dawn. On the fifth morning keen passengers would surface early to glimpse the Manhattan skyline coming up through the mist: easily the best way to see America first.

Queer From the time it was first noted in America during the 1920s, 'queer' as the slang word for homosexual was standard usage in England for nigh on half a century, and was used almost universally in light-hearted badinage without giving offence ('Cheers my dears, we're all queers'). Then, as the homosexual world came out into the open, the word queer began to give offence, and must now be replaced in polite usage by the politically correct term 'gay'. Somehow, though, it does not quite have the same comic clout, as in the story of the sexually ambivalent Harold Nicolson's first words on entering the House of Commons as a newly elected MP: 'Not much of a place for queers, is it?' Nor, now, is England: gay's the word.

Queue It was George Mikes who first pointed out that a man in a queue was the image of a true Englishman just as a man at a bullfight was the image of a true Spaniard. The Second World War saw the apotheosis of the queue and dramatised the bovine stickability of the island race in a rather ludicrous way.

Yet, even in an age of plenty, the English still like to queue for special treats like Wimbledon* tickets, standing room to hear Domingo sing, or the last night of the Proms*. Indeed they sometimes seem to enjoy this curious ritual more than the pleasure it is designed to achieve; bringing their sleeping bags and Primus stoves, and setting up world records by queuing for days and nights on end.

Bizarre though this English sport may seem it probably links demand and supply with less fuss than the continental equivalent (rioting) or the American (payola).

Quite Another of those English words that has been not only changing but is now even reversing its meaning. Thus, while it originally meant 'totally' ('I was quite alone'), it also meant 'actually' ('she was quite ill'); and out of this second sense has grown the use of quite to mean 'fairly' or 'somewhat'. So when we say 'his work is quite satisfactory' do we mean it 'somewhat' or 'totally' satisfies? Americans still, and not only in this instance, tend to prefer the old sense; in England the original meaning now sounds distinctly affected – and not just quite affected.

Quotation   What the English are good at is not so much quotation as misquotation. Thus, Wellington did not say 'Up Guards and at 'em'; Milton did not say 'Fresh fields and pastures new'; Congreve did not say 'Hell hath no fury like a woman scorned'; Acton did not say 'All power corrupts'. What we carry around in our heads is a vast jumble of half-remembered lines which our minds simply elide to the shape that suits them best.

It must be manfully faced that the Irish have given the English far more than their share of their best quotations. From Wellington himself – 'Publish and be damned' – through Wilde – 'Work is the curse of the drinking classes' – to Shaw* – 'Every man over forty is a scoundrel' – they have shown the English how to polish epigrams till they glitter.

True, great Englishmen like Samuel Johnson* have left a whole treasury of inimitable and enchanted lines that still chime in the mind; but he was fortunate in a Scottish amanuensis of genius. In politics, the exotic Jewish adventurer Benjamin Disraeli – 'Never complain and never explain' – is far better value than the pious Liverpool Old Etonian William Ewart Gladstone – 'Time is on our side'.

In our own century, meritocrat Harold Wilson may have shown the richer sense of metaphor – 'The gnomes of Zurich' – but it was left to patrician Alec Douglas-Home, mocked by Wilson for being the four-teenth earl, to come up with the perfect riposte: "When you come to think about it, I suppose he is the fourteenth Mr Wilson.'

Indeed, the gift for picking precisely the right phrase out of the air does not require a great quantity of formal education. Thus nineteen-year-old Mandy Rice Davies, told in court during the Profumo scandal that Lord Astor had denied her allegations, gave a reply that has passed into the language: 'He would, wouldn't he?' Political parties and big business pay fortunes nowadays to advertising agencies to fail to come up with lines half as good as that. Yet in politics as in literature, the best lines are often the work of that prolific word-spinner Anon*.

Rabbits 'Once upon a time there were four little rabbits whose names were Flopsy, Mopsy, Cottontail and Peter,' wrote Beatrix Potter in *The Tale of Peter Rabbit*. She was not the first author to exploit the winning qualities of the common or garden *Oryctolagus cuniculus*, nor the last – Richard Adams made a substantial fortune from the heart-rending story of the rabbits in *Watership Down*.

Still, to the countryman the rabbit is a pest, and an exceedingly persistent one. He will shoot, wire or ferret them on a Saturday afternoon or Sunday* morning most seasons of the year; residually perhaps as a bit of a sport, but principally to keep them down, for they are a voracious menace to grass, crops, trees and gardens.

Ever since the worst epidemic of myxomatosis, they have been unpopular as a dish; and though they have grown resistant to the horrible disease, rabbits can still be found stricken down by it in the briar, when the only recourse is to dispatch them as speedily as possible. The gap between the gentle creature of fiction and the noxious vermin of reality remains unbridgeable.

Radio Times   It was born in 1923 when a hostile press refused to print BBC* programmes (ironically newspapers have since spent a fortune trying to get that right). It has always been the highest-selling magazine in the country; the Coronation issue of 29 May 1953 sold nine million copies; and over the whole year in 1955 it averaged sales of more than eight million a week. It was also profitable from the beginning and at one time in the thirties was contributing a quarter of the BBC's entire revenue. This wealth and power attracted some talented people; Maurice Gorham, editor from 1933 to 1941 went on to be head of BBC Television; Eric Maschwitz, his predecessor in the chair, went on to become not only head of BBC Variety but a playwright and lyricist who would be remembered, if for nothing else, as the author of *These Foolish Things*. It was also able to call on a wide range of gifted illustrators: Edward Ardizzone, Peter Brookes, Robin Jacques and Ralph Steadman among them. Though its circulation is now well below that great fifties peak, it remains one of the highest-selling magazines in the land. Radio is now squeezed into smaller type after the coloured bezazz of the television programmes each day, but the *Radio Times* remains an item in the everyday diet of English life; and is as harmless and anodyne as Ovaltine*.

The RAF   They have no traditions, they only have habits, remarked a naval petty officer in a letter to *The Times** as recently as 1977. There is some truth in the thrust; but no shame either. Manifestly the RAF is the most free-and-easy of the three services simply because it does not have centuries of tradition to inhibit it. Unlike the others it cannot claim to have been in battle against most of the world at some time or other; indeed, it has effectively had only four enemy air forces to contend with, the German, the Italian, the Japanese and the Argentinian; and it has given a good account against all four.

It is hard for those not alive at the time to understand the hero-worship in which the RAF was enveloped at the time of the Battle of Britain. This was a scrap which the English saw unfolding directly above them in the great diorama of the skies; and nothing was more heart-stopping than the sight of the British fighter squadrons climbing high into the cirrus to meet the silver shoals of German bombers. No fighter pilot had to pay for his taxi back to RAF Biggin Hill; the London cabbies saw to that. Though the RAF did not shoot down quite so many German planes as it had thought (all air forces exaggerate their kills in the heat of battle) it destroyed two German aircraft for every one it lost. This ratio, if not the three to one claimed at the time, was quite enough to prove decisive, and to deter the German invasion. If it had not been for the toughness of Hugh Dowding, the supremo of Fighter Command, who steadfastly refused all blandishments from Churchill and others to squander his planes and pilots over France and particularly at Dunkirk, it might have been a different story.

Bomber Command had a less happy war. The total cost to Germany of British bombing was one per cent of production – if that. The strategic air offensive of 1940–41 killed more members of the RAF than Germans. Still, the effect of that campaign on British morale was vast; and the bomber crews were heroes too.

The trouble with men made demi-gods by war is that they have to learn to cope with peace; not all of them did. Men who had been mythogenic had to earn their livings as schoolmasters or salesmen again. They became merely mortal; even ludicrous. Thus Group Captain Max Aitken, who was in the air the day the war started and still flying the day it ended, led the victory fly-past; but lived on to earn the mocking sobriquet Biggles (airman hero of a hundred schoolboy yarns) from *Private Eye**, none of whose staff were old enough to have any clear recollection of the war in the air and quite naturally had no especial regard for the men who had fought it. Every hero, as Ralph Waldo Emerson reminds us, becomes a bore at last.

Rain   The myth that England is a rainy country dies hard. The heaviest rainfall ever recorded here in a day (9.56 inches at Bruton, Somerset in 1917) is a mere trickle compared with the several feet in a tropical downpour.

London in January has an average monthly rainfall of two inches compared with Johannesburg's 4.5 and Jerusalem's 5.2. Nevertheless England's climate is intensely humid (not quite the same thing) and it is this which gives English grass its preternatural glory and English women their gorgeous skins.

Melancholy images of rain abound in English writing all the way from Medieval Anon's 'Western wind, when wilt thou blow / The small rain down can rain? / Christ if my love were in my arms / And I in my bed again!' In modern times, though, rain is seen as principal killjoy on sporting occasions.

'Rain stopped play' is perhaps the most lowering of all sports reports in the summer papers; and it was these gloom-filled words which, on their return from their shenanigans with various Nazi bounders in the classic Hitchcock thriller *The Lady Vanishes*, greeted the silly-ass, cricket-mad, archetypal Englishmen, Charters and Caldicott*.

Redbrick   For six hundred years there were just two universities in England (Scottish education has developed quite differently. The tradition of the lad o'pairts, the poor boy who comes from his village to study at the four historic Scottish universities with his pack on his back goes deep into antiquity.) In England it was not till 1832 that Durham* was founded; London followed four years later. By 1945 there were ten English universities. Then came the real explosion; now there are ninety-five in the United Kingdom.

Six hundred years is a long lead. When David Lodge, one of the most interesting novelists now writing (and one of the most fashionable English professors now teaching), went to University College, London, soon after the last war, he did not know that any other university apart from his own and the two ancient ones even *existed*.

His close friend, Malcolm Bradbury, another distinguished novelist and professor of English, began to write *Eating People is Wrong* – already established as a modern fiction classic – while an undergraduate at what was then University College, Leicester: 'It was late redbrick, verging on white tile, and still a constituent college of the University of London; it had some seven hundred students. It was located in the old county asylum ...' Leicester then did not offer glittering prizes: 'What it offered was sober futures, in low or middle management or school teaching ...' All that was to change precisely because men like Bradbury and Lodge brought their considerable gifts to the service of universities like Birmingham and East Anglia.

An informal dozen or so universities seem to be grouping themselves in the English mind as an unofficial first division rather on the lines of the American Ivy League. Oxbridge, Durham, and London are fairly obvious entries, but so too are a number of the well-dug-in, old-established redbricks. No name on this list is sacrosanct. Universities must compete for students just as students compete for places. With men like Lodge and Bradbury in them, the redbricks have everything to play for.

Rice Pudding   One of those dishes that every Englishman knows from the days of his youth, it is hated by some and adored by others, for it is redolent of English childhood and thus, according to the spin of the coin, of hell or heaven. Though the sophisticated Englishman will claim to have put it away with his toys, it mysteriously surfaces at places like the Guards Club and the ultra-chic Connaught Hotel in London, where they say there is a steady demand for it. The dish also stars in one of the most colourful and contemptuous English images of moral or physical feebleness: 'he couldn't kick the skin off a rice pudding'. But see too *Afters* and *Pudding*.

Rolls-Royce   If the Rolls-Royce owned by Lord Berners, which had a piano built in the back, had some claim to be the most glamorous of its breed, the Rolls-Royce owned by the Duke of Westminster – which he used to charge a platoon of German cavalry in the First World War – has a claim to be the most gallant. We should not be too surprised to learn that not only did Tsar Nicholas II of Russia run a Rolls but also Lenin, Stalin and Brezhnev. Yet even in these austere times, a third of all Rolls-Royces are bought by the island race; another third by Americans; and the rest of the world takes the rest. It must be allowed, though, that the best customer over the years for the Rolls has been the Scottish Co-operative Society. Images of Co-op customers quietly piling up their divvies till they can afford the £118,557.50 currently required for the cheapest Rolls are, however, misplaced: the Rolls is top of the pops north of the border as a hearse. Most Scots take their first ride in one horizontally.

Rose   It is probably a fair comment on national proclivities that while the Welsh emblem is the unlovely leek, the Irish the uninteresting shamrock, and the Scottish the positively repulsive thistle, all three plants will be much on display in England on the national day of each small country. The Englishman, however, who boasts as his emblem the most beautiful flower in the world, does not deign to wear it on his national day, being self-conscious about such displays of naked chauvinism. He can, however, grow it rather well.

The Royal Family   It has long ceased to be the seat of power and is increasingly the hub of show business. Not only is a royal presence the *sine qua non* of any grand film première; in a real sense the royals are playing in their own soap opera. No script writer could wish for a better cast: a large, variegated family with everyone's favourite mum (Lilibet), a super Gran (the Queen Mum), a wilful aunt (Margaret), a cantankerous father (Philip), interesting children (cheerful Charlie, randy Andy, educated Edward and angular Anne), all sorts of in-laws (divine Diana, feisty Fergie, problem-girl Princess Michael), grandchildren galore – but one could go on for ever. Add a string of polo ponies, helicopters, fast cars and castles, and the stage is set for a run that could well last for centuries. See also *Queen, Pheasants.*

Rude Songs and Verses   This is the province of Anon*, that prodigal wordsmith who has contributed so bounteously to English literature, for in the entire panoply of those rude songs and improper verses which are every Englishman's birthright, few if any can be attributed with any authority, though A.P. Herbert is often credited with the saga of 'Eskimo Nell'. It is indeed a zestful narrative that occasionally rises to great lyrical heights. The theme is phallic voracity matched by uterine insatiability, and was clearly written by somebody who could string a few words together. Some improper songs are parodies ('Little boy kneels at the foot of his bed / Lily white hands are caressing his head / Oh my, couldn't be worse / Christopher Robin is screwing his nurse') and some derive from famous hymns. Thus, 'There's a Street in Cairo' goes to the tune of 'Abide with Me'. Some have political undertones, as in the famous parody of 'The Red Flag' ('The working class can kiss my arse / I've got the foreman's job at last'), but many purvey a brooding sense of melancholy ('It's the same the whole world over / It's the poor wot gets the blame / It's the rich wot gets the pleasure / Ain't it all a bleeding shame?').

Though perhaps the most celebrated repository of these songs is now the rugger club, and some clearly have a rugby provenance, many had their origin in the barrack or on the mess deck in the long watches of the imperial night. Prominent in this subdivision of the great genre is 'The Good Ship Venus' ('The Captain's daughter Mabel / As soon as she was able / Would fornicate with the second mate / Upon the chart-room table'). Some are cleaned up and surface as popular songs ('Roll me over in the clover') and some improbably transmogrify to advertisements, most recently 'Ivan Skavinsky Skavar', who is now selling lager.

Many of these underground ballads are not to be underrated. Thus 'Cats on the Rooftops' contains verses of real power ('Long-legged curates grind like goats / Pale-faced spinsters shag like stoats / And the whole damn world / Stands by and gloats / As they revel in the joys of copulation') would not be unworthy of Auden* on a so-so day, while some make short self-contained poems drawing on reservoirs of true desire ('Flo, Flo, I love you so / I love you in your nightie / When the moonlight flits / Across your tits / Oh Jesus Christ Almighty'). Comic, pessimistic, ingenious and above all subversive, the improper song has been a harmless safety valve for men without women wherever the English writ ran. Today it may have little or no social role; but should be preserved and probably will, if only for its charm, eccentricity and vigour.

Rugby It is hard to believe that *all* the main varieties of football – American, Australian, Association, Gaelic, Rugby Union, Rugby League – stem from the same game. But they do.

In 1863, at the first meeting of the Football Association, every possible attempt was made to frame laws for a universal game that would satisfy both those who liked to carry the ball and those who liked to dribble it. The rugby men walked out; the games began to diverge. Yet all footballers are kin, and no boy should be taught the rules of rugger until he has mastered the basic skills of soccer.

The first clue we have to that oval shape comes in *Tom Brown's Schooldays* when there is a passage about the ball *pointing* towards the goal. The first person to catch the ball and run with it (in 1823) was a Rugby schoolboy called William Webb Ellis, later Rector of St Clement Dane's, the RAF church in the Strand. His eventual resting place was a mystery till Ross McWhirter, founder of the *Guinness Book of Records*, later to be murdered by Irish gunmen, traced his grave in 1971 to Menton in southern France. Since then the French Rugby Union have been proud to tend it. The English Rugby Union placed fifteen red roses on the grave with a card thanking him for his pioneer act of 1823.

They have reason: the game is now played by seventy-nine countries. The Russians are getting useful at it; the Americans have played at Twickenham*. The Romanians have beaten France, one of the most fizzing and formidable of all modern sides. The secret of rugger is that it is a joy to play (the *furor scrumicus* or ecstasy of the scrum is said by those who have tried both to be second only to the act of love itself) and a delight to watch. A majestic try fashioned from a jewelled movement can be so perfectly timed that it conveys the illusion of being executed in slow motion.

Rupert Bear Although he has qualified for his old age pension, Rupert maintains his perennial charm for the young and is still one of the basic ingredients that keep the *Daily Express* selling. In 1920 the *succès fou* of Teddy Tail in the *Daily Mail* had the *Express* badly worried. It had searched high and low without success for a suitable counter-attraction. Finally, the night news editor at that time tentatively volunteered that his wife, Mary Tourtel, could draw, and in desperation they asked her to have a go. She came up with Rupert Bear. In the thirties Rupert, till then a bit listless, was given a shot in the arm by a brilliant artist called Alfred Bestall, who put Rupert on level terms with Teddy Tail. The continuing Rupert Bear sagas both in the paper and Christmas annual still reflect his idiosyncratic genius. For a less appealing sprig of *Ursus arctos*, see under *Winnie-the-Pooh*.

Sainsbury's   When John James Sainsbury and his young wife Mary Anne started their first dairy in Drury Lane back in 1869 their ambition was to have a branch for each of their sons. In the upshot there were always rather more branches than sons (they had six boys – and five girls). Today, their great-grandson, David Sainsbury, runs a business with 364 supermarkets and a group profit of £712 million last year. He is the largest butcher, and the largest retailer of fresh fruit and vegetables in the UK.

Sainsbury's was not always so paramount. At the turn of the century Maypole Dairy had 200 shops, Home and Colonial 400 and Liptons 500. Even by 1914, Sainsbury's still had a mere 115 branches; but they were already going for slightly different goals. A prewar Sainsbury's, like that at Croydon, as Englishmen and women of mature years will recall, was a baroque temple consecrated to space, cleanliness and order. There was always room for a woman to push her pram down the full length of the shop. There would be room for shelves along the walls and a work area for the assistant behind the counters on each side. Huge mounds of butter were kneaded to hypnotically interesting shapes with wooden spoons. The windows were framed by marble-faced pillars, wood, and stained glass spandrels; the fascia was crowned with wrought iron and displayed the Sainsbury name in gilded glass. The floor, walls and counter fronts were tiled in the lush designs of the period and the counter tops were made of marble slabs. The office was built of polished teak, and the customer's side of the counter furnished with bentwood chairs. You never quite shook off the feel of the place.

It would have been comfortable to stop there; but when Lord Sainsbury, grandson of John and Mary, went to America in 1949, he came back convinced that self-service stores were their future. So he opened the first experimental supermarket at Croydon in 1950; the largest supermarket in Europe at Lewisham in 1955; the first hypermarket in 1975. In 1987 they bought 50 supermarkets in America and now own 96 there. When John James Sainsbury died in 1928, he exhorted his successors to keep the shops well lit. They have done that – and rather more.

Saint George   He was a native of Cappadocia (now part of Turkey) and died in about AD 303. It was a thousand years later that Edward III made him England's national saint, and for a while his name was actually invoked by the English in battle, as in Henry V's 'Cry, "God for Harry, England and Saint George!"' (note the batting order). He has since, however, become something of an embarrassment to the English, most of whom do not even know what their national flag, the Cross of St George, looks like and instead rather half-heartedly wave the Union Jack, which of course represents the amalgam of all four countries and is often as not upside down.

Salvation Army   At one moment in 1983 there were two plays running side by side at the National Theatre with the Salvation Army as their themes: in the Olivier, Frank Loesser's joyous musical *Guys and Dolls*; in the Lyttelton, Bernard Shaw's delicious comedy *Major Barbara*. Both derive gusts of belly laughter from the interaction between the Army and the sinners it is bent on saving: in New York, Runyonesque gamblers with names like Harry the Horse and Brandy Bottle Bates; in London the down and outs and drudges of the East End. In both however, the laughter is good-natured; even respectful. As Shaw points out: 'It is the army of joy, of love, of courage … it marches to fight the devil with trumpet and drums, with music and dancing, with banner and palm … it picks the waster from the public house and makes a man of him; it finds a worm wriggling in a back kitchen and lo! a women.'

The movement took off when its founder, William Booth, a Nottingham evangelist, picked up a pen and struck out one word in a printer's proof. It was the 1878 Report of his Christian Mission, founded in 1865 and, till that time, doing quietly conscientious good. The proof described the Mission as a Volunteer Army. Booth made it read Salvation Army and ignited the movement.

Today the Sally Ann (as it is known among those it most helps) may seem a faintly eccentric survival of Victorian philanthropy; but not to anyone whose job it is to cope with the underside of affluent England. The old battles against, for example, child prostitution may have been largely won; but the fight to help the alcoholics and the homeless goes on. In its centenary year of 1965 a Salvation Army report found 400,000 children in need of love and care, 400,000 social misfits, and 675,000 old people who were underfed, lonely and cold. It traces 1,200 vanished husbands and 3,500 missing persons each year. Nobody else can or will do these thankless jobs.

To move with the times, the Army's eighth general, Frederick Coutts, urged that the gospel should be carried into the coffee bars and disco clubs. In four months the Sally Ann's own pop group, the Joystrings, were in the charts with their first record: 'It's an Open Secret'. The scheme illustrates perfectly the Army's knack of getting at people the Church is unable to reach. Booth refused an overture from the Archbishop of York to amalgamate. At first intent on turning his converts over to the churches, he found that churchwardens in fashionable parishes looked askance at worshippers without Sunday suits; and only one man in thirty at Booth's meetings even owned a collar.

Sausages   They range from the coarse-textured, spicy Cumberland, the veal-flavoured Oxford and the highly seasoned Cambridge to the meaty Gloucester, the herby Suffolk, and the mutton-based banger of Aberdeen. No doubt they do not seem as good as they once did; though in truth by law they must now contain 65 per cent meat if pork and at least half meat if not. There is a famous passage in Orwell* when he bites into a sausage and finds it disgustingly ersatz; it is in truth a homely index in the English subconscious of honesty; when the bangers* are off something is rotten in the state of England.

The Savoy   Though Claridge's is more discreet, the Connaught's cooking better, and the Ritz ritzier, most Englishmen asked to think of a great London hotel say the Savoy. This may be partly due to the pervasive folk memory from the days of early radio when the Savoy Orpheans under Debroy Somers and later Carroll Gibbons broadcast nightly on the pioneer station 2LO. Even if he has never crossed its threshold, your ordinary Englishman knows that the Savoy is the natural showbiz hostelry; the place where Noël Coward* sang 'Let's Do It' in cabaret and George Gershwin played for the first time in Europe his 'Rhapsody in Blue'.

Maybe it is this showbiz connection which gives the Savoy its American feel; but the times of the QE2 sailings in the lobby help. It must also please American hearts to know that the Savoy was the first hotel in England to have electric light, the first to install lifts, the first to have air conditioning. Quite separate from the technology, though, the Savoy people are renowned flatterers who keep a famous card-index system noting each guest's personal whims and preferences.

However, certain things are still not done, even in the breezy transatlantic world of the Savoy, and one is entering the bars or restaurants without a tie: but they keep a stock of ties to get you out of the jam.

It's not only Yanks who get the treatment. A Battle of Britain pilot left his hairbrushes there one hectic night in 1940, was shot down and taken prisoner next day. When he called for them in 1945 they were still there waiting for him – of course.

Scotland An Englishman, ruled the historian and Londoner Philip Guedalla, was a man who lived on an island in the North Sea governed by Scotsmen. There is just enough truth in the thrust to permit Englishmen a rueful laugh; and every Sassenach worth his salt knows Samuel Johnson's* celebrated crack about the noblest prospect a Scotsman ever sees being the high road that leads to England. Yet there is hard reason behind the pleasantries.

The Scots, under the inspiration of John Knox, have for centuries believed in comprehensive, compulsory, democratic and free education for all who can profit by it, and at the turn of the twentieth century, when only one English child in 1,300 was at a secondary school the corresponding figure for Scotland was one in two hundred: a ratio which only Prussia could then equal.

This great cornucopia of intelligence had no choice but to emigrate in order to be fulfilled; and Scots went to every corner of earth marked pink on the map to play key roles in servicing the British Raj. In politics the Scottish influence may not have been quite so charismatic as the Welsh, divided as it is between the great patrician Etonian Scots (Balfour, Home, Macmillan) and the working-class demagogues (Willie Gallacher, Jimmy Maxton, Keir Hardie, Ramsay MacDonald).

Yet the Scottish middle class is neglected at our peril, and its contribution to science and technology is massive. The Napiers founded marine engineering, Nasmyth devised the steam hammer, Macadam gave his name to modern roads, Dunlop to tyres. Lord Kelvin and James Clerk Maxwell dominated physics in their time; Alexander Graham Bell gave us the telephone and John Logie Baird has the best claim to be the inventor of television. And so on.

Yet the benefit of interaction between Scotland and England only slowly became clear. At the time of the Union in 1707 the London mail bag sometimes reached Edinburgh with only one letter in it. Scots looked to their old allies the French rather than the auld enemy England; Jacobite exiles lived in Italy and France; Presbyterian clergy and lawyers went to Dutch universities; Scottish merchants dealt with Holland and Scandinavia, but were excluded from trade with the English Colonies. Not any more though. The huge bonanza of North Sea oil and gas has brought new wealth to Scotland but not noticeably thinned the legions of Scotsmen who sit high in English places.

The Englishman finds the Scots less mercurial than his Irish and Welsh neighbours; duller, perhaps, but steadier and a sight less trouble. Scottish nationalists may occasionally do something romantic and dashing like purloining the Stone of Scone from Westminster Abbey; but they do not use arson like Welsh nationalists nor murder like the Irish. Besides, they have introduced him to one of his favourite games (golf*) and favourite tipples (whisky), a gill of which even Dr Johnson had to try on his Hebridean journey to see what it was that made a Scotsman happy. In this curiosity he had reason, for as P.G. Wodehouse* observed, it is never difficult to distinguish between a Scotsman with a grievance and a ray of sunshine.

The Season   Strictly, the period of the year during which a particular place is most frequented for business, fashion or amusement; especially the time (now May to June) when the fashionable world is assembled in London. That was how the *OED* defined it fifty years ago, and to most English people the definition made perfectly good sense then. Since then, however, the Season has mushroomed with bewildering speed until it is now quite possible to see a year-long cycle all the way from the rugby internationals at Twickenham in January to the hunting and shooting of December.

At one time any satisfactory definition of the Season would have involved the idea that some member of the royal family took part: the Queen at Ascot; Prince Philip at Cowes; Prince Charles at the Guards Polo Club in Windsor Great Park; the Kents at Wimbledon. And indeed they do lend glamour and focus to the traditional events in the old Season. They are not, however, so thick on the ground at more cerebral moments like the Royal Academy Summer Exhibition or Glyndebourne. They have, on the other hand, indelibly put their stamp on relatively new events in the Season like Badminton – now approaching its fiftieth year.

Just about every event in the Season involves the English predilection for dressing up (or down, against the weather) and indeed it might most elegantly be defined as the sum of all those parties to which the English wear fancy dress. It nearly always involves a contest (even at the Chelsea Flower Show, there is always keen interest in which rose or rhododendron will win first prize). And it always seems to involve lashings of drink: notably champagne. It has been fiercely argued recently that money is ruining the Season; but it has been doing that ever since the Russian Czarevitch wrote home in 1894 telling his mother, the Empress Marie, that the Prince of Wales was entertaining horse dealers. In fact, money makes the Season increasingly classless. Any bounder can hire a morning coat at Moss Bros; and many do.

The Seventies While it is clearly too soon to attempt a proper perspective on the decade, one perceptive writer, Christopher Booker, has argued already (in his book, *The Seventies*) that it was quite different in mood and meaning from all that had gone before in the century. Certainly there was a daunting crop of world-scale disasters. There was Watergate, and the first resignation in history of an American President. There was the ignominious débâcle in Vietnam, the rape of Cambodia, and the worst economic recession since the war. In Britain inflation rose to an appalling 27 per cent and the prime minister, Harold Wilson, so recently the new hope of the new left, now warned against 'a catastrophe of unimaginable proportions'.

The British people had to cope with a series of strikes by low-paid workers who, it was noticed too late, did jobs essential to the survival of any modern civilised state. Hospitals were closed, ambulances failed to run, water was shut off, sewage was untreated and bodies unburied. It was a bitter aftermath indeed to the 'Swinging Sixties'. Yet all decades can be shown to have spawned a string of catastrophes. The difference in the seventies, Booker argues, is that for the first time *homo sapiens* lost confidence in his ability to overcome material obstacles by his own innate intelligence: 'It was the decade when our bluff was called.'

In Britain this new mood found political expression in the election of a new conservative administration led by Margaret Hilda Thatcher, which embodied the precepts of the radical right: a massive swing away from the hegemony of central government and the shelter of the welfare state, towards private enterprise and self-help. The smack of firm government was heard in the land. The British people had opted for a dramatically new direction, and they had got it. How would it work out? No one knew; except, that is, the formidable dowager in one of Osbert Lancaster's inimitable cartoons. 'Mark my words,' she opined, ramrod-straight in her high-backed chair as the decade ended, 'The eighties will be worse. They always are.'

Sex   *No Sex Please, We're British* was the title of a West End comedy which ran for seventeen years. The joke was, of course, on the legions of foreign visitors, who flocked to see it; for what it meant was 'Oodles of sex, please, we're British'. As we have already noted under *Love*, the Brits have some claim to be the randiest race on earth, and celebrate their partiality on St Valentine's Day* with a profusion of printed erotica unknown anywhere else. Nightly on British television sexual themes are explored, sexual references insinuated, and sexual jokes cracked that would bring on instant cardiac arrest in the higher echelons of broadcasting on the other side of the Atlantic. The raunchy end of the Sunday papers dissect the amatory follies with a gusto no other press can approach in scale; while in most newsagents now whole shelves of girlie magazines compete for favour with the still popular coloured seaside postcards, garnished with the bums and tits of yore.

The English language serves the English predilection nobly. Take, for example, 'a bit of the other', first noted in Joyce's *Ulysses* where the context perhaps explains how it arose: 'They would be just good friends like a big brother and sister without all that other.' D.H. Lawrence shows the line of thought even more clearly in *Lady Chatterley's Lover.* 'She loved me to talk to her and kiss her ... But the other, she just didn't want.' However the average Englishman has forgotten the context if he knew it and uses the phrase as a bit of humorous and arcane code. It predates the permissive society, which demolished the barricades between the one thing and the other, and may therefore be doomed; though the thrust of mocking allusion is a powerful one in modern English.

Then there is the racy phrase 'to have it away', an interesting example of a phrase changing its sense in mid-journey. Modern usage in either sense, it is first noted by the *OED Supplement* as late as 1958 as criminal slang for escaping from prison. Even more recently though, and first in 1970, the *OED* notes its use in the sense of making love. Quite possibly the term went over the points through a simple misunderstanding. Did you have it (while you were) away? In any event, the sexual use now seems to be winning. Is it, though, quite such an anonymous affair as Germaine Greer suggests in *The Female Eunuch*? 'The vocabulary of impersonal sex is peculiarly desolating,' she complains. 'Who wants to have it away?' One would have thought she would have known. Increasingly, though, the phrase suggests not so much apathy as abandon.

Sometimes, though, the wholesale revolution of the English sexual behaviour leaves words stranded. 'Are yer coortin'?' Wilfred Pickles, the BBC's token northerner, used to ask on the air, thus eliciting gales of giggles. Still, that was already a long time ago, and such a query today might well be greeted by blank incomprehension: cohabiting is fast replacing courting and the old convention of the front parlour where young couples of the respectable classes got to know each other between kisses has been usurped by the galvanised gavotte of the disco. Whether this is an advance is anybody's guess. Another enchanting term from the vanished era of courtship is 'walking out': the custom by which young servant girls were allowed to take a stroll with their beaux on Sunday afternoons. The phrase has however been borrowed by the sophisticated young to mean a riotous and usually illicit affair. Their walking out now means they're having it away, like everyone else in modern England.

Shakespeare, William (1564–1616) To his contemporaries he is gentle, sweet, and honey-tongued Shakespeare. A fellow actor leaves him a ring for remembrance. 'I loved the man', says his great coeval, rival and friend Ben Jonson, 'and honour his memory this side idolatry.'

What kind of man? Someone obsessed with the fragility of life, the transience of beauty and the brevity of love. A man who found sleep elusive: night and day blurring into one fevered dream. A man, above all, haunted by the pervasive and sinister menace of Time.

He returns to the charge again and again. Time, he cries, is a bloody tyrant. Time is sluttish, devouring, thieving. He shakes his fist: 'No Time, thou shalt not boast that I do change ... thy Registers and thee I both defy.' He has a sovereign remedy: his own words. 'So long as men can breathe or eyes can see / So long lives this, and this gives life to thee.'

He speaks to us directly as the living, breathing, suffering man – I, Shakespeare – only in the Sonnets. We are compelled to listen. The finest among them reach for perfection and sometimes touch it. They contain a naked testimony of passion and loss which comes to us at white heat over the centuries. They are made in a quick forge. They hold the distillation of life and the quintessence of love.

What nightmare he was living as he poured them out we can only conjecture. We must hope that he came through the storm to calmer seas. ('Poets are tough', Auden* reminds us, 'and can profit from the most dreadful experiences.') Shakespeare had a sure sense of his own power and destiny: 'Your monument shall be my gentle verse / Which eyes not yet created shall oe'r read.' He has held his great argument with Time; and won.

Shaw, Bernard (1856–1950)   In his will, Shaw stipulated that for the first twenty-one years after his death his royalties should be devoted to the new alphabet which had long obsessed him. Then they were to be divided among three institutions which had rendered him much service: the British Museum, the National Gallery of Ireland, and the Royal Academy of Dramatic Art. (He liked to say, with some truth, that he had been educated by wandering around galleries and museums in his youth.) The three residual beneficiaries took the alphabet to court on the grounds that it was not in the public interest. In the end the alphabet got £8,300. A competition was held, and *Androcles and the Lion* was duly set in the resulting version. The three were then free to split Shaw's royalties, which have lightened their load now for nearly half a century. Such is the thrall of Shaw nearly fifty years after his death.

Yet it was not till he was forty-eight that he began to gain authority in the West End theatre (America had recognised his worth much earlier). He thought he was a novelist, and before turning to the stage wrote five books, which are now largely unread. He had already proved himself an elegant and incisive music and theatre critic. His correspondence with the actress Mrs Patrick Campbell, a woman who could match him line for line as a wit, is an abiding delight. 'It's too late to do anything but accept you and love you,' she wrote to him in 1912, 'but when you were a little boy somebody ought to have said hush just once.'

Though we see what she was driving at, we would not nowadays require too much hush from Shaw: the fact that the West End stage still thrives on a steady diet of Shaw plays is testimony enough not just to his genius but also to his skill as an entertainer. Plays like *Pygmalion* have been turned into films, into musicals (*My Fair Lady*) and then into filmed musicals. Despite the changing shape of society, his rapier still goes home. 'All professions are conspiracies against the laity' is as true now as it was when he first wrote it. 'Assassination is the extreme form of censorship' has a chillingly modern ring.

What distinguishes the wit in Shaw – what lends it that clean edge and sharp glitter – is his gift of verbal counter-point. 'I wouldn't have your conscience, not for all your income,' cries Peter Shirley, the down-and-out, to Undershaft, the munitions millionaire in *Major Barbara*. 'I wouldn't have your income, not for all your conscience,' returns Undershaft courteously, and there is no more to be said.

The most celebrated opportunity for this coruscating counterpoint was offered him on a plate by a mysterious lady writing from Zurich. 'You have the greatest brain in the world, and I have the most beautiful body; so we ought to produce the most perfect child,' she proposed. To this there was only one possible riposte. 'What,' inquired Shaw, 'if the child inherits my body and your brains?' The English have cause yet again to give heartfelt thanks for their Irish writers. 'He hasn't an enemy in the world, but is intensely disliked by all his friends,' quipped his contemporary Oscar Wilde. Not true, actually, but the epigram sits well on Shaw's bony shoulders. He was a vegetarian most of his life. 'God help us if he would ever eat a beef-steak,' opined Mrs Patrick Campbell.

'I delighted in Shaw, the formidable man,' wrote William Butler Yeats. 'He could hit my enemies, and the enemies of those I loved, as I could never hit, as no living author that was dear to me could ever hit.' Those hits still go home, night after night, all over the civilised world, and the royalties rattle in to the museum, the gallery and the academy. Indeed, student fees at RADA would be double without Shaw's bequest. That would have delighted him. 'The trouble, Mr Goldwyn,' he wrote to the movie mogul, declining to sell him his screen rights, 'is that you are only interested in art and I am interested only in money.'

Shopkeepers   A nation of shopkeepers, opined Napoleon of the English with some truth; but the jibe no longer has any force (if it ever did). After all, Margaret Thatcher's father was a grocer. True, retail trade has become socially acceptable only as the century has advanced (Raymond Asquith, himself a prime minister's son, complained bitterly about having to hob-nob with retail tobacconists at country house parties in Edwardian England) but the right kind of shop has been a chic side-line for the upper class since after the First World War (Victoria Sackville-West's mother opened a hat shop).

Indeed, with the patina acquired by long years of affluence and patronage some stores, like Harrods* and Fortnums* have become centres of chic in themselves, while eminent shopkeepers like the Marks and Spencer* and Sainsbury* families have played an attractive role in the social and artistic life of the country. Gradually, however, with the rise of the supermarket, the small trader, satirised so memorably by Dickens* and H.G. Wells, is being driven out of business – or is selling out to a new wave of talented Indian immigrants prepared to invest time and effort on a scale no English shopkeeper would contemplate. (See *Mr Patel.*)

Sir and Madam   Once in continuous use between male equals (see Boswell's *Life of Samuel Johnson* passim) 'sir' is now used in that context only in slightly obsolete mockery ('my dear sir') or emphasis ('yes SIR').

It is used by retailers soliciting custom and parliamentary candidates soliciting votes, but decreasingly now as a mark of social deference.

Professor Alan Ross, in his celebrated essay on *U and Non U*, remarked that he kept 'sir' only for men of great age and/or distinction. Even here it rather depends on the man. Thus, most Englishmen would have had no great difficulty in calling Harold Macmillan, at ninety, sir, while few would have found it necessary so to address the chummy Emanuel Shinwell, who was nearly ten years his senior.

It is generally thought unnecessary for women to address men as sir except in shops, and contrariwise, the language is deficient in a word with which to address great ladies. 'Ma'am' (rhyming with charm) is reserved solely now for royal females, and 'madam' too is obsolete outside shops. Thus Mrs Thatcher could be addressed only by her full name or as 'Prime Minister'. Perhaps the reluctance to use madam stems from its other meanings: as the owner of a brothel or a hoity-toity female – 'she's a proper little madam'. Similarly 'madam shops', boutiques selling ready-to-wear to older women, pre-empt the ground.

On the other hand, in informal situations (restaurants, buses, pubs) the English now increasingly address each other without the slightest embarrassment as *love* (or *luv* in the north) while a young girl can now be addressed without offence by older men in similar contexts as *dear* or even *darling*. So much for the allegedly icy island race.

The Sixties Those who say decades do not have characters of their own face a dilemma in explaining away the sixties. For nothing could be more idiosyncratic and separate, original and different than that decade. It began with the election of a charismatic new American president, John F. Kennedy, who seemed to symbolise and embody all the shining hope of a new Camelot. It was soon garnished and seasoned at home by the birth of the new satire movement: the pyrotechnic debut of the four unfairly gifted young men who brought *Beyond The Fringe* from Edinburgh to London, and placed a conceptual bomb under all the old shibboleths: patriotism, religion, monarchy.

This anarchic tidal wave was quickly transmuted into a television mode of unquantifiable power as *That Was The Week That Was*; a weekly snook cocked at the Establishment with great vim, under the benevolent aegis of the new and libertarian director general of the BBC, Hugh Carleton Greene, whose term of office in that key job ran with almost runic precision from 1960–1969. It was the decade when Rachmanism – the strong-arm eviction of slum tenants – was first revealed to an astonished nation; and when the Great Train Robbery created a new race of anti-heroes, some of whom flourish outside bars to this day.

It was the decade of Dr Strangelove and Dr Beeching. It was the era when the London Hilton was built, Mary Quant made a million, and the new liberal, concerned, middle class, affluent yet faintly absurd in their self-questioning self-deprecation, took up residence in London's NW1. It saw the launch of the colour supplement*, the birth of the drug culture, the advent of flower power, the cult of youth, the craze for the mini-skirt, and the jackpot for Carnaby Street and Kings Road. The high octane roar of the E-type Jaguar* was the most characteristic sound of the decade.

It was the era that saw Gaitskell's death and Macmillan's resignation; politically in England it was the high summer of Harold Wilson and the white-hot heat of technological advance he proclaimed from the commanding heights of the economy. It was the era that first heard the plangent minor chords of the most potent popular sound the world has ever known: the songs of four Liverpool* troubadours who called themselves The Beatles*.

It was high noon for the new wave of fashion photographers, born in the East End of London, who soared to fame through the phallic power of their camera lenses. Brian Duffy, Terence Donavan, and David Bailey were earning £100,000 a year between them when the pound was a pound, and had in their *macho* tow some of the most scrumptious models in christendom. It must also be said that it was the era of the Profumo scandal and the great spy sensations – Philby, Blake, Vassall – mirrored in the scarcely less real world of the top spy writers – Deighton, Le Carré, and Fleming*.

It was the heyday too of the psychopathic East End arch-criminals: the Krays and the Richardsons. All these seamy underworld figures moved easily and without comment in and out of polite society; there was a surrealistic feel to life that was exemplified by the launch of the Monty Python show. The slow motion death of Jack Kennedy on the Magruder movie film and the meaningless agony of Vietnam on everyone's colour television confirmed the diagnosis: the western world had suffered a collective nervous breakdown; from which even the phlegmatic English were not immune.

Soho   When this book first appeared, it looked as if Soho's number was up. It had become one of the most desolate parts of London. A wilderness of amusement arcades and sex shops had swallowed up the bookshops and *ateliers;* and the *Good Food Guide* could recommend just one of its restaurants. The change in the last few years has been dramatic and heartening. New laws have pushed the sex shops out. New restaurants have opened up; notably Alastair Little, a brilliant English chef, in Frith Street; Bistrot Bruno, with its minimal design and hearty helpings; and Soho Soho, with its French Mediterranean food providing, as the *Good Food Guide* noted, a welcome taste of Provence on a cold and dreary Monday night. Meanwhile, the Gay Hussar still cooks mightily for the lunchers of the left, while the Escargot flourishes under its cool and colourful new ownership. Peter Boizot, who runs the Pizza Express group, has shown how to roll with the punches by turning Kettner's, once a trad, plush place patronised by Edward VII, into a crowded and popular pizza house. The Venice in Peril fund still gets 20p for each Veneziana sold. So there's life in the old place yet.

Spender, Sir Stephen (1909–95)   When he was made a knight in the 1983 Birthday Honours list, it was objected by one detractor that he had not written one memorable line of poetry. This is demonstrably untrue. 'I think continually of those who were truly great' is a magnificent opening line which resurfaces constantly.

By outliving his contemporaries – Auden*, MacNeice*, Day Lewis – Spender had to accept a curious foreshortening in the look of his work. Broadly speaking, most of his best poetry was written by the end of the war, but since then he has done excellent work as critic and teacher. Nor should we forget that he was joint founder and co-editor with Cyril Connolly* of that required reading for the age of longing, the literary magazine *Horizon*, and fourteen years co-editor of *Encounter* too.

With his strong Liberal background, part-Jewish ancestry, doughty anti-fascist record, curiously appropriate war service (in the London fire service) and consistent decency, Spender, though perhaps not so truly great as his dead friends Wystan and Louis, has signed the vivid air with his own honour.

Spitfire   '... The machine was sweeter to handle than any other that I had known. I put it through every manoeuvre that I knew of and it responded beautifully. I ended with two flick rolls and turned for home. I was filled with a sudden exhilarating confidence. I could fly a Spitfire, in any position I was its master. It remained to be seen whether I could fight in one.'

So said Richard Hillary* RAF fighter pilot in the Battle of Britain, who went on to prove he could. Nearly nineteen thousand Spitfires were built; its grace, delicacy and speed were never in doubt. It owed its thoroughbred qualities to its descent from the racing aircraft designed by R.J. Mitchell for the Schneider Trophy. Just as Sidney Camm and his team at Hawker's went ahead with the Hurricane* without waiting for government blessing, so Mitchell at Supermarine first built a fighter to Air Ministry specifications, found it mediocre, scrapped it, and built the exquisite aircraft he wanted on his own initiative.

The Spitfire began its career with a speed of 346 m.p.h. and went on to an eventual maximum of 460 m.p.h. The wing was an almost perfect ellipse; there were no excrescences. The engine was completely cowled and the radiator little more than a slot under the starboard wing. The eight guns made it as lethal as it was lovely.

The early versions were delicate and sensitive, later marques sophisticated and dangerous. The danger to the enemy came from the improved weaponry; to the pilot from the extra power in the Griffon engine which, mishandled, could turn it on its back with sometimes fatal consequences at low altitudes. Later, that problem was ironed out. The Spitfire was a triumph; and the most renowned fighter to fly in the Second World War.

Spoonerisms So called after Warden Spooner of New College, Oxford, who really did announce a hymn one day in chapel as 'Kinquering Kongs their Titles Take.' He was an albino, and suffered from a slight speech impediment which, lovingly proliferated among generations of undergraduates (he was at New College for sixty-two years), gave a new word to the language.

Almost certainly he never perpetrated any of the legions of spoonerisms coined after his initial lapse. That is, he did not, alas, really say: 'You have tasted two whole worms, you have hissed all my mystery lectures: you must leave by the town drain.' Nor did he ever propose the health of our Queer Old Dean.

Yet he has another claim to our respect and affection; for during his wardenship (1903–24), and largely at his instance, a plaque was put up in the college chapel which read: 'In memory of the men of this college who coming from a foreign land entered into the inheritance of this place and returning fought and died for their country in the war 1914–19.' Three German names follow.

Spring The most treacherous of English seasons – providing perennial short measure and dashing uncounted high hoped: April is the cruellest month. However, there is a subdivision of spring which might most properly be called the fifth English season. It is what H.E. Bates called the sudden spring: that moment when the English countryside is caught by surprise and spring breaks a month before its time. When this happens,

Bates remarked, 'the English have the occasional satisfaction of gathering flowers long before people living a thousand miles to the south of them'.

On the February day (in 1941 during the bleakest stretch of the war) when he wrote that: 'The grass was luminous with rain and from daybreak there was a bright call of birdsong everywhere. Thrushes sang without rest, and even a cock chaffinch lifted a warm claret breast to the sun ... leafless crocuses, pale mauve touched with fawn and small alpine anemones, pink and white, were pushing away the drifts of light sepia oak leaves ... here and there a touch of vivid blue, an early grape hyacinth showed up an eye of magenta-purple, a primula pushing up from wine-veined leaves.'

He concludes that in England, spring, like summer, has no official date, as in other countries. Indeed, the seasons interweave, and he sees the winter as a series of miniature springtimes. Here, perhaps, is the true explanation of spring's persistent elusiveness in England: is it not a season in its own right, but a sport of all the others; a love-child of winter, a decoy used by summer; a *Doppelganger* of autumn.

Squash Just as cricket* has been called chess on grass, so squash has been called chess played fast. A descendant of rackets and fives, archetypal public schools games, squash has now spread to all classes and most countries, and is one of the most concentrated modes of taking exercise in huge dollops known to man; and yet another legacy to the pantheon of sports devised by the island race.

Stock Exchange 'A low wretch who makes money by buying and selling shares in funds', Samuel Johnson* wrote of the jobber in his Dictionary, and the broker has not done much better, being associated in the English mind principally with a certain kind of house; a large, comfortable place in the stockbroker belt or outer suburbs with manicured lawns and a name like Seven Acres, built in the Edwardian era in a style known as stockbroker Tudor.

The Stock Exchange is renowned for its chauvinism (women were not admitted till 1973, foreigners in 1971), for its cliquishness, and for being the principle source of improper stories. Orwell* predicted its abolition; instead, it has grown steadily more technical and remote, dealing increasingly with the big institutions who now account for ninety per cent of the business in gilts and two-thirds of all the trade in equities.

There are nevertheless thought to be still some two million private investors in the country, but little is heard of them until they are courted in a takeover bid, one of those moments in English life when sporting considerations are put on one side and the English businessman is seen at his most steely, ruthless, venal and greedy.

Suburbs   They are the great undiscovered areas of England. They have attracted little literature, and hardly any art. Whoever wrote a symphony to a suburb? They have no real past, and no clear future. They are homogenised politically, economically, culturally and racially. Frederic Raphael put the point well in *The Glittering Prizes*: 'I come from suburbia ...I don't ever want to go back. It's the one place in the world that's further away than anywhere else.'

So the aspiring suburban young head for the inner city, where they will find jobs, contacts, ideas, money, power; perhaps even fame; but at the very least excitement. When they have carved out their piece of pie they will move right out far beyond the suburbs, to the deep country again. The suburbs are thus the one part of England no one is proud to be coming from. It is one thing to hail from Sherborne or Smethwick, suggesting as they do tranquil rural arcadia on the one hand, or gritty northern reality on the other, and quite another to come from Surbiton or Sutton which seem to stand for nothing.

But is it quite as simple as that? Where did these suburban millions come from, thronging the mock Tudor houses along the great and ghastly ribbon developments of the thirties? From agricultural labour and domestic service, to turn the cogs of the great banks and insurance companies of the City of London just before the computers came; conventional, law-abiding, aspiring men and their wives. Unconscious exemplars of the territorial imperative, they put fences round their little plots and filled them with flowers. They lived, worked, loved, played, dreamed and died there, these New Pooters; nine million nobodys. Perhaps one day they will be noticed.

Suffolk   Though it has its fair claim to poets (George Crabbe, Thomas Nashe, Edward Fitzgerald) the flat brooding landscape and wide dreaming skies of Suffolk have worked potently on the imagination of two English painters and one English musician of genius. Benjamin Britten was born at Lowestoft and died at Aldeburgh, where with his friend Peter Pears he had instituted a world-famous music festival and built a splendid concert hall in the Maltings at nearby Snape. He used local themes and characters in his work, most notably in his opera *Peter Grimes*, whose first night was a triumph in the annals of English music to rank with the début of Elgar's *Enigma Variations*. Yet the visual thrall of Suffolk has been the most remarkable of all.

John Constable, greatest English landscape painter of the nineteenth century, declared roundly that it was the Suffolk countryside in which he grew up which had made him into a painter. As the *Dictionary of National Biography* records, he was 'the first to paint the greenness and moisture of his native country, the first to paint the noon sunshine with its white light pouring down through the leaves and sparkling in the foliage and the grass ... the first to paint truly the sun-shot clouds of a showery sky, the first to represent faithfully the rich colours of an English landscape ... the first to suggest so fully not only the sights but the sounds of nature, the gurgle of the water, the rustle of the trees.'

Gainsborough, his great precursor, bore the same testimony to the spell of that hypnotically empty landscape. Sent to his uncle's grammar school, he spent all his holidays sketching, and declared that there was not 'a picturesque clump of trees, nor even a single tree of any beauty, no, nor a hedgerow, stem or post' in or around his native town of Sudbury in Suffolk that was not from his earliest years treasured in his memory.

To this day people visiting old Suffolk market towns like Lavenham with its characteristic orange-washed half-timbered houses, and un-spoiled Suffolk fishing villages like Orford, are taken by their sense of isolation and preoccupation; not so much with time past as time lost; and the country between these dreamlike places still retains that other-worldly aura which moved Gainsborough in his time, Constable in his, and Britten in ours.

Summer   'Summer has set in with its usual severity,' wrote Samuel Taylor Coleridge, thus encapsulating what every Englishman knows: that summer's lease hath all too short a date. Indeed, there is a curious short circuit in the Englishman's mind which allows him to believe that summer does not really exist: or rather that it used to exist but has recently become extinct. Every Englishman remembers the great summers of the past and most noticeably, even if he was not alive at the time, the summers of 1914 and 1939. 'Before the war, and especially before the Boer War, it was summer all the year round,' remarked George Orwell*.

The hard reality behind this myth is that the capricious English climate dishes up vile and sweet weather with an impartial hand; in 1975 snow stopped play at a game of cricket in June, while the next year a temperature of 110 degrees Fahrenheit on the centre court at Wimble-don caused four hundred spectators to faint. Given these baffling parameters, the English have simply elected to *pretend* that summer will come and have put the Derby* and Royal Ascot* in June, Henley* and the British Open in July, Cowes Week and the Glorious Twelfth in August.

Sometimes, of course, these high festivals of alfresco England take place in torrential monsoons and sometimes in a glinting glory of summer sun. The English mind then simply erases all the former experiences from the tape of memory and joins up the others to make up one vast, collective recall of shimmering heat, strawberries and cream, and hearts at peace under an English heaven. 'Summer afternoon – summer afternoon', said Henry James, 'to me those have always been the most beautiful words in the English language.'

The Sun   It started life as the *Daily Herald*, the voice of trade unionism in Britain. In the 1930s it had the largest daily sale in the country; but was going downhill steadily when the Mirror Group bought Odhams Press, which owned it, in 1961. In 1964 Hugh Cudlipp, chairman of Mirror Newspapers, masterminded a major revamp in which the *Herald* was renamed the *Sun*. At that point it was still selling 1,500,000; but even throwing the union allegiance overboard had no effect on its fortunes. By 1969 it was down to 850,000 and had cost its new owners £12 million. It was sold to Rupert Murdoch for under a million pounds. When the first copy of the *Sun* under Murdoch was delivered to Cudlipp, smudgily printed and full of literals, he shouted: 'We've nothing to worry about.' Within a year the *Sun's* circulation had doubled; and today stands at 3.97 million to the *Mirror's* 2.4 million. This astonishing turnabout has been achieved by jettisoning the *Mirror* theory that the day of the working class tabloid was over and something far more sophisticated was needed. The *Sun* thrives on shameless hedonism (best symbolised by the topless daily page three girl), chauvinism (its headlines during the Argentine war included STICK IT UP YOUR JUNTA) and populism. It is against inherited wealth, the House of Lords, public schools and Oxbridge. It is not so much pro-Tory as passionately populist. It believes in putting across its message in the vernacular. When the church of England decided to allow homosexual clergymen to continue their ministry, its front page proclaimed: PULPIT POOFS TO STAY. It can also headline stories of mind-bending nullity: FREDDIE STARR ATE MY HAMSTER. It gives blanket coverage to television and sport. Its vast success is achieved with few big by-lines (as the *Mirror* in its heyday starred Cassandra and Marjorie Proops), but it is a tightly edited paper dominated by its back bench of key production executives. Its most famous editor, Kelvin Mackenzie, boasted just one O level; but the *Sun* still has a minor genius for knowing what that man in the street wants.

Sunday It has had a bad press in England; not unnaturally, for in the racial folk memory its traditional melancholy is pervasive. 'Bugger Sunday, I say,' declares Gregory Gladwell, the forty-four-year-old black-smith in Ronald Blythe's modern classic *Akenfield*. He did not use the words lightly: he was born in 1925, but could remember people in the village as recently as the thirties going to chapel at nine in the morning and not coming home till eight at night. 'It's a fact. They were nothing but a lot of bloody hypocrites. Suffolk used to worship Sunday, not God.'

Even among the godless, the English Sunday hardly sounded more attractive; it was the time, as Alan Bennett wrote in *Forty Years On,* for washing the car, tinned peaches and Carnation Milk. It was also, certainly in the working class, the time to send the children off to Sunday School in the afternoon and use their absence to procreate some more.

However, all these stereotypes are dissolving as religion weakens its hold and affluence seeps through the land. You have, for a start, a choice no other country can offer, of eight national newspapers delivered to the door. They range from some of the very worst to some of the very best in the world, and you will be reclusive indeed if you find nothing in any of them to interest you. At noon the pubs* will open to receive you and now are empowered to stay open all day. A few jars of ale or gin and tonic will fortify you for the roast beef and Yorkshire pud* of old England and then if the garden* does not call there are museums and galleries, fishing* or football*, concerts or cricket*.

When evening comes you will be a dullard indeed if nothing can hold your interest in the four national television stations and four BBC radio channels, not to mention the cornucopia of the satellites. Then, thanks to the great family of Patel* you can shop all day long as if it were a weekday. The great superstores open on Sunday too: not much fun for shopworkers, highly convenient for working mums. If you have a rotten Sunday in England nowadays you frankly have only yourself to blame.

Sussex Though Sussex has its fair share of famous sons (Cobden, Shelley) and associations (H.G. Wells went to Midhurst Grammar School; Keats began 'The Eve of St Agnes' at Chichester), it has two stentorian champions: Belloc and Kipling. Hilaire Belloc lived from 1906 till his death in 1953 at King's Land in Shipley, West Sussex, a house dating from the 15th century. Much of his immense *oeuvre* – verse, essays, novels, and history – was written here, and it was no doubt of this house that he was thinking when he wrote in 'The South Country', his great hymn to Sussex: 'If I ever become a rich man / Or if ever I grow to be old / I will build a house with a deep thatch / To shelter me from the cold / And

there shall the Sussex songs be sung / And the story of Sussex told.'
Belloc never became a rich man, though he became an old one, and the
house at Shipley never had thatch, though it had stunning views of the
Sussex downs. But here the story of Sussex was undoubtedly told.

Kipling bought Bateman's at Burwash in Sussex in 1902 and lived there
till he died in 1936. Here he wrote *Puck of Pook's Hill* – he could see the
hill of the title from the house – *Rewards and Fairies* and *A School
History of England.* Here, too, he wrote his most quoted poem, 'If', and
'The Glory of the Garden', most recently quoted by Sir William
Rees-Mogg, Chairman of the Arts Council, with some effect in his report
on the future spending policy. Kipling also weighed in with his own
hymn to Sussex: 'God gives all men all earth to love / But since men's
hearts are small / Ordained for each one spot shall prove / Beloved over
all / Each to his choice, and I rejoice / This lot has fallen to me / In a fair
ground – in a fair ground / Yea, Sussex by the Sea.' With two lyricists of
this power, Sussex has scant need for public relations men.

Tarzan   What is a healthy outdoor all-American hero like Tarzan doing in an English companion? Tarzan was, of course, an Englishman, indeed, an English aristocrat: heir to Lord Greystoke when shipwrecked as a baby and left to be brought up by the apes; later he succeeded to the title. He is not the first member of the House of Lords to swing from a rope, though we must trust he will be the last.

Taylor, A.J.P. (1906–90)   He was the epitome of an English radical. He never appeared in a New Year or Birthday Honours List and may well have turned down the invitation. He was not honoured by his old university of Oxford with either a chair or an honorary degree (though both his old colleges there made him an honorary fellow). No matter. His distinction came not from what others made of him but from being his own man: a Lancashire cotton merchant's son, born to wealth, liberalism, nonconformism and conscientious objection, who became historian to the man in the street, the first academic to find fame on television, and the only one to give a half-hour lecture without note or prompter.

He wrote some thirty books, including a highly engaging autobiography in which he manfully interweaved the tangled story of his private life and three marriages (his first wife Margaret fell hopelessly in love with both Robert Kee and Dylan Thomas). His most notable book, though, is his volume in the Oxford History of England, *English History 1914–1945*. He very nearly gave up when he got to 1931, depressed by the bleak politics of the era, when his bosom friend Beaverbrook* simply got out of his chair one night and walked up and down, talking off the cuff so compellingly about the men and issues – Baldwin ('what a rascal'), the Hoare Laval plan, the Abdication – that Taylor, shamed, took up his pen again.

It is the only one of the fifteen Oxford volumes to tell its story through the lives of ordinary people and was well called by Max Beloff a populist history. The style is crisp, racy, idiosyncratic. The last paragraph gives a vivid taste of the whole; of great learning lightly worn: 'In the second world war the British people came of age. This was a people's war. Not only were their needs considered. They themselves wanted to win ... The British Empire declined; the condition of the people improved. Few now sang "Land of Hope and Glory". Few even sang "England Arise". England had risen all the same.'

Tea   The English national drink has evolved its own rites and myths. Thus, there is the snobbery over whether the milk goes in first or not. It makes a better mix if it does, but is not deemed quite OK socially – the point is memorably made by John Betjeman* in his celebrated poem 'How to Get On in Society' where the wretched *nouveau riche* lady, having already committed any number of howlers, asks, 'Milk and then just as it comes dear?' There is the snobbery over which tea to use, Earl Grey being decidedly upmarket and China tea smarter than Indian. There is the snobbery which says tea after lunch* or dinner is decidedly socially inferior to coffee.

Tea has been a social catalyst in England for three hundred years, though the teashop is no older than the 1880s, when an enterprising ABC manageress, finding her friends enjoyed coming to the back of her shop for a cup of tea, put the table in front, thus launching a nationwide vogue. The tea-dance of the twenties seemed to have died, but is now having a spirited revival; to meet it Lyons recently reopened one of their flagships, the old prewar Corner Houses that seemed to have gone under with 78 r.p.m. records and double-breasted suits. Indeed, up and down England, inflation has driven people back to the teashop from the restaurant; to that calorific cornucopia that ranges from Westmorland parkin, rum nicky and Bakewell tart in the north, through cream teas in the Cotswolds, cucumber sandwiches in the Thames valley, and Lincolnshire shortbread in East Anglia to the toasted crumpets, home-made scones and buttered muffins of the south.

Whatever the vagaries of fashion in English tea-drinking, however, one institution remains inviolable and rock-solid: the early morning cuppa which dissolves sleep and prepares the Englishman for the day ahead.

Traditionally and quite properly made by the man in the house, it has clarified the minds of great generals like Monty who worked out his battle plans while sipping his char, and soothed the hangovers of equally great and only slightly fictional characters like Bertie Wooster.

Team Spirit   Though the principle itself clearly goes back to Arnold and the kind of public school he engendered with its aura of muscular religion, cold baths and loyalty to house, school and country, the phrase itself is curiously little chronicled. Indeed in the *OED Supplement* it is first supported by a quotation as recently as 1928, and then in an industrial context. Frank Muir was much nearer the mark when in 1976 he wrote of schools 'sending forth … superbly fit chaps, light on imagination but strong on team spirit'.

Perhaps the most absurd yet memorable extension of team spirit to real life occurs in Sir Henry Newbolt's poem 'Vitaë Lampada' with its celebrated opening: 'There's a breathless hush in the Close tonight'. There was, that summer evening, as every Englishman knows, a bumping pitch and blinding light, ten to make and the last man in. 'And it's not for the sake of a ribboned coat, / Or the selfish hope of a season's fame / But his Captain's hand on his shoulder smote / Play up! Play up! and play the game!'

Whether in truth a captain at Clifton, Newbolt's old school, would ever have uttered words so monumentally daft at such a moment is hard, a hundred years on, to know. What is quite certain is that the scene in the second stanza, where the action has shifted to some desperate outpost of the Raj, is simply not credible. 'The sand of the desert is sodden red / Red with the wreck of a square that broke / The Gatling's jammed and the Colonel dead / And the regiment blind with dust and smoke.'

Things look pretty grim. England's far, and Honour a name. 'But the voice of a schoolboy rallies the ranks / "Play up! Play up! and play the game!"' This is intolerable. Newbolt never heard a shot fired in anger or he would hardly have perpetrated such patent balderdash. Nevertheless the absurdity, set in the aspic of the age when it was written, was to bring him instant fame. He was made a Companion of Honour, won honorary degrees from Bristol, Glasgow, St Andrew's, Sheffield, Toronto, Oxford and Cambridge, and the esteem of such eminent contemporaries as Robert Bridges, A.J. Balfour, H.G. Wells and Sir Edward Grey. He died in 1938, full of years and honour: but would not have been so honoured in modern England.

This is not because teams have ceased to exert loyalties, but because to spell out such allegiances publicly is to invite your team's belly laugh.

When Montgomery, at an Eighth Army reunion soon after the war, urged his former troops to remember in peace the tow-ropes they had used in the desert (only owing to an unfortunate impediment he called them tow-wopes) he got a ribald response. This is not to say that no Desert Rat would never extend a tow-rope to another, only that he would not want the gesture, or the frame of mind, ratified and promulgated.

Team spirit, in short, has become a rather private matter, in England, referred to allusively, almost apologetically. The only exception to this rule of modern English life occurs in the 'team talk', a dire American importation in which international teams are worked into a state of perfervid excitement by an impassioned address just before the game. The Welsh, with their passion for the *hwl*, are past masters at the team talk and it is said that an address by the former rugby star turned BBC boss, Cliff Morgan, in which the welfare of wives and families was invoked, would cause men to try to break down the doors to get at the opposition. However, the English are shy about such naked displays of emotion, and reluctant to talk about either 'team spirit' or the 'team talk' which is said to engender it.

Tennis Originally a game for bored monks, real – or more properly royal – tennis, an indoor cult game now played at only a handful of clubs in America and England by dedicated enthusiasts, seems to have been transmogrified into lawn tennis at Hampton Court. Here there had long been (and still is) a real tennis court; but those waiting for a game began to amuse themselves by knocking a tennis ball around on the lawns outside. Certainly a rudimentary form of lawn tennis was played in the sixteenth century, for the pleasure of Queen Elizabeth I, by servants of the Earl of Hertford in Somerset. However, as in so many sports, it was left to the Victorians to put the modern game on the map.

In 1872 two Birmingham enthusiasts called Gem and Pereira, abetted by two local doctors, set up the first lawn tennis club at the Manor House Hotel in Leamington Spa. It was two years later that a Major Wingfield applied to patent the game of lawn tennis, which he at first envisaged as being played on an hour-glass court. This curious shape was supported by the MCC who at that stage still had some parental authority over the new game. In that same year, however, the All England Croquet Club began to play lawn tennis, and the MCC's days as controllers were numbered. In 1877 the *Field* magazine put up twenty-five guineas for a new cup to be played for at the All England Club, and a sub-committee was set up to modify the rules. What they decided still governs the shape of modern tennis: a rectangular court 78 by 27 feet, with a net lowered to

3 feet 3 inches at the centre, thus giving to the fearsomely fast server the early advantage which has never really deserted him.

Wimbledon*, despite all the tantrums and rows, remains the mecca of the game; but it is played at all levels and in all parts of England by English people of all ages and kinds. It has never been more lovingly enshrined than in the poem 'A Subaltern's Love Song' by John Betjeman*, where the laureate imagined himself taking on one of those archetypal outdoor girls who is much too good for him: 'Love thirty, Love forty, Oh weakness of joy / The speed of a swallow, the grace of a boy ... How mad I am, glad I am, sad that you won / I am weak from your loveliness / Joan Hunter Dunn.' Betjeman takes his beating like a man: 'Her warm-handled racket is back in its press / But my shock-headed victor / She loves me no less.'

The celebrated words 'Anyone for tennis?', stock augury for the sort of play Aunt Edna would have loved, were never uttered in that order by anybody. Amazingly, the youthful Humphrey Bogart, in his first walk-on part as a Broadway *ingénu*, may have got as close to uttering them as anyone.

The Thames The entire undergraduate population of Oxford* jumped into its waters and drowned for love of Zuleika Dobson*. The three little Liddell girls first heard the story of Alice in Wonderland as Lewis Carroll* rowed them along it one golden day in 1862. Jerome K. Jerome came paddling rather inexpertly along it often in the 1880s with his friends George Wingrave and Carl Hentschel, thus providing him with the raw material for his immortal *Three Men in a Boat*. By its banks Kenneth Grahame first told his four-year-old son Alastair the story of *The Wind in the Willows**.

The Thames *Zeitgeist* is clear enough: whimsy, romance, mystery and scandal. William Morris played out his celebrated *ménage à trois* at Kelmscott with his wife Jane and Dante Gabriel Rossetti; the eccentric and dissolute Francis Dashwood conducted his obscene rites with his debauched friends John Wilkes and the Prince of Wales at Medmenham Abbey by the Thames; while not far down the river at Cliveden, at one of Lord Astor's lavish parties in 1961, the Secretary of State for War, John Profumo, met a girl called Christine Keeler. Its hospitable banks accommodate the Palace of Westminster, St Thomas's Hospital (whose students have been able to land missiles from their side of the water on the Mother of Parliaments with a giant home-made catapult), two universities (Oxford* and Reading), three famous schools (Eton*, Radley and St Paul's), a film studio (Shepperton) and a plethora of pubs ranging from the ritzy Rose Revived at Newbridge (built c.1250) to the metropolitan Dove at Hammersmith, haunt of Ernest Hemingway, Sylvia Plath, Graham Greene, A.P. Herbert and many generations of rowing men. Fun is the name of the game: see also under *Maidenhead.*

Thank-you   It takes four *thank-yous* for a ticket to be bought in an English bus. First the bus conductor heaves in sight and calls out *thank-you* (I have arrived). The passenger then hands over his fare with an answering call of *thank-you* (I note that you have arrived and here is my fare). The conductor then hands over the ticket with another *thank-you* (I acknowledge receipt of your fare and here is your ticket in return) whereupon the passenger replies *thank-you* (thank-you).

This elaborate and formal ritual amazes Americans, who can do the whole transaction with hardly a single *thank-you* being exchanged. It certainly slows life up, but oils the gears of everyday intercourse. It is also the curious custom in English pubs for the customer to say *thank-you* on receiving his beer and *thank-you* again on leaving the pub. The well-mannered publican, if he hears, will respond to each in kind.

Even on railway trains, the guard will thank his passengers for listening to him, as will the British Air pilot after communing with his. All this archaic ceremonial probably reflects the gradual escape of a very old feudal society from its medieval chrysalis. It also reflects another curious hole in the English language; for whereas a Frenchman can say *de rien* neatly and politely when someone says *merci* to him, the English vernacular is defective in the reciprocal.

'Don't mention it' is dated, and 'don't mensh' positively Edwardian in its masher-like larkiness. The American riposte, 'you're welcome', sounds too folksy on this side of the Atlantic. So it is 'thank-you', 'thank-you, 'thank-you', and 'thank-you'.

They   One of the most troublesome words the Englishman has to cope with; and in more than one way. It is a grammatical trap (everybody has *their* price). It is also a handy portmanteau word for the anonymous hosts of invisible authority ('they're building a new airfield down the road'). *Pace* the feminist movement, everybody has *his* price. As for that new airfield, aren't *we* building it? The latter difficulty is profound, and may have a lot to do with the fallible nature of a democratic society that is still only skin deep.

The Thirties   It was a mean and shoddy time. It was the decade of the hunger marches and the Left Book Club, of gormless comedians like George Formby and guileless comediennes like Gracie Fields*, of George V's silver jubilee and Edward VIII's abdication. It was the decade that Hitler came to power and Chamberlain flew to Munich; of the 1936 Olympics, when the flashing black legs of champion sprinter Jesse Owens made mincemeat of Nazi theories about race supremacy. It was the era of civil war in Spain and the ominous, distant war in China. It was the golden age of wireless and high summer for the popular press. It was vintage time for motor racing at Brooklands and joyriding at Croydon airport. It was the era of Amy Johnson, everybody's favourite girl, who took to flying too high with some guy in the sky (in this case the dissolute and cack-handed Jim Mollison). It was the heyday of the socially conscious novel: A.J. Cronin's *The Citadel* and Richard Llewellyn's *How Green Was My Valley*. It was the time when Bernard Shaw* and Julian Huxley went to Stalin's Russia and liked what they saw; or more accurately what they were shown. It was prime time for the thirties poets Auden*, Spender* and MacNeice*: hard-nosed, unsentimental, worldly men who saw the canker in the rose. It was for every schoolboy one endless summer in which to savour the majestic batting of Donald Bradman and the bodyline bowling of Harold Larwood. It was the famous time when Tommy Farr, the boy from Tonypandy, went the distance with the previously unstoppable heavyweight champion of the world Joe Louis, and countless Englishmen sat up in the small hours to hear the epic battle on their crackling, whistling radios. It was cocktail time for those who could afford it. It saw the fight for the Blue Riband of the Atlantic, the birth of the Dorchester Hotel* and the launch of Penguin books. It was the heyday of the Reverend Dick Sheppard at St Martin in the Fields and Charles Laughton at the local Odeon as Henry VIII, or Quasimodo or Captain Bligh. It was the decade that began with the great Stock Exchange crash and ended with the Second World War. Through it all, and in ironic counterpart to the increasingly sombre scene, men like George Gershwin, Cole Porter and Noël Coward* wrote the most carefree popular music, full of fizz and with the music and poetry were two of the very few products of the thirties worth remembering.

The Times   It is not what it was, say the Jeremiahs; but then it never has been. These prophets of woe should be asked to give a clear account of the golden period from which *The Times* has lapsed. They do not mean, surely, those early years two centuries ago when both owner and managing editor did spells in prison, and the government paid secret sweeteners to ensure favourable coverage. Nor, surely, do they mean a century ago, when *The Times* was made a laughing stock and very nearly ruined by publishing a series of palpable forgeries it alleged to be in the hand of the Irish leader Parnell. Nor can they mean surely the early twenties, when *The Times* had a proprietor, Lord Northcliffe, who had clearly lost his marbles; and most certainly of all, not, surely, the thirties, when its editor, Geoffrey Dawson recorded in his diary for posterity to see that he was doing his utmost to keep out of the paper anything that might hurt the susceptibilities of the Nazis.

Yet of course there have been shafts of light and triumph between the years of gloom and folly. The brilliant despatches of William Howard Russell from the Crimean War saved an army and destroyed a government. When Russell went on to report the Civil War in America he was received in Washington by President Lincoln himself. 'Mr Russell,' said the President, 'I am very glad to make your acquaintance. The London *Times* is one of the greatest powers in the world – in fact I don't know anything which has much more power – except perhaps the Mississippi.' Yet Russell's coverage of the Battle of Bull Run incensed the North, who had lost it. He was never allowed south, and came home in 1862, to be replaced by Charles Mackay, a fanatical advocate of the South, who was to cover the war from there in a totally partisan fashion.

Still, *The Times* played a crucial role in bringing down Asquith in 1916 and came out of the General Strike with credit: not only was it the only independent paper to continue to publish (the *British Gazette* was a government mouthpiece); it even drew praise from the left-wing *New Statesman* for the fairness and balance of its coverage.

One of its problems has been that foreigners have understood it to be the voice of the British government; in truth, as we have seen, it has been at its best in bringing down governments; and earned its nickname, 'The Thunderer', for the passion and the power with which it advocated the great Reform Bill of 1832. Yet not even the most scrupulous drafting has been able to secure *The Times* a future combining editorial independence with financial viability. The Astors, who had bought it from Northcliffe, were compelled to sell it to the Thomsons, who threw their hand in when they were £70 million down. In 1979 it was shut for nigh on a year; since then it has acquired another new owner in Rupert Murdoch, and has had five editors. What it clearly needs now is a long stretch of peace. What it has had is a ferocious price war, principally with its arch-rival, the *Daily Telegraph*, which has narrowed the gap between them dramatically. The *Telegraph* at the time of writing is struggling to stay over a million. *The Times* is three-quarters of the way there. See also *Wapping*.

Traitors Though England has had its refugee traitors like Fuchs and Pontecorvo, the names that still haunt the English imagination are the diplomats, Donald Maclean and Guy Burgess, who disappeared together one day in May 1951 and surfaced four years later in Moscow. They were upper-middle-class Englishmen, public school and Cambridge*, alcoholic and fatherless, who were traitors to their country but who, it seemed to the man in the street, had been protected by their class long past the point of reasonable doubt.

Persistent murmurs that there must have been a third man, much higher up, who had made their escape possible by warning them it was time to go, reverberated until Kim Philby (Westminster and Cambridge) was unmasked; and then came the sensational disclosure that Anthony Blunt (Marlborough and Cambridge), principal adviser on the Queen's pictures, no less, had been a traitor too. What incensed the ordinary Englishman was that all four seemed still to live within the invisible web of Establishment connection even *after* they had been rumbled; Blunt, for example, was even given an excellent lunch in *The Times** boardroom.

The notion of the well-bred traitor imprisoned in the aspic of Russian life, still loyally English in all but one crucial regard, has fascinated English writers like Cyril Connolly* (who saw Maclean on the day he disappeared and wrote a short book, *The Missing Diplomats*, on the theme) and Alan Bennett (who has written two excellent plays on it: *The Old Country* and *An Englishman Abroad*).

Bennett in particular has explored the ironies with delicate skill: in *The Old Country* the traitor Hilary is living in a nondescript country house set in a landscape which could well be Aldershot*, and is revealed only halfway through the first act as somewhere outside Moscow. He still wears his Garrick Club tie, reads *The Times*, and plays Elgar* incessantly on his gramophone. Meanwhile Burgess, in *An Englishman Abroad*, asks the actress Coral Brown (who played herself on BBC TV) to order a new suit from his London tailor and a fresh Old Etonian tie to replace his worn one.

What he misses in exile from London is the gossip* ('How is Auden? Have you seen Connolly?') and he, too, has a theme tune for his gramophone: Jack Buchanan singing over and over again 'Who Stole my Heart Away?' Bennett put into Burgess's mouth his own position: 'I can say I love London. I can say I love England. I can't say I love my country, because I don't know what that means.'

Tunbridge Wells All nine English spas, in the nature of things, symbolise the status quo, though one (Bath*), has now become so cosmopolitan that the faint aroma of reaction has been long drowned in headier scents, and two (Droitwich and Woodhall) are really too small to have impinged much on the national consciousness at all. The remaining six (Buxton, Cheltenham*, Harrogate, Malvern, Leamington and Tunbridge Wells) will all strike the average Englishman as bastions of bourgeois conformity; but of the doughty half-dozen only one has entered the language. Disgusted of Tunbridge Wells has become the notional signatory of countless cod letters (most typically to the *Daily Telegraph*) railing against the collapse of what he sees as civilisation. What Tunbridge Wells did to get lumbered with Disgusted is not totally clear; but lumbered it assuredly is. Some four years ago, the borough designed a new logo and launched a slogan: 'Yours delightfully, Tunbridge Wells.' It cut no ice at all.

The Twenties The grievous domestic problems that had obsessed English life before the First World War afterwards came back again unsolved and exigent: the future of Ireland; the status of women; the fate of the miners. As England knows to her cost, they have still not gone away as the century draws to its close. There were watersheds: the union with Ireland was ended in 1922, but the festering sore of Ulster remained; women over thirty got the vote in 1918 though the so-called flappers, or women in their twenties, had to wait till 1928 till they were enfranchised too; the miners were defeated when they struck in 1921 and again when they led the General Strike in 1926; they would have to wait till 1974 when they smashed the Heath government for their revenge.

Yet 1926 was the last year in which a clear class struggle was fought; after the two inconclusive minority Labour governments of the 1920s, a sizable part of the middle class threw in their lot with the working class to form the great reforming Attlee Labour government of 1945–51. Back in the twenties the fear of red revolution was real enough; returning ex-servicemen who had the training – and the motive – to precipitate revolution were bought off with generous welfare settlements until they were resettled.

Ex-officers, who were supposed to have private means, frequently spent their gratuities on businesses that went bust; and the discontented unemployed ex-officer was to play the hero in the thrillers of Sapper and the detective stories of Dorothy L. Sayers. He was also, in the real world, to officer the brutal Black and Tans, whose appalling reign of terror in

Ireland just before independence created a bitter urge to revenge that is still being worked out.

The fear of revolution remained real enough: an Oxford undergraduate and ex-officer was asked to leave Balliol, of all places, because he had passed his vacations in Russia. It was the era of the bottle party and the Bright Young Things; the Charleston and the shimmy; of swindlers like Jimmy White and Horatio Bottomley; cocktails and cigarette holders; Noël Coward* and Somerset Maugham* had four plays apiece running in the West End. It was the era of ribbon development and mock Tudor, silent films and lawn tennis.

Despite the incursion of the dreadful *nouveaux riches*, the hard-faced men who had done well out of the war, the upper class carried on as if nothing had happened; it was the age of the great society hostesses like Lady Cunard and Lady Sybil Colefax. It looked as if the Jazz Age had come to stay: but the collapse of the New York stock market on 29 October 1929 spelled goodbye to all that.

Twickenham   It was Philip Toynbee who once remarked that a bomb under the West Car Park at Twickenham would end fascism in England for a generation. The fact is that it is not the jackboot but the car boot which is the symbol of rugby football's international headquarters, and on the day of a big game it is instructive to stroll between the lines of parked Rovers and Jaguars inspecting the cornucopia on display: barbecues and *boeuf en croûte*, salmon and sandwiches, chicken and cheddar, plonk*, Scotch, bubbly and barrels of beer. A conscientious appraisal of the massed revellers would suggest that any lurking fascists are effectively drowned in the shoals of schoolmasters down from the north, Welsh miners, Scottish salesmen, Frenchmen on a weekend spree from the Dordogne, and Irish priests. Say what you will, a Twickers crowd is typically in high good humour, and despite the huge quantities of booze put away, outbreaks of fisticuffs and chauvinistic set-tos are rare indeed. As big money inexorably seeps into this traditionally amateur game, the goodwill may seep out at the other end: it usually does.

Undergound   It is easy to forget how old it is. The Metropolitan, oldest underground line in the world, was opened in 1863. There is a photograph of Gladstone sitting in an open carriage wearing a top hat. These early undergrounds were served by steam trains and were only just below the surface: channels over which new building would later form a roof. With the coming of electric trains far deeper shafts could be dug, but only at some expense; many streams had to be channelled and the river Westbourne, for example, can still be seen carried in pipes above the station at Sloane Square. The Bakerloo line is said to have originated in the desire of City businessmen to see the last hour's cricket at Lord's without leaving their offices too early (if so, they might have placed St John's Wood station rather closer to the ground).

Today the Underground has proliferated till it thrusts deep into outer suburbia: to High Barnet and Upminster; Wimbledon, West Ruislip and most recently Heathrow. Though underground travel offers a womb-like intensity – and indeed at rush hours a well-documented adventure playground for frottage – it has not precipitated such a rich literature as the railway. Nevertheless, it floats in the Englishman's mind as the backdrop for some of Henry Moore's most memorable wartime paintings of Londoners sheltering from the bombs above.

The poet of the Underground is John Betjeman* ('Gaily into Ruislip Gardens / Runs the red electric train / With a thousand ta's and pardon's / Daintily alights Elaine.') Alas, the early innocence of the Underground has been swallowed up by bomb alerts and casual muggings; the scene for grisly suicides, inexplicable crashes, a dreadful fire, and one or two fine cops-and-robbers chases along the tunnel. It has been a political arena, as when Ken Livingstone, leader of the GLC, drastically lowered all the fares as a populist gesture; an industrial cockpit when closed by strikes; and an exhibition gallery for the display of new and bold forms of poster art.

United States   When Mrs John Bull's Westclox alarm goes she puts on her Maidenform bra, Playtex girdle and Max Factor lipstick. She breakfasts on Weetabix, washes up with Fairy Liquid, and Hoovers the house. Then she goes shopping in the Ford, buys Campbell's soups in the Safeway supermarket, and in the afternoon makes a dress on her Singer sewing machine. Later she answers the children's questions from the *Encyclopedia Britannica*, pays the Diner's Club account, and watches a Columbia film on television.

Her husband comes home in a Hertz hire car. They retire to bed under their Monogram electric blanket, and her husband swears he will dream of his firm, the advertising giant J. Walter Thompson. This scenario – much scaled down here – forms the preface to a book called *The American Take Over of Britain* by James McMillan and Bernard Harris. The point they are making is that every single brand named is American. Does it matter? Would England be a better place without Fords or Hoovers? The debate can go either way; but the fact of the American domination cannot be gainsaid. It soaks through every crevice of English life.

Insofar as this American suzerainty is economic most Englishmen outside the committed left accept or even welcome it. Insofar as it is political their attitude is ambivalent. On the one hand, they know perfectly well that only American intervention won two world wars. As Winston Churchill put it after Pearl Harbor: 'To have the United States on our side was to me the greatest joy ... So we had won after all! ... England would live.' On the other, incidents like the Grenada action remind them uneasily that when the chips are down America is perfectly prepared to go it alone; and whatever the political disclaimers no English restraining hand held a key to the horrendous American missiles which once pointed into the Russian heartland from English soil.

This political collision is not new. 'The Great Republic was the chief foreign threat to the well-being of the British Empire', wrote James Morris in his imperial trilogy *Pax Britannica*. 'Time and again since Victoria's accession the two Powers had quarrelled ... over the sovereignty of Oregon, over British naval supremacy during the American Civil War, repeatedly over Newfoundland fishing rights, incessantly over Canadian frontier issues.'

Still, none of this mattered much if, like many Englishmen of the time, you saw America as hardly a foreign power at all. The *Illustrated London News*, in its Christmas issue of 1849, said that though the British race would undoubtedly continue to rule the world, it would presently be from the other side of the Atlantic. Well, it has not worked out like that, and even the romantic notion propounded by Harold Macmillan that England is playing Greece to America's Rome is as condescending as it is simplistic. The interplay between the two cultures is so intricately woven that it can no longer be disentangled, and perhaps this is the most reassuring point about it.

The Royal Shakespeare Company may slay them on Broadway; but the best modern life of Shakespeare is by a professor of English at Northwestern University (Samuel Schoenbaum) just as the best edition of Shakespeare's Sonnets is by a Berkeley professor (Stephen Booth). The *Oxford English Dictionary* remains the greatest reservoir of the English language; the *New Yorker* the most scrupulously tended mill through which it courses. Meantime the Hoovers seem destined to prevail in England, at least until Hondas go into the business: but that, thank heaven, will be for a future edition of this companion.

Up   An English adverb of enormous power. It lends spectacular magnification to otherwise unremarkable words; thus to be 'beaten up' is far more comprehensive than to be merely beaten, a 'fry-up' more enticing than a fry, a 'ton-up' (100 m.p.h. for the unworldly) on a motorbike far more dashing than doing a ton, a 'balls-up' a far greater disaster than making a mere balls of something can ever be; to be 'done up' far more thoroughgoing than to be done. And note how in the Harrow* school song, 'Forty Years On', which Winston Churchill* so delighted to sing even in old age, up makes all the difference. 'Follow up, follow up, follow up' is a call to action and to arms; 'follow, follow, follow' is something you do when dreamily pursuing the merry merry pipes of Pan. Up, on its own, is moreover an expletive of great if coarse power, as in 'up yours, mate'. It is also used poignantly in the vernacular verdict, 'he can't get it up any more' or more personally, 'he can't get it up for her'.

Valentines Nothing is so calculated to overthrow a national stereotype as the behaviour of the English on St Valentine's Day. Some eight and a half million Valentine cards are dispatched, and newspapers groan under the weight of a great gallimaufry of bizarre, arcane and often unashamedly erotic messages. 'Petalbum sends nuzzles and kisses to his favourite duck', says one in the normally po-faced *Times*. 'Pin', declaims a *Guardian* troubadour, 'nibble my nose and I'll follow you anywhere.'

Even the stern comrades on the communist *Morning Star* are not immune: 'James. This is more than just a petty bourgeois, individualist, ideological construct. Your relatively autonomous Jackie.' Images of small and furry animals abound: 'Pooh Bear. Will you be my valentine. Your small, squeaky-voiced but highly intellectual piglet.' Sometimes past glories are relived: 'Wally Mumblatt Thank you for revolutionising my knicker collection. Love Pole Pole.'

The point about this collective English February folly is that nothing similar is known in France or in Germany, or even in America. It is yet more evidence of the total unpredictability of the English.

Victoria Station It was in fact two stations, one serving the Brighton* line, the other Dover*. The former was thought the smarter and in *The Importance of Being Earnest*, Oscar Wilde made a point of the fact that, though Jack Worthing had been found in a handbag at Victoria, it was at least on the Brighton side. Though all great stations have what Cyril Connolly called *angoisse des gares*, giving us that stab of anxiety as we arrive or depart, he felt it most keenly at Victoria and worst in the evenings. It was the scene for the uncounted partings as the troop trains left.

In a happier context, Victoria is the symbolic gateway to the start of immeasurable adventures abroad, and Ernie Bevin spoke for all Englishmen when he defined his foreign policy as being able to buy a ticket at Victoria Station and going anywhere he damned well pleased. It was, for instance, the place from which the Golden Arrow, that magical train with the chocolate and cream Pullman cars and engines bearing names like *Excalibur* and *Tintagel*, began its daily run to Paris.

It made its last run on 30 September 1972. The buxom *Brighton Belle* has gone too, and with it those breakfast kippers which famously sustained Lord Olivier as he journeyed up to Victoria.

Village   It is in a sense the most interesting focus through which to study modern England: exemplar of a past which never really existed; snapshot of a present which shifts as we try to understand it; blueprint of a future which is essentially unknowable. It is a cluster of country dwellings, with something between a hundred and a thousand inhabitants: less would make it a hamlet; more, a small town. Typically, it will contain one pub*, one church, and one post office* (which may double as the village grocery). It might well be blessed with a green, a square or triangle of turf on which cricket* is played in the summer, football* in the winter. Yet, if we look a little closer, we may well see that the church is open only fitfully, if at all, its parish having been amalgamated with several neighbours* in some Church of England reshuffle; the pub may have been taken over by some giant chain, and feature juke boxes and space invaders with the fizzed beer and potato crisps; the post office may be moribund and its grocery losing ground to the supermarket in the nearest town. Things are not what they were. The village approximates to an ideal way of life the further one is away from it. Certainly to the original inhabitants, there was nothing particularly romantic or desirable about a tied cottage* where tenancy turned, more or less, on the whim of the owner and the compliance of the tenant. Who found Arcadia in a two-up, two-down hovel with no dampcourse, no heating and no running water? Love in a hut, with water and a crust, as Keats reminds us, is, love forgive us, cinders, ashes, dust. So the original denizens of the village with any get-up-and-go got up and went. The people they left behind tended to be slower and gentler; if they are still there they tend to be mavericks, quietists, misfits or fatalists; the new village dwellers have come, for a wide spectrum of reasons, from outside.

These modern inhabitants of an English village may well include (a) a sprig of the titled family who once owned all the land as far as the eye can see and still own a sizable slice of it; (b) the original villagers, much depleted by emigration to America, the Commonwealth, London, and even nearby big towns, but still in a skeletal sense, its inheritors; (c) a new meritocratic middle class: accountants, engineers, lawyers and computer experts who make their livings in the big towns within driving range; (d) a few daily commuters who do not mind the grind of the journey to London in return for the first lungful of God's good air when they get home in the evenings; (e) the neighbourhood farmers and their employees who actually still work the land round the village; (f) a number of retired admirals, colonels and air commodores who have decided that this will make a good last posting; and (g) the weekend Londoners, who like to hit the M4 or whichever motorway* it is at 4 p.m. on Fridays and recharge their batteries for a new assault on the corridors of power early Monday morning. Now of all these groups, only a, b and e have any long-term emotional rights in the village, and it is this grievance that has precipitated burnings in Wales* and bombings in Ireland* (an extension of the problem). In truth, the original villagers never owned their own cottages, and hated them when tenants; but that does not stop them resenting the arrival of the new villagers (see also under *Cottage* and *Class*). The best villagers are those who learn to get on with as many of the groups here specified as is tenable; but that is a hard trick. Meantime the contemporary English village is as much the nodal point of change, flux, tension and collision as the big city from which it is popularly supposed to be a portmanteau refuge.

VIP   First noted in a 1933 novel of Compton Mackenzie (when it stood for Very Important Person*age*) VIP has come to be associated with air travel under privileged conditions and, though once taken quite seriously, is now used increasingly in a mocking context to mean a very unimportant person.

V-Sign   Patented by Winston Churchill in the last war as symbolic shorthand for Victory, the V-sign is an ambiguous gesture in unworldly hands, for while it expresses the Churchillian mode right enough palm outwards, it means something quite different palm inwards; something of vast and uncharted antiquity, but to the worldly totally unambiguous in its import. Up yours mate, is what the palm inward V-sign signifies or even more directly, get stuffed (see *Up*). Hugely popular with schoolboys and soldiers as a universal expression of derision, the palm-in V-sign does not yet seem to be used widely, despite the onset of women's lib, by women; though that, no doubt, is to come.

W

ales 'This chap has a certain natural gift of rhetoric', observes Professor Higgins of the eloquent dustman Alfred Doolittle in Bernard Shaw's* *Pygmalion*. 'That's the Welsh strain in him. It also accounts for his mendacity and dishonesty.' The notion that the Welshman is a bit too quick for him is deeply ingrained in the Englishman's mind, and the edge is rationalised as a proclivity to light-fingeredness. 'Taffy was a Welshman', says the nursery rhyme, 'Taffy was a thief.' And as Evelyn Waugh* remarked in *Decline and Fall*, 'We can trace almost all the disasters of English history to the influence of the Welsh.'

Yet if the English image of the Welsh is unflattering, it is as nothing to the Welsh view of the English. The word *Sais* in Welsh does not just convey Englishman; it is also a term of profound obloquy. For generations now the Welsh have seen the Sais as a distant, po-faced tyrant who has rifled his land of its vast mineral wealth and forced him to sweat for his bread in the bowels of the earth. But Welsh revenge has been sweet.

They have sent up to Westminster* a series of wizards who have put a spell on Parliament. David Lloyd George was not only the most gifted politician of his time (perhaps of the century), he was also one of the funniest. 'The Honourable Gentleman has sat so long on the fence that the iron has entered into his soul', he famously remarked of John Simon; and less famously, but just as shatteringly, of Herbert Samuel: 'When they circumcised him they threw away the wrong bit.'

He was succeeded as chief thorn in the side of the English Establishment by Aneurin Bevan ('Fascism is not a new order of society. It is the future refusing to be born.' Still, most Englishmen conceded, there was nothing quite like a Welsh Speaker of the House of Commons (most recently George Thomas) to thunder out the lesson at a royal wedding: while the poetry of the young Dylan Thomas and the voice of the young Richard Burton still work their powerful magic on English minds.

There are only 2,807,000 Welshmen in Britain; if they sometimes seem ten times as many it is because of the passion and pride with which they push their luck. They are a classless people; and they believe in self help. Lord Elwyn Jones, for example, was Lord Chancellor of England from 1974 to 1979; he started at Llanelli Grammar School and made his way to Cambridge on scholarships; when he went away to college his father, a furnaceman, pushed his luggage to the station on a cart. His brother became a professor; his sister a headmistress.

Another example of the incidence of Welsh prestidigitators is at the BBC; while on the rugby field generations of Welsh players endowed with quicksilver bewitched, bothered and bewildered the plodding English for decades. That dominance came to a close with the renaissance of English rugby in the 1990s. Perhaps the end of amateur rugby means that many of those preternaturally gifted Welsh players who went north to play the professional game will play for their country again. Many have already come south, but often to play for rich English clubs. How it works out, only time will tell.

Wapping   The newspaper plant Rupert Murdoch built in the London dockland cost him £100 million. It was, he announced, designed to print his new paper, the *London Post*. For six years he tried to get a viable deal with the print unions; and for six years failed. One union negotiator told Murdoch his best plan was to blow the plant up. At some time during that long travail – no-one knows quite when – he decided on a far more revolutionary plan. He would print his existing titles – *The Times, The Sunday Times,* the *Sun*, and the *News of the World* – there. Eddie Shah had got a foot in the door when he succeeded, after a bitter fight, in printing his free sheets in the north without traditional union agreements. Murdoch kicked it down. He printed a section of *The Sunday Times* there without a single print worker. His workforce – all, that is, except management and journalists – struck. They were never to work for him again. Electricians bussed in each morning from Southampton ran the high-tech machines. The journalists were split into refuseniks, who would not agree to the move, and those who would. There were quite enough of the latter to run the papers. The dispute lasted a year.

Throughout that time, despite determined picketing and ugly clashes with the police, the print unions spectacularly failed to prevent the four papers getting out. In the end, they settled for £60,000,000 compensation. The rest of Fleet Street followed suit, moving en masse to dockland and able at last to settle with the previously entrenched unions on the new technology. While much of Fleet Street's troubles stemmed from the cowardice, avarice and stupidity of management and owners, and much from deep historical roots, the unions displayed a stunning lack of imagination in not making a deal before it came to war. They had always won their battles with the owners; they thought they always would. The vast economies engendered meant that the newspaper industry had ensured its survival for another generation. The barbed wire was taken down at Wapping; the bitterness remains.

Waugh, Evelyn (1903–66)   The point about Waugh was that he got it right. He knew exactly what his target was, and hit it smack in the centre. He saw his characters with the high definition of a batsman who has thoroughly played himself in, and wrote about them in a prose of the most pleasing and elegant clarity. All the way from his sparkling début in *Decline and Fall*, through the darker chords which are heard in *A Handful of Dust*, to the plangent melancholy of *Brideshead Revisited*, there are no *longueurs* in Waugh. He never showed off, never belonged to a school, never worked for effect.

He considered that he had allowed the exigencies of wartime life in England to lead him into an extravagance in the writing of *Brideshead* which he sought to excise later; his *aficionados* were not best pleased. Even infidels who are obliged to reject in its entirety the religious basis on which *Brideshead* is predicated – in his own words, the operation of divine grace on a group of diverse but closely connected characters – are seized by its sumptuous settings, ineluctable plot and characters who walk out of the page.

When Waugh opened his notebook to record the foibles of his time and place he could draw on incomparable raw material. There was Lord Berners, who had a piano built in the back of his Rolls, and E.S.P. Haynes, solicitor in Waugh's divorce, who seldom finished lunch till 4 p.m. and died when his shirt-tails caught alight as he stood before his gas fire. Other writers and artists lived in the same *milieu* but did not have the divine grace to convey these foibles to us for all time. Waugh may not have been a saint – he could be abominably rude to the world, though he was kind in private – but he was an English writer of unquestionable genius.

The Weather In England it has taken on the anthropomorphic quality of a licensed jester whose latest caper is universally discussed daily with wry resignation. Indeed, as David Lodge observed in his novel *Changing Places*, to a visiting American, the English weather forecast sounds like nothing more than some bizarre extension of the satire industry: 'some kind of spoof, predicting every possible combination of weather for the next twenty-four hours without actually committing itself to anything specific.' Though popularly renowned for its fickleness, English weather is in truth more properly distinguished by its gentleness. The extremes of temperature observed in England (about +38°C to −27°C) are under half the world's widest; English rainfall is a quarter of the world's wettest. True, between these mild parameters, it displays an infinite capacity for surprise that means all English farmers, cricketers, builders, sailors, street vendors and holidaymakers are perforce gamblers who must accept the caprice of the weather with unflinching resignation and humour. The only answer, therefore, in England, seems to be to enjoy whatever heaven sends. 'There is really no such thing as bad weather,' observed Ruskin, 'Only different kinds of good weather.' But see *Spring, Summer, Autumn,* and *Winter.*

Wessex Literally, the domain of the West Saxons who settled in Hampshire early in the sixth century and pushed north and west till, under Egbert and Alfred, they first created the Kingdom of England. Its perimeter encompassed what we now call Dorset, Wiltshire, Berkshire, Somerset and the original settlement in Hampshire. That was all it meant till 1874 when Thomas Hardy*, groping for a word to describe the stretch of England he would be celebrating in *Far from the Madding Crowd* and the series of novels that followed, hit on the idea of reviving the word.

'The region designated was known but vaguely, and I was often asked even by educated people where it lay', he recalled. 'However the press and public were kind enough to welcome the fanciful plan, and willingly joined me in the anachronism of imagining a Wessex population living under Queen Victoria – a modern Wessex of railways, the penny post, mowing and reaping machines, union work-houses, lucifer matches, labourers who could read and write, and national schoolchildren.'

It was a simple but brilliant device. The map of Wessex which decorates the endpieces of the Wessex novels blurs fact and fiction as his prose did: from the Isles of Lyonnesse (Scilly Isles) in the far west to Castle Royal (Windsor) in the east, and from Christminster (Oxford*) in the north to Sandbourne (Bournemouth*) in the south. Very big places like Bristol and Southampton stand as they are; but Melchester is of course Salisbury and Wintoncester is Winchester*.

Within this ambitious framework the wide, stark tapestries of his books are marvellously woven; and the actual texture of the Wessex landscape is central to their triumph. In the majestic opening scene of *Far from the Madding Crowd* 'the kingly brilliance of Sirius pierced the eye with a steely glitter, the star called Capella was yellow, Aldebaran and Betelgeux shone with a fiery red. To persons standing alone on a hill during a clear midnight such as this, the roll of the world eastward is almost a palpable movement.' Such is the thrall of Hardy's Wessex.

Westminster   'I have always thought that to sit in the British Parliament should be the highest object of ambition to every educated Englishman', wrote Anthony Trollope in his Autobiography. His view was not shared by his great contemporary Dickens*, probably the best and fastest shorthand reporter the Commons had ever known, who heartily despised the pandemonium beneath him. Trollope stood unsuccessfully for the first and last time when he was fifty-three, thus fortunately giving himself the time to write some of his best books: notably *Phineas Finn* and *The Prime Minister.*

'The government of your country', cries the armaments millionaire Undershaft to his son Stephen in Bernard Shaw's* *Major Barbara*, 'I am the government of your country; I and Lazarus. Do you suppose that you and half a dozen amateurs like you, sitting in a row in that foolish gabble shop, can govern Undershaft and Lazarus? No, my friend, you will do what pays us ... Be off with you my boy, and play with your caucuses and leading articles and historic parties and great leaders and burning questions and the rest of your toys. I am going back to my counting house to pay the piper and call the tune.'

A brutal speech, and no doubt a simplistic analysis. Still, the modern House of Commons is a dull place. It contains few politicians of undisputed world rank, and has not heard a truly great speech for years.

Wet   Though the word has been used as slang for a ninny for a good fifty years now, it found a new surge of popularity as a contemptuous description of anybody who opposed Margaret Thatcher's hard-line monetarist economic policies then, indeed, anyone who opposed her at all. In consequence there was soon a whole alternative cabinet of Tory wets sitting on the Conservative back benches, most notably and vociferously the former prime minister Edward Heath. With the departure of Maggie, her favourite term of contempt has been quickly marginalised. The battle between the wet and dry wings of the Tory party nevertheless rages on.

Who's Who   It has been coming out for 149 years now, this perennially fascinating guide to the great and the good in national life. The annual invitation from Messrs Adam and Charles Black is the ticket for an agreeable and harmless ego trip during which far more is revealed about the traveller than might meet the casual eye. Some give father's name but not mother's; some give university but not school; some list current wives but drop all record of previous ones; some compress their lives into half a dozen laconic lines; others ramble on for a column of densely set type. Recreations provide one obvious opportunity for fun and games. Thus Christopher Booker offers among his pastimes the psychology of story telling and following the Somerset cricket team; Andrew Boyle used to watch bad football matches from public terraces, especially at Fulham. Cartoonist Mel Calman vouchsafed that he spent his leisure hours brooding and worrying, while musician/writer Fritz Spiegl lists his hobbies as printing, cooking, inventing and several deadly sins. Writer Russell Hoban ruefully contributes rewriting yesterday's pages. Writer Keith Waterhouse offers a one word diversion: lunch. Science-fiction doyen Brian Aldiss is even more randomly arcane: his recreations are fame, obscurity, and trances. Famous entries from the past include Osbert Sitwell's ('educated Eton; mainly self-educated') while John Betjeman*, who used to describe himself as poet and hack, grew grander after he became Laureate and dignified himself as poet and author. The most manful entry in the great compendium, though, must surely have been that from poet Chistopher Logue: 'Private in Black Watch, two years in Army Prison, discharged with ignominy.'

Wimbledon   Within an hour of the Wimbledon Championships finishing, a small army of officials are on their knees examining every inch of the Centre Court. The scattered divots are lovingly replaced with ladies' hairpins, the grass is re-seeded at once and then again in the spring. Apart from four hand-chosen ladies who play half an hour of doubles before Wimbledon to test the turf it stands unused for all but the two frenetic weeks of the Championships. It is tender loving care like this that makes Wimbledon, even to those who continuously tour the great tennis venues of the world, still the most beautiful, traditional, and disciplined tournament there is.

The word disciplined may sound odd in the era of loudmouths like John McEnroe, but even he moderated his behaviour at the All England Lawn Tennis and Croquet Club; and in any event his famous disputations with the umpires were due as much to a change in the rules allowing for a dialogue between players and officials as anything else.

Yet as we have noted throughout this book, when the money comes in one end of the sport, the fun tends to leave by the other. That prince of the ticket touts with the unimaginably apt name, Stan Flashman, for example was ordered to pay £3,000 damages to an American tennis tour organiser for selling £42 tickets at £125 each.

The royals have taken a lively interest in the game since King George V gave a cup for the men's singles championship and his son, then Duke of York, played in the 1926 Championships: and every year the Kents are there to give the prizes on the last days.

Perhaps the escalating price of the strawberries and the press of humanity may deter some fans; certainly the draw for tickets seems a little less over-subscribed now than once. Besides, there are no action replays to be seen from the Centre Court seats. Yet, not to have been to Wimbledon at all is not to have known one of the key ingredients of the English summer: as maddening as it is magical.

Wimp Yet another of those handy pejorative slang terms that is still settling down. It was first recorded as a word for a girl, and the verb to wimp, or look for girls, was in use at Oxford as early as 1917. But in that context it failed; and by the 1960s was being used in America for a feeble or ineffectual man. Its etymology is obscure; perhaps it comes from whimper; perhaps the resonance with limp lends it strength. Whichever, the wimp became a familiar figure in Thatcherite England, along with his near cousin the wet*.

Wimsey, Lord Peter In his youth Dorothy L. Sayer's aristocratic sleuth was oddly like Bertie Wooster*. Both were sprigs of the nobility, both had manservants worth their weight in gold: the indispensable Bunter, the incomparable Jeeves. Both were at Oxford, but whereas Wimsey took a first in modern history, Wooster's exploits were confined more to taking off his clothes at Bump Suppers and diving into the college fountain. Wimsey was a real goer in bed, while Wooster never seems to have gone the whole hog with any girl; though often as near as dammit. The main difference between them would seem, on superficial analysis, to be that while Wooster looked an ass and was an ass, Wimsey looked an ass and had one of the best brains in Europe (for a fairer and truer account of Bertie's intellectual powers see under *Wooster*).

Wimsey, on the other hand, was intolerable in his accomplishments. He rode superbly, shot expertly, drove a car at grand prix level, played the piano beautifully, was a connoisseur of wine and so on. Perhaps Dorothy L. Sayers modelled him on Eric Whelpton, with whom she had been in love (like Whelpton, Wimsey had 'a long narrow face, like a melancholic adjutant stork'); perhaps on the mysterious and cosmopolitan John Cournos, whom she had loved too; perhaps on the Chaplain of Balliol, for whom she also had a soft spot. Probably, though, she should be believed when she claimed that Wimsey was a composite.

There can be no doubt, however, about Harriet Vane, heroine of many Wimsey tales, Lord Peter's mistress and eventually his wife. Harriet, like Dorothy, was tall, dark, and no great beauty. She too wrote detective stories, and she too signed herself with a middle initial: Harriet D. Vane, echoing Dorothy L. Sayers (the L stood for Leigh, her mother's name, and denoted her descent from one of the founders of *Punch*, a provenance of which she was very proud). The actual circumstances of Peter's acceptance by Harriet in *Gaudy Night* still set a high-water mark in self-indulgence which will take some beating: 'With a gesture of submission he bared his head and stood gravely, the square cap dangling in his hand. "Placetne, magistra?" "Placet."'

Whatever Wimsey's defects, there is no doubt that Harriet doted on the man. At a performance of the Bach Double Violin Concerto at Balliol 'Peter, she felt sure, could hear the whole intricate pattern, every part separately and simultaneously, each independent and equal, separate but inseparable, moving over and under and through, ravishing heart and mind together'. Perhaps Wimsey was the ideal husband Dorothy would have liked. The one she actually got was Oswald Fleming, a captain in the Royal Army Service Corps, later motoring correspondent of the *News of the World*, a snob, a hack and a drunk. Yet if she had found a real-life Wimsey, there might well have been no need for her to write the detective novels, and the world would have been a much poorer place.

Winchester 'The ancient city of Winchester, city of Alfred, once capital of England, perhaps even the Camelot of Arthur': so writes A.G. Macdonell in the last chapter of his flawed masterpiece *England Their England* (1933). Its hero, fledgling writer Donald Cameron, a young Scottish ex-officer and a dead ringer for Archie Macdonell himself, has nearly completed his quest for the hearts and minds of the English. The immortal cricket match at Fordende has been played, and now Donald, seduced from Lambeth by the scents and sounds of the imminent English spring, is playing truant from his book.

He has taken a train to Alton, hitched to Alresford, drunk some Hampshire beer, then hitched again until the water meads of the river Itchen lie beneath him, not to mention the city of Alfred. In truth it was never undisputed capital of England (though certainly an important royal centre and the seat of treasury in Norman times) and its claims on Camelot, if they rest on the Round Table in the Great Hall, are slim indeed: though old, maybe six hundred years old, it is nowhere near old enough to have served Arthur, who flourished, if at all, a good eight hundred years before the table was made.

The book is a love letter to the auld enemy and though the last chapter simply will not do ('the muted voices of grazing sheep, and the merry click of bat upon ball, and the peaceful green fields of England') Macdonell seems to know his Winchester. He takes us into the Cathedral, to the chantry of William of Wykeham, defended by a Wykehamist captain in Cromwell's army with drawn sword against his own pillaging troops; and the memorial to Jane Austen* ('kindliest and gayest and gentlest'). He leads us through the Deanery and the Canonries and the Tithe Barn into the College itself, where the newest of new boys is called a Winchester man and the school motto is the best known of all: Manners Makyth Man. Every other motto he'd ever heard of, Macdonell remarks, called on an unspecified Supreme Power to allow the institution to flourish or prosper or to wax strong: 'In general to get on in the world.' This school, however, put kindness before power or fame.

From the College Archie Macdonell takes us on to the Abbey of St Cross, which still disposes its traditional bounty, the wayfarer's dole of bread and ale, to any who ask for it. Then we go up St Catherine's Hill, where he falls into a rather embarrassing trance in which the whole tapestry of English history rises before him out of a cloud of steam like a telly ad for Watney's Ale. What a rum place.

Winchester has turned out a handful of military men like Wavell, Dowding and Portal, politicians as disparate as Gaitskell and Mosley; mavericks like A.P. Herbert and Cecil King. In six hundred years, it could have done better. Never mind, we shall forgive Winchester for giving us Archie Macdonell, a Wykehamist himself, of course, and that immortal chapter seven of *England Their England*.

The Wind in the Willows The Secretary of the Bank of England – for that is what Kenneth Grahame (1859–1922) was, no less, when he wrote this enchanting story, published in 1908 – had much on his side. First, he had hit on a title of spellbinding power. It sounds like an invocation. When A.A. Milne, another skilled artificer, turned it into a play, he could choose from Grahame's text a title of well nigh equal charm: *Toad of Toad Hall*.

Next, Grahame had hit on a phrase for a form of time-squandering that was always, and remains still, dear to the island race: 'messing about in boats'. The river and its thrall are central to the fascination of *The Wind in The Willows*. Again, foreshadowing *Watership Down* by more than half a century, he had seen the appeal of using anthropomorphic animals to animate his plot. 'In reading the book', wrote Milne, 'it is necessary to think of Mole, for instance, sometimes as an actual mole, sometimes as such a mole in human clothes, sometimes as a mole grown to human size, sometimes as walking on two legs, sometimes on four. He is a mole, he isn't a mole. What is he? I don't know. And, not being a matter-of-fact person, I don't mind.'

Indeed, all the animals have distinctly human foibles: naive Mole, kindly Rat, worldly Badger and capricious Toad. A visitor to the Grahame house at Cookham Dean by the Thames paused entranced outside the night nursery, hearing 'two of the most beautiful voices, one relating a wonderful story, and the other, soft as the south wind blowing, sometimes asking for an explanation, sometimes arguing a point, at others laughing like a whole chime of bells – the loveliest duet possible'.

It was his only son Alistair for whom Grahame spun the magical story of the river animals, just as on the same river Dodgson had spun his story for Alice. But Alistair was destined to die at twenty on an Oxford railway line in what may well have been suicide. The story written for him lives on, still enchanting new generations of children and grown-ups who have never quite shaken off the spell cast by the mist on the river.

Winnie-the-Pooh   The name of a rebarbative bear owned by Christopher Robin, infant son of the English writer A.A. Milne (1882–1956). Bear and boy are extensively celebrated in Milne's books, notably *When We Were Very Young, Winnie-the-Pooh, Now We Are Six,* and *The House at Pooh Corner*. These books with their illustrations by E.H. Shepard have found an enormous audience on both sides of the Atlantic and in many translations from Japanese to Bulgarian; but the applause has not been universal. Reviewing *The House at Pooh Corner* for the *New Yorker* in 1928 Dorothy Parker opened by printing the song on page five: 'The more it / Snows – tiddely – pom, / The more it Goes – tiddely pom / The more it / Goes – tiddely – pom / On / Snowing.'

Pooh explains that he put in the word pom to make the little lyric 'more hummy'. We shall concur with Dorothy Parker's verdict: 'And it is that word "hummy", my darlings, that marks the first place in *The House at Pooh Corner* at which Tonstant Weader Fwowed up.'

Winter   The English achievement was to turn it from a noun into a verb. No one in his right mind denies that an English winter at its most vile is an unencompassable horror; though even at its most unspeakable it will suddenly throw out at random days flooded with a cold and golden sunlight which are among the most casually beautiful the English year can afford.

Still, well-to-do Englishmen long ago learned the knack of heading south as the winter solstice approaches. Not for nothing did the Promenade des Anglais at Nice get its name and it was here, two centuries ago, that Tobias Smollett first amazed the locals by actually swimming for fun in the sea. For good measure, an Englishman called Arnold Lunn taught the Swiss to slalom and winter sport is now the alternative diversion that rescues tens of thousands of the island race from the horrors of an English Christmas.

For the unadventurous and the stick-a-beds, even the inspissated gloom of the English midwinter can be suddenly illumined by the miraculous winter jasmine, the innocence of the first snowdrops, the blaze of the early crocus. By February the national folly of St Valentine's Day* signals the emotional start of a thaw that may well continue to midsummer.

Wodehouse, P.G.   (1881–1975)   Perhaps the most interesting point about his enormously long working life (seventy years) is his relationship to George Orwell*. On the face of it, no two English writers could be more inimical. Wodehouse lived in an imaginary world in which politics, crime and sex hardly obtruded; Orwell in a wincingly real world where they manifestly did.

Oddly similar in their family backgrounds (Wodehouse's father was an English upper-middle-class judge who served the British Raj in Hong Kong, Orwell's father an English upper-middle-class civil servant who served the British Raj in Bengal) one made his name by celebrating the eccentricities of the English upper class; the other by dramatising the predicaments of the English working class. In the upshot, they had much more in common than either of them might have cared to admit.

When Wodehouse gave five broadcasts from Berlin in 1941 as a civilian prisoner of the Germans he aroused the fury of A.A. Milne and Duff Cooper, but the sympathy of more understanding men like Compton Mackenzie and George Orwell. Though there is nothing in the five talks now which causes the slightest offence, he was clearly unworldly to make them. However, being unworldly was his stock in trade. He belonged indeed to another world where time had stood still since the summer of

1914. Orwell, penetrating as ever, and a Wodehouse fan since the age of eight, saw that Bertie Wooster*, who made his début in 1917, was already late and really belonged to Edwardian England.

Even here though, the matter is somewhat more complicated than it appears. Was Edwardian England quite as sun-kissed and C major as all that? Of course not; it was a bitter and divided era (strikes, suffragettes, Ireland*, the Lords) and a notedly inhuman one (forced feeding, the cat, capital punishment). It was just that Wodehouse took what suited him from the golden days

Orwell argued that since Wodehouse's mental clock had stopped in 1914 it was pointless to blame him for the German gaffe; the entire *oeuvre*, he went on, was innocent of any reference to fascism. This was not quite so, for in *The Code of the Woosters*, P.G.W. specifically mentioned the Black Shorts, a farcical outfit to which the beefy lout Roderick Spode belonged; and in a spate of sudden awareness he even let in the dire word fascism. Still, it must be allowed that this is merely a dash of realism in the immense confection.

The Wodehousian world is a remarkable one; enclosed, logically quite consistent, yet at an angle to reality. It is like one of those alternative universes postulated by theoretical physicists. Within, it is always spring, and at the Drones Club in Dover Street Bertie Wooster is harmlessly passing the noon hour with young men in spats: Catsmeat Potter-Pirbright, Dogface Rainsby, Bingo Little, Oofy Prosser, Gussie Fink-Nottle, Pongo Twistleton-Twistleton and Barmy Fotheringay-Phipps. *Se non è vero,* as the Italians so well put it, *è molto ben trovato.* If it didn't actually happen, it sounds as if it did.

No doubt, as Orwell complained, Wodehouse made the English aristocracy nicer than they really were. He could not have made them more odd. Besides, it was done with such glittering panache. Open the books anywhere, as Evelyn Waugh remarked, and you will find three brilliant and original similes leap at you from the page: 'He writhed like an electric fan' or 'He was uttering odd strangled noises like a man with no roof to his mouth trying to recite "Gunga Din"' or 'Uncle Tom always looked like a pterodactyl with a secret sorrow'. With the unequalled purity of his style went a matching penchant for the delineation of character; and he would be remembered, if for nothing else, then alone by the creation of the great Jeeves*.

Wog Originally an offensive term for an Indian or Arab or anyone not white; more lately, for any European who is not British ('wogs begin at Calais'). It was popularly supposed to be the acronym for Wily Oriental

Gentleman; but Egyptians working on the Suez were issued with special shirts bearing the legend Working On Government Service, and this seems to be the true, or at any rate earlier acronym.

Women   'He glanced at her feet – being an old stager; she was perfectly shod.' Thus does Bulldog Drummond first appraise his future wife Phyllis in the Carlton one day in 1919. Can a woman be shod like a horse? Drummond clearly thought so, but then he was an English sportsman and a gentleman*. Whether he knew much about women is another matter.

It is an evident absurdity to take any general stance about half the race; especially when it must contain human beings as disparate as the late Diana Dors and Margaret Thatcher. Nevertheless, the formal outer framework within which women's lives are lived is clearly changing fast. In a country with a woman on the throne and another so memorably in 10 Downing Street, it might well be argued, parity has been found. Still, feminists will argue, with some force, that these are cosmetic changes which conceal the real imbalance still surviving.

We do have women priests and women judges, and nobody raises an eyebrow; women members of the Stock Exchange* and women dining as of right at high table in Oxford* and Cambridge*. So a start has been made. Still, it may take a generation or so before the mental bias has been ironed out; and not least in the minds of women themselves.

They face a bewildering world. The invention of the Pill, the laws on sex equality, the gradual onset of equal pay, and the rise of militant feminism have overturned the old verities. The transient partner, the lesbian alternative, the commune and the crèche, have replaced the old certainties. Whether this has made Englishwomen any happier is a nice point; but they clearly have the right – and must have it – to choose the nature of their own happiness or unhappiness.

Meanwhile the English woman, in the eyes of the Englishman at least, seems a sight less neurotic than the American woman, far less daunting than the Russian woman, and much less of a handful than the continental woman. She remains, in short, very much his cup of tea*.

Wooster, Bertie   'As far as brain is concerned,' says the great Wodehousian scholar Richard Usborne, 'he is as near to being null and void as makes no difference.' We know that his manservant, the great and inimitable Jeeves* concurred, and Bertram seemed to have some faint inkling of his own limitations too. 'Providence looks after the chumps of this world; and personally I'm all for it,' he remarked in 1925.

Yet have we been underestimating the chump all this time? After all, he was a bit of a goer with the racquets, and had even got his half-blue in the arcane sport. Then there is his strong moral sense, the celebrated Code of the Woosters. This manifests itself in two principal rubrics: (1) Thou shalt not let down a pal and (2) Thou shalt not scorn a woman's love. It is his manful adherence to these two doctrines, his over-riding sense of *noblesse oblige*, that has landed Bertram Wooster in so many tight corners.

As that other great Wodehousian Geoffrey Jaggard has noted, Bertie has been saved by the gong from matrimony times without number. Aunt Agatha failed to marry him off to a prim, missionary type of girl who turned out to be a gangster's moll. Tough intellectuals like Honoria Glossop and Florence Craye tried to mould him for marriage only to find his clay disintegrated into sand and slipped through their fingers. And so on.

He was engaged to Pauline Stoker, and all but figured in a shotgun wedding at the hands of her father after she had found refuge in (the absent) Bertie's bed. As Jaggard observes: 'It was clearly one up to Pauline, since the only other sensate beings ever discovered in Bertie's bed were a hedgehog and a lizard (up the left pyjama leg).' He has, according to Jeeves, a pleasant light baritone voice in which he sings (in the bath or at smoking concerts) 'Sonny Boy', 'Roll Out the Barrel' and 'Every Morn I Bring You Violets'. Still, let us not damn Bertram with faint praise. The man can string a few words together when all is said and done: 'She wriggled from base to apex with girlish enthusiasm', or 'Bingo swayed like a jelly in a high wind', or his fine portrait of the dreaded Honoria, 'who read Nietzsche and had a laugh like waves breaking on a stern and rockbound coast.'

Once, alarmed at the prospect of the coming revolution, Bertie took a course in self-survival, and actually got a prize for sock darning (though to tell the truth he had smuggled an old woman in to do it for him and was expelled in consequence). Yet, come the revolution, Bertram could surely make a few bob by stringing those few words together. After all he has been doing just that for over three-quarters of a century already, and shows no signs of strain yet, chump or no chump.

Xenophobia It was not that the prewar Englishman did not like foreigners: he generally did not know any. After all, he lived on an island, and unless well-heeled, holidayed at Brighton* or Blackpool*. The war, and its economic aftermath, changed all that. Your modern Englishman is a far more sophisticated citizen of the world. He has to be. His firm, most likely, is owned in America, his car is from Japan, his camera from Germany, his CD player from Hong Kong. His son has gone to seek his fortune in Saudi Arabia, his daughter is an *au pair* in Marseilles, his lunch-time pizza was cooked by an Italian, and his newspapers sold to him by an Indian. He holidays in Spain or Greece, and is beginning to think about a package to Guadeloupe. His football teams are full of foreigners, his cricket teams of Jamaicans. The one unchanging consolation in all this flux is that all these foreigners speak his lingo, which relieves him of the necessity of speaking theirs. To this indulgence he owes the ruthless energy and greed of his forebears, who colonised a quarter of the globe and left their language behind even when their writ had ceased to run. But see under *The English Language*.

Yob Originally a back formation from 'boy', it seems likely to supersede lout and loafer as the natural term for any teenage layabout. *Private Eye** invented a character called Sid Yobbo who edits one of the more raffish daily papers. He is not over-hard to identify; though some would argue that there are many Sid Yobbos in the Street of Shame.

Yomping The term invented by the Royal Marines to describe their disconcerting habit of marching seventy miles a day during the Falklands* conflict, a distance thought to be well outside the ambit of possibility by the Argentinians. The practice is a vivid example of the truth that in conventional war the English military, with their much-tattooed soldiers, brass-lunged sergeants and po-faced officers, all doing the job because they feel like it, are still not to be taken on unless it is absolutely essential.

Yorkshire 'There's nowt so queer as folk' goes the Yorkshire adage; but to the Englishman there's nowt quite so queer as the folk from the dales. Yorkshire has been called the Texas of England; but in a profound sense it seems more English – more Anglo-Saxon at any rate – than any part of the country. The most celebrated characteristics of the Yorkshire-man are his bluntness, his hard-headedness, and his stubbornness; all virtues for which the English have some grudging admiration. Admittedly, there is a less attractive side to this stereotype. 'Hear all, see all, say nowt; sup all, eat all, pay nowt', is said by detractors to be the Yorkshireman's motto; in truth, the lines probably owe more to his well-developed if earthy sense of humour.

When a Yorkshireman finds fame, it seems if anything to accentuate his roots; no one in England has been left in any doubt about which county politicians like Harold Wilson and Denis Healey came from; nor have the English ever been in the slightest doubt about the provenance of writers like J.B. Priestley* or John Braine. Yorkshire has some claim to be the home of the working-class hero, wincingly on the make in Braine's *Room at the Top* or articulating his passion in David Storey's *This Sporting Life* with a clump round his lady-love's lug-hole. Rugby League football is the improbable strand round which Storey weaves his novel, and the game is played with dedication there; but the prime Yorkshire obsession is with cricket.

All England watched bemused as Yorkshire was rent in twain by the great Geoffrey Boycott controversy. Was Yorkshire's greatest and dourest batsman exacting too great a price in morale and unity from his team-mates and would he have to go? He went; but a palace revolution at Headingley, the county's cricket Mecca, brought him resoundingly back. Every Yorkshireman worth his salt, from Westminster's Roy Hattersley to television's Michael Parkinson, felt impelled to pronounce on the grave dilemma. But then, a kind of psychic steam seems to drive all Yorkshire people: from writers like the Brontës* to reformers like William Wilberforce, explorers like Captain Cook, composers like Frederick

Delius and conspirators like Guy Fawkes.

Fortunately, that dour and laconic sense of humour, laced by the inimitable dialect, never deserts your Yorkshireman for long. Thus, there is no doubt where we are when a courting couple sit long hours by the fire in the front parlour till suddenly the young man blurts out: 'Wilt th' marry me, lass?' To this she has her reply ready: 'Ay, I will lad.' After that the clock ticks away and for an hour there is a deep silence in the parlour. At length the lass inquires: 'Hast th' nowt else to tell me?' Her intended thinks this over in the way Yorkshiremen will, and at long last replies: 'Nay: I've said too much already.'

Yorkshire Pudding   'It is an exceeding good pudding; the gravy of the meat eats well with it,' wrote the Elizabeth David of her day, Hannah Glasse, in *The Art of Cookery Made Plain and Easy*, published in 1747. It still is. In a typical small English country inn, for instance, three quarters of all lunches ordered on Sunday are still roast beef and Yorkshire pudding.

The original *raison d'être* of the pud was undoubtedly frugality: the batter of eggs, flour and milk was placed under the roasting spit to catch and soak up the dripping and juices as the meat turned. In Yorkshire then and now the pudding is often served first. Here again necessity was the motive. Mother would offer most meat to whichever child ate the most pud: but when the pud had been demolished, there was that much less room left for the beef, so it went further.

George Orwell* maintained in 1945 that you were more likely to get a good rich slice of Yorkshire pudding in the poorest English home than in a restaurant. There is still a lot of truth in this, for the wretched little buns served often in restaurants with roast beef, full of air and innocent of gravy, are but pale travesties of the home-made pud.

For true delicacy, the batter should be allowed to stand after it has been mixed; and a perfectly made Yorkshire pud should be able to stand up to the most sophisticated French soufflé in lightness of texture. Every Englishman worth his salt knows that the interior of a Yorkshire pud is moist and saturated with the juices of the joint; the outside light, brown and crisp. The art of the true pud connoisseur is to be sure of being served a little of both.

Yuppie   He entered the language just twelve years ago and now seems unlikely to go away. At first he was the yumpie, or young, upwardly mobile person: but soon yuppie, or young urban professional, over-hauled him, probably because of the resonance with puppy. He found his unlovely apotheosis in Nick Leeson, the derivatives dealer from nowhere who made a fortune for the aristocratic merchant bank of Baring's until his luck changed, sending them to perdition and himself to jail. It would be rash to assume from this fascinating fable about the interplay of class and wealth, greed and stupidity, that the yuppie's days are numbered. He is alive and well and thriving in the City. He may indeed be seen best as a bit player in the mighty drama that has shaken the English upper middle class to its foundations as stately homes and broad acres are bought by those who have struck it rich in currencies and commodities from those who have effortlessly lost the lot at Lloyd's.

Zizz   A short nap or snooze, a useful word for the language, and a vivid example of the thrall of onomatopoeia. It probably derives from the z-z-z- used in balloons by cartoonists to indicate the gentle sound emitted by someone asleep and, because it acts out its sense, seems bound to prevail.

Zonked   A newish word, probably echoing the sound of a heavy blow, and used for utter exhaustion brought on by drink, drugs or even work.

Zoo   To most Englishmen it is the headquarters of the Zoological Society in Regents Park, a fashionable port of call these last one hundred and fifty years and a favourite with many celebrated Englishmen, notably Cyril Connolly*, who was given a surprise seventieth birthday luncheon there and was found hours later wandering amid the cages which housed his beloved lemurs. It was also a happy haunt for the infant Christopher Robin Milne, who used to visit a favourite polar bear there, the *fons et origo* of Winnie-the-Pooh*. In 1981 a middle-aged Christopher Robin unveiled a statue in the zoo to Winnie-the-Pooh – arguably the most famous bear in the world, though this will be disputed by adherents of Rupert Bear*, and indeed Paddington.

Zuleika Dobson   The story of Max Beerbohm's divine temptress is yet another illustration of the profound truth that the Thames is a magic river, Oxford an enchanted city, and England, as may be seen throughout this book, an imaginary land inhabited by improbable people.

Index

Index

Index